ALSO BY JONATHAN RAUCH

Kindly Inquisitors:
The New Attacks on Free Thought

The Outnation:
A Search for the Soul of Japan

DEMOSCLEROSIS

DEMOSCLEROSIS

THE SILENT KILLER OF AMERICAN GOVERNMENT

Jonathan Rauch

TIMES BOOKS

RANDOM HOUSE

Portions of this work were originally published in different form in the April 25, 1992, September 5, 1992, and August 7, 1993 issues of *National Journal*.

Library of Congress Cataloging-in-Publication Data

Rauch, Jonathan
    Demosclerosis: the silent killer of American government/
Jonathan Rauch.
        p.   cm.
    Includes bibliographical references and index.
    ISBN 0-8129-2257-3
    1. Pressure groups—United States.   2. Entitlement spending—
United States.   3. Government spending policy—United States.
4. United States—Politics and government.   I. Title.
JK1118.R38   1994
324'.4'0973—dc20   94-489

Book design by MM Design 2000, Inc.
Manufactured in the United States of America

9 8 7 6 5 4 3 2

First Edition

ACKNOWLEDGMENT

My special thanks to Richard Frank, John Fox Sullivan, and the staff of the *National Journal,* who have made this and so much else possible.

CONTENTS

DEMOSCLEROSIS

1

THE TRAP

ETWEEN THE TIME when the results became clear and the moment when the new president-elect emerged to acknowledge his victory, two long hours passed. A crowd of fifty thousand stood waiting for their man in front of the Old State House in Little Rock, Arkansas, shivering in bitterly cold weather which, being unseasonable, caught people in their shirtsleeves. Millions of members of the public waited, too. Younger people could barely remember a Democratic presidency and wondered how the first Democratic president-elect in sixteen years would sound. Their elders wondered whether the new man would show he had learned from his Democratic predecessors' mistakes.

At 11:22 P.M. central time, on November 3, 1992, Bill Clinton finally emerged, looking exhausted but happy. He had made history and he knew it. His speech was short and began with thank-yous for the crowd, the family, the voters, the running mate. Then came what was, in effect, the first substantive statement of the Clinton years. He said that he would "face problems too long ignored," and that people needed to be brought together "so that our diversity can be a source of strength." Then he said:

3

"I think perhaps the most important thing that we understand here in the heartland of Arkansas is the need to reform the political system, to reduce the influence of special interests and give more influence back to the kind of people that are in this crowd tonight by the tens of thousands. And I will work . . . to do that."

Campaigning against special interests, railing against them and deploring them and promising to break them, is a venerable American tradition. In 1948, President Harry Truman cried out from his railway car that his campaign was "a crusade of the people against the special interests," and the people cheered. In private, twenty years earlier, Calvin Coolidge warned his successor, Herbert Hoover, about the armies of interested parties who would be coming to see him. "You have to stand, every day, three or four hours of visitors," Coolidge said. "Nine-tenths of them want something they ought not to have. If you keep dead still, they will run down in three or four minutes. If you even cough or smile, they will start up all over again." Long before Coolidge, James Madison thought hard about how to contain the undue influence of what he called "faction," by which he meant "a number of citizens . . . who are united and actuated by some common impulse of passion, or of interest, adverse to the rights of other citizens, or to the permanent and aggregate interests of the community." If he had known the term "special interest," no doubt he would have used it.

The curious thing is that ever since Coolidge's day, and especially since Truman's, interest-group activity has increased. The more the public complained and the more the politicians promised change, the more the lobbies seemed to thrive and the more powerful they seemed to become. And so the president-elect stood there in 1992, promising "to reduce the influence of special interests," as so many had promised before him. The promise was the easy part. Delivering would be much harder.

Hard not only because all politicians must reckon with inertia and human frailty, but because today all politicians must also reckon with a kind of Chinese puzzle which traps you if you try to escape by brute force. If you want to pass a few bills and hand out a few new benefits and pay for them by running up the budget deficit a little more, then that is not really so difficult. You can almost always add a few more programs here and there. But that neither weakens special interests nor solves government's long-term problems. Politicians like Bill Clinton and his successor and *his* successor cannot hope to keep their promises to "reduce the influence of special interests" until they un-riddle the paradoxes of a political malady whose perverse dynamics are undermining government and enraging voters.

Why does the "special-interest" sector grow year after year, despite the politicians' promises and the public's disgust? Why does this sector feed on its own growth, with no limits in sight?

Why does the richest body politic in the history of the human species feel poorer than it felt thirty years ago, even though its wealth then (adjusted for inflation) was less than half as great as it is today?

Why is it that, despite America's extraordinary wealth and the advent of all kinds of new problem-solving technology, the American government's capacity to solve problems appears to have sharply diminished since the 1960s?

Why does "getting things done" in the short run often make problem-solving more difficult for the government in the long run? Why does the government work at an ever more frantic pace and yet seem to produce ever fewer successes?

Why are many liberals and Democrats, with their greater proclivity to use government to right wrongs and correct flaws, paralyzing the very government that they believe they are championing? Why are many conservatives, with their no-new-taxes stance and their rhetoric of blame, actually feeding the governmental appetites that they constantly decry?

Why was Bill Clinton's own election-night rhetoric, which promised to reinvigorate the system by reducing the influence of "them" (the special interests) and increasing the influence of "us" (the American people), a cause rather than a cure of the problem he sought to solve?

If politicians and the public do not understand the answers to those questions, they will not have a chance.

"The clear mandate of this election," Clinton remarked a few days after winning, "was an end of politics as usual, an end to the gridlock in Washington, an end to finger-pointing and blame." The new president was given a mandate for change by an electorate that was beside itself with frustration at Washington's failure to solve problems. And so a window of opportunity opened. I remember thinking, on that night when he stood before the Old State House in Little Rock, that we would soon see whether he knew how to exploit his chance, or whether the chance would slip by. The very first hint, namely his attack on "special interests," was not particularly encouraging, because it implied that the problem was "them." Wrong. The problem is us.

SIGHS AND MOANS

For me, the first inkling that something malign was happening came in February 1985, only a few months after I arrived in Washington. Having just left my job with a newspaper in the South to become a reporter for the *National Journal,* I wandered into the Senate press gallery and beheld the tall, gangly figure of Senator Alan Simpson. The Wyoming Republican was doing what's known as "holding the floor" while the majority and minority leaders worked behind the scenes on some compromise or other. In this case, holding the floor consisted of haranguing an almost entirely empty chamber (and this was before TV came to the Senate). I sat down in the gallery, at first listening idly and then becoming absorbed. To this day, I have never witnessed another political speech like that one.

Simpson was complaining about the partisan games that go on in the Capitol. "Out there in the American public," he said, "are people who are watching us go through this, trying to see who can hook the anchor on the Democrats or who can hook the anchor on the Republicans, who look upon that as a childish activity." Well, that was certainly true, but it was hardly new. Simpson went on, however, to talk about the political uses of fear.

"We are frozen in place," he said. "We are frozen in place because there are enough of us who get a coterie of people and interest groups and media about us and say they are going to do a number on this issue or are going to do this or that." He talked about a veterans' lobbyist he knew. "We have had some very earthy discussions, the two of us. He is a delightful, pleasant guy. But the emphasis was to get the two million members; and you do that . . . just like we do things here—by juicing up the troops. . . . What happened to us was we got a $200 billion deficit by juicing up the troops." And then he said:

"One of the things . . . that we do here so beautifully . . . is the use of fear, raw fear. You can do a lot with raw fear. You can do a lot with raw fear with people who do like nuclear power or do not like it. You can do a lot with raw fear with farmers. You can do a lot with raw fear with uranium workers. You can do a lot with raw fear with oil and gas workers. You can do a lot with raw fear with veterans. You can do a lot with raw fear with Social Security recipients.

"And that is what we do beautifully here in this place, because I guess we really are all impelled by a raw fear—and that raw fear is, I would guess, a fear of what the electorate will do to us, and, of course, maybe that is the primal raw fear in this place. It may well be."

This was more than just an oration; it was an outburst. The striking thing about it, besides its candor, was the level of frustration it exposed. At that point, "gridlock" had yet to become a political cliché. The same party controlled the Senate and the White House (though not the House) under an extraordinarily popular president. Yet here was rhetoric of stagnation and defeat: "We are frozen in place." Simpson's complaint went deeper than the parties or personalities in the White House or the Congress, deeper even than the difficulty of getting things done. The founders, after all, intended that personalities clash and that getting things done be difficult: better safe than sorry. Simpson's complaint seemed to be that individuals and groups had become adept at mobilizing fear to achieve political goals. His tone suggested the pain of one who is in a trap and does not understand why he can't get out.

In May 1985, three months after Alan Simpson's speech, one Democratic representative from Texas, a former banker and high school teacher named Marvin Leath, rose in the House to propose a budget package that would have significantly reduced the deficit. In it he included most of what the experts agreed needed to be done: reductions in Ronald Reagan's defense buildup, some increases in taxes, and the abolition of one year's increase in Social Security payments. This last provision was especially courageous, because in today's political world a Democrat proposing to dock Social Security is like a hemophiliac volunteering for a swordfight. On the House floor, Leath gave a gutsy speech that deserved to be remembered, though it wasn't:

"As you could most certainly expect," he said, "conservatives are pointing fingers and telling liberals, 'It's your fault. All the years of massive social and domestic spending are responsible for these deficits. Let's gore your ox, and we can solve the problem.' And just as certainly, as you might also expect, liberals are pointing fingers and telling conservatives, 'It's *your* fault. These massive defense buildups and these massive tax cuts are responsible for these deficits. Let's gore your ox, and we can solve the problem.'

"The . . . truth is, we all know who is to blame. Democrats and Republicans are to blame. Liberals and conservatives and all in between are to blame. The people are to blame for believing all the garbage they get bombarded with through the mail raising money from both parties and a thousand special-interest lobbies who circle this Capitol in their Mercedes automobiles after leaving their million-dollar homes in northern Virginia."

Here again, as in Simpson's speech, were the undertones of rage and entrapment. Politicians have a poor image, but anyone who knows them knows that by and large they are hardworking people who want only the best for their country. They do not want to make things worse; they want to make them better. Yet increasingly they feel that they *cannot* make things better. Increasingly they play the blame game without wanting to but without understanding why they play it or how to escape. They feel their country is poor, far poorer than it actually is, and they wonder why the swelling crowds of aides and lobbyists and campaign consultants seem not to empower them but to hem them in. And in all of those feelings, they mirror the feelings of the people who elect them.

Many people in the capital admired Leath's budget package, because it made good sense. Practically everyone admired Leath, who stood up and told the truth and stuck his neck out. Practically everyone voted against him, too. His package was defeated, 372 to 56. In 1990, disgusted with his and Congress's inability to solve problems, Marvin Leath announced that he would not seek reelection to a seventh term.

For thirty years, the American public has increasingly expressed feelings of frustration and entrapment similar to Alan Simpson's and Marvin Leath's. In 1958, 75 percent of the public said it trusted the government in Washington to "do what's right" always or most of the time. After the assassination of John F. Kennedy, a long decline of confidence began. By the early 1990s, the trust level had fallen by more than half, to around 35 percent—and in February 1993 it reached a new low, with only one in five Americans expressing trust in government to do the right thing. Other data tell the same story of disillusionment. Seven in ten Americans say that the government creates more problems than it solves, rather than vice versa; by more than two to one, people say that abuses by the federal government are a bigger problem than abuses by big business. Between the early 1950s and the early 1990s, the proportion of people saying that government wastes "a lot" of their tax money rose from fewer than half to 75 percent. By the time the 1980s came, politicians routinely campaigned against "Washington" and "government," even as voters demanded more from both places. People felt they deserved more, yet they felt they received less, and they didn't understand why. The more they struggled, the more they felt beset.

By 1992, the word "gridlock" was well established. "Our people are pleading for change," Bill Clinton said at the Democratic convention in July 1992, "but government is in the way." In 1960, very few people, and least of all a Democratic presidential candidate, would have said that government was "in the way." Why, in the 1990s, was government "in the way"? After all, it didn't use to be. "We have a government that doesn't work," the independent presidential candidate and business tycoon Ross Perot declared again and again in 1992. Millions of people agreed with him and shared his bewilderment and disgust at what they saw as a government that was servile but had ceased to serve. Why didn't government "work"?

RED HERRINGS

The easiest way to refer to government's problems is as "special-interest gridlock." That description isn't completely wrong, but it is far enough off target to be badly misleading.

For one thing, the "gridlock" metaphor implies that nothing gets done. It implies, in other words, that the problem is lack of governmental motion, or lack of activity. One of the main goals of this book is to refocus attention away from the quantity of motion in Washington and toward the effectiveness of results. The central issue is not "Why does Washington get so little done?" It is "Why has Washington's activity become so ineffective at solving problems?"

In Washington, after all, things always get done. Despite all the talk of "gridlock" in the years prior to Bill Clinton's election, in that time the government passed scads of laws and scads more regulations and, by any objective measure, got a lot done. The do-nothing, gridlocked days of George Bush were in fact neither do-nothing nor really gridlocked. Those years saw passage of the sweeping Clean Air Act and other environmental measures, the almost equally sweeping Americans with Disabilities Act, new money for child care, a major highway bill, and much else besides. In just the field of civil rights, during the "gridlocked" Bush period the government enacted, among other new programs and laws, the Civil Rights Act of 1991, the Voting Rights Language Assistance Act, the Civil Liberties Act Amendments of 1992, the Minority Farmers Rights Act, the Japanese American Redress Entitlement Program, the antiredlining provisions of the banking-reform law, the Hate-Crimes Statistics Act, and the aforementioned Americans with Disabilities Act. According to congressional figures, the number and page count of laws enacted during "gridlock" remained well in line with the post-1970 norm.

The question is not the quantity of activity, but how effectively a given amount of activity solves problems on net. That phrase "on net"—meaning "on balance," after the wins and losses are tallied up—is important. In life, every solution creates at least some new problems. The trick is always to find solutions which create fewer problems than they solve. In the classic example, if you kill a fly with a flyswatter, you come out ahead on net. If you kill a fly with a cannon, you create more problems than you solve. To the extent that an institution can reliably solve more problems than it creates, it has problem-solving capacity.

Problem-solving capacity is precisely what seems to have been shrinking for the federal government. Political activity has become a kind of flailing which creates frenzy but does little good, or even makes problems worse. Wheels spin and gears mesh, but the car goes nowhere, or goes everywhere at once, or shakes itself to pieces. More problems seem to be created than solved.

The other problem with the term "special-interest gridlock" is its implication that a few fat cats manipulate the system for their own narrow advantage. But the fact is that the American system of governance today is much less at the mercy of any narrow, manipulative few than at any time in the past. The era of the backroom bosses who called the shots, of the rich patrons who could buy the system, is over. The Leath budget was not defeated by any cigar-chomping industrialist with an interest in protecting his western mining interests. It was defeated by a coalition of interests representing virtually everybody. The American Association of Retired Persons alone boasts well over thirty million members, or one of every six adult Americans; and, because most of us have aged relatives, most of us are among the group's indirect clients; and, because we all grow old, each and every one of us is among the group's potential members. If you add the farmers and veterans and oil workers and all the others whom Simpson mentioned and Leath took on, you see there is no longer anything particularly special about "special interests." Today everyone is organized, and everyone is part of an interest group. We have met the special interests, and they are us.

If, however, the interests are no longer special, they are not quite general, either. And here is a puzzle. Conventional wisdom has suggested that as more Americans got organized, and as the process was opened up to more groups and classes than ever before, the claims of all of those competing interests would be weighed and mediated in the political process, producing a more balanced and satisfactory result than the fat-cat system had ever done. But that is not what has happened. The public today is *less* happy than before, and problems are *less* likely to be solved. Government, as Clinton said, is "in the way," despite the desultory but sincere efforts of leaders to lead.

It is possible to cook up all kinds of ad hoc explanations for what is wrong. And many of them have some truth in them. But most of them are finally unsatisfying.

A standard complaint has been of a lack of leadership. But that diagnosis does not explain enough. There is little evidence that the people are electing poorer leaders now than in the past, or that a worse class of person runs for public office, or that human leadership capacity has deteriorated over time. Some politicians are fools and rogues, but many more are bright, hardworking, and honest. In times of crisis—the debate over whether to authorize war in the Persian Gulf in 1991, for instance—the system still can and does rise magnificently. At exceptional moments, leadership can still be found in abundance, even in the rank and file of politicians. Marvin Leath's ill-fated 1985 budget proposal was just one example.

Some people, mainly liberals, would say that the public has been brainwashed by Ronald Reagan and other Washington-bashing conservatives into hating government, and that the result has been to render government ineffective. Yet the decline in confidence began well before Ronald Reagan and his conservatives came to town. The wave of disgust with government brought Jimmy Carter into office before it swept Reagan to power. Moreover, these days you would have to be brainwashed *not* to have doubts, or worse, about government. Even among thoughtful observers who were no fans of the Reaganites, the feeling has been growing that government really *is* in the way.

I, for one, am no government-basher. I know an anti-government activist who said he got physically ill just looking at the edifices of Big Government in Washington. For me, the effect is always the opposite. As many times as I have been in the United States Capitol, I can't enter it or even look up at the great dome without catching my breath a little in awe. Yet, as time goes on, I have a steadily harder time denying that government's effectiveness is decaying.

One day I had a conversation with William Niskanen, who had been acting chairman of the Council of Economic Advisers in the Reagan Administration. "Congress," he said, "is the most reactionary institution in American life. Congress is basically trying to prevent change in the economic structure of the country, to protect declining industries against rising industries, to protect existing firms against new firms, to protect weak regions against strong regions." Niskanen may have been overstating his case; he had been a Reagan appointee, after all, and was no friend of government. By contrast, I find much to admire in Congress: it works hard, it means well, it is close to the people, it has done much good. Yet I left Niskanen's office feeling disquieted, because there was much truth in what he said.

Here again was something strange, which ruled out another ad hoc explanation, namely that jellyfish and Neanderthals were getting elected. Today's politicians include a few genuine reactionaries, but also a quantity and range of activists whose commitment and talent yield nothing to the abolitionists of 150 years ago or the Progressives of eighty years ago or the labor left of fifty years ago. Moreover, today's activists hold positions of power, whereas in the 1950s and 1960s they were mostly locked out by the powerful old men who controlled Congress. If the government is becoming unable to solve problems, that is not because it's filling up with weaklings and reactionaries. The change has to be on the *system* level. And, to judge by the frustration and bewilderment expressed by Simpson and Leath and others, the problem must be of a sort that is not transparent to the people within the system.

The growing influence of money in politics is often held up as the problem. That may be a problem, but there is nothing remotely new in it. There is more money in politics today than before, but money by itself need not lead to gridlock. If the money is wielded by a few powerful interests who agree on what to do, then money greases the skids and things get done. Anyway, blaming money begs the real question: *Why* is there more money in politics? Why does political activity suck up a growing share of the country's resources? The rising expenditure on politics is itself as much a symptom as a cause of whatever is wrong.

Some liberals, such as the writer William Greider, complain that the problem is the power of corporate lobbying to block changes that are in the public interest. Here many of the same reservations apply. There was no lack of corporate influence in the days of Andrew Carnegie and J. P. Morgan, and those magnates were unable to stymie the trustbusters. Corporate influence is nothing new. What is new is the proliferation of nonbusiness activist groups, many of them representing what they take to be the public interest. Some of those, such as the environmental groups, have large amounts of money and wield enough power to put through, for instance, the massive Clean Air Act of 1990, which most corporations would happily have done without. Ask a business lobbyist if he feels he can control what government does, and he will look at you with incredulity.

Still another diagnosis in recent years blamed divided control of the government, in which Republicans held the White House and Democrats held the Congress. Unquestionably, divided control can make the process stickier. However, Democrats held both branches under Carter and had plenty of problems; Republicans held effective control of both branches in 1981, and rather than defeating the interest groups they rolled over for them, handing out tax breaks as party favors. Moreover, a number of countries with parliamentary systems, under which the ruling party or coalition always controls the whole government, have had "special-interest gridlock" problems comparable to our own. In France, much as in America, opinion polls in 1993 found that a record share of the public (82 percent) was dissatisfied with the way the country was being governed. In Japan, decades of single-party control turned government ministries into special-interest protectorates and made policy gridlock a way of life, leading at last to an electoral rebellion *against* single-party control in the summer of 1993.

"Publics all across the industrial world don't know what to do about modern government," writes the public-opinion expert Everett Carll Ladd. "They see no alternative to its playing a large role, but they are increasingly frustrated as they see it malperforming and increasingly doubtful that it can be made to work better." Whatever has happened does not seem to be wholly peculiar to the American system of government.

In January 1993, the Democrats took control of both branches, and their record will provide a test of whether divided government is at the root of government's ills. The record of the Clinton Administration's first few months—its difficulty passing even a modest economic program, for instance—suggests that there is more to the story. Over the course of several years, I have come to believe that ad hoc explanations based on personalities or political parties are too superficial to explain what has happened. I have come to suspect that the conventional wisdom is backward: the worrisome thing is not so much that American society is in the grip of its gridlocked government, but that American government—and the American economy, too—is in the grip of powerful and broad changes in American society. Alan Simpson and Marvin Leath, without quite understanding how, were squeezed by tectonic forces which are very deep and very difficult to resist, and which, importantly, are *directional.* That is, the situation, if left unattended, tends to get worse.

My view may be wrong, but I have little doubt that Americans would be wise to confront squarely and unflinchingly the possibility that it is right. To do so is to confront demosclerosis.

TOCQUEVILLE'S SHADOW

This book is about side effects of the postwar style of politics, a style that emphasizes interest-group activism and redistributive programs. As such, the book may be most congenial to conservatives, who have always resented programs that take money out of some pockets and put it in others. I hope, though, that nonconservatives will also think hard about what follows, since the argument itself is neither partisan nor ideological.

To understand demosclerosis and see that it is a serious problem, you don't need to believe that government is evil and all programs should be abolished. Redistributive programs are in use everywhere, and should be. Aid to the unemployed provides security against the most bruising trauma of capitalism; aid to the elderly gives security in old age. Aid to farmers can help maintain a base of food production. Aid to veterans repays a public debt to those who serve. All of those goals are worthy, and all of those programs serve real social purposes. The problem is understanding and then minimizing the programs' cumulative side effects, which turn out to be both nasty and inherent.

By definition, government's power to solve problems comes from its ability to reassign resources, whether by taxing, spending, regulating, or simply passing laws. But that very ability energizes countless investors and entrepreneurs and ordinary Americans to go digging for gold by lobbying government. In time, a whole industry—large, sophisticated, professionalized, and to a considerable extent self-serving— emerges and then assumes a life of its own. This industry is a drain on the productive economy, and there appears to be no natural limit to its growth. As it grows, the steady accumulation of subsidies and benefits, each defended in perpetuity by a professional interest group, calcifies government. Government loses its capacity to experiment and so becomes more and more prone to failure.

Calcification

That is demosclerosis: postwar government's progressive loss of the ability to adapt.

A lot has happened to American government and politics since 1960, when the public's esteem for Washington stood so much higher. There were the expansive promises of the Johnson and Nixon years, and the subsequent disappointments; the Watergate scandal and the disillusionment it spawned; the growth of a Washington press corps that became more independent and more aggressive, often adversarial; the professionalization of the Washington political class, which filled up with full-time campaign consultants and public-relations experts and direct-mail impresarios and fund-raising wizards. Outside Washington, there was the bitter reaction against the war in Vietnam, and the reaction against the reaction; there was the spread of an entitlement mentality among the voters, who increasingly looked upon government benefits as inherent rights rather than as earned privileges or temporary assistance; there was television, the civil rights revolution, and much else besides. To focus on demosclerosis isn't to imply that it explains everything that has happened—far from it. However, modern government's failures cannot be fully or even adequately understood unless demosclerosis is taken into account. Its implications are broad and unsettling:

The process is destructive. Though probably not fatal, it saps the vitality of the economy and ravages the flexibility and problem-solving capacity of the government.

It is inherent. Democracies are necessarily vulnerable to demosclerosis (though not uniquely vulnerable). The problem is encoded in democracy's DNA.

It is progressive. Unless you work to control it, the disease gets worse. Resisting it requires constant effort and attention. You can't coast or relax.

It is cunning. Demosclerosis thrives on the more-benefits-for-me mentality that self-interested voters often use. It ensnares the unwary in a trap baited with attractive subsidies and

well-meaning programs. Coping with it will require a more sophisticated level of thinking than the political debate has yet
produced.

It is not someone else's fault. Demosclerosis renders obsolete all
political scapegoating of the customary sort ("Liberals did it!"
"Conservatives did it!" "Business did it!" "Labor did it!" "Republicans did it!" "Democrats did it!"). The problem is not any
kind of "them." It is not the political group you most despise,
whoever that may be. It is you and me and many people like us.

A century and a half ago, Alexis de Tocqueville came to
America and concluded that democracy's Achilles' heel was tyranny of the majority. "The majority in the United States has
immense actual power and a power of opinion which is almost
as great," he said. "If freedom is ever lost in America, that will
be due to the omnipotence of the majority driving the minorities to desperation and forcing them to appeal to physical force."
But democracy, here and elsewhere, has not succumbed to majoritarian tyranny. In fact, America has probably done a better
job protecting minorities than any other society in history.

A hundred years after Tocqueville, many people worried
that democracy's vulnerability lay in its lack of resolve in the face
of totalitarianism. Dictators, after all, could make decisions almost instantaneously, while democratic institutions dithered
and deliberated. That fear, too, was misplaced. American democracy saw the dictators to their graves. It saw the Cold War
through in a display of consistency and resolve which history
can hardly match. Dithering democracies turned out to have
the better side of the deal: they turned out to be much better
than dictatorships at finding and correcting their mistakes before mistakes became cataclysms. Nothing that follows in this
book is meant to imply otherwise.

Today it appears that democracy's truer vulnerability lies
closer to home—in the democratic public's tendency to form
ever more groups clamoring for ever more goodies and perks
and then defending them to the death. Free and stable societies,

it seems, tend to drift toward economic cannibalism and governmental calcification, unless they make a positive effort to fight the current. Demosclerosis may now represent the most serious single challenge to the long-term vitality of democratic government.

One reason democracy wasn't done in by majoritarian tyranny or by the dictators' resolve was that people became worried about both threats, and so managed to defeat them. The current threat is more insidious. It operates quietly and slowly from within, giving us no belligerent "them" to bravely stand up to—no majoritarian lynch mobs with nooses, no implacable Stalins with armies. It is a crisis of American appetites.

This book, then, is about a change in American society and behavior over the past thirty or so years which is compromising our ability to govern ourselves and to solve common problems. It is about the way Americans have trapped one another in an escalating game of beggar-thy-neighbor that damages the economy and chokes the government. We cannot escape the game until we understand how it captures us. Then we must choose, despite strong incentives to the contrary, to make for the exit.

The book is, finally, a request that people like you and me stop our resentful scapegoating of liberals, conservatives, government, business, foreigners, wealthy elites, the poor, politicians, and everyone else, and that we shoulder the blame ourselves, like grown-ups. We demand ever more of our politicians and our government, yet it is we who are hemming them in and circumscribing their ability to satisfy us. The book is not an apocalyptic tirade about the imminent death of American civilization or democracy or prosperity; I believe in no such thing. It is rather a warning. A nation of expectant whiners cannot break out of the trap that I am about to describe.

2

MR. OLSON'S PLANET

I N THE MID-1950s, a young American traveling in Europe was struck by an economic oddity. The United Kingdom had won two great wars and enjoyed all the splendors of empire, yet it suffered from economic anemia—so much so that people came to speak of the "British disease." Germany had been defeated in two wars and then was broken in half, yet West Germany was booming—so much so that people came to speak of the German "economic miracle." Why would two European economies, of roughly comparable size, with well-educated populaces, and with similar technological bases, behave so differently?

That question led the young man to ponder a broader one. Why do stable societies seem to wind down over time? Great Britain was only the most recent example of a society that emerged rapidly, flowered brilliantly, and then sank into torpor and decay. Germany, on the other hand, had suffered cataclysmic destabilization, yet was full of vigor. Most explanations resorted to specific events like wars, or spun vague theories about culture, or resorted to clichés about countries' becoming "tired" or "lazy" or "old," as though countries were people. The young American, still fresh out of university and on his way to a career

21

in economics, was unsatisfied. There ought to be a more systematic answer, a regular mechanism to explain a regular pattern. He turned the problem over in his mind for years. In 1982,
he proposed a striking solution.

THE LOGICIAN OF COLLECTIVE ACTION

Mancur Olson was born in 1932, sixty miles north of Fargo,
North Dakota, on a farm by the Red River, which forms the
border with Minnesota. His forebears migrated from Norway,
but the peculiar first name is not Norwegian. It was passed down
from his father, and probably comes from the Arabic name
Mansur, meaning "victorious"—thus is pronounced "Mansir,"
not "Mankur." The name is all the odder in that Olson himself
could not look less Arabic: his face is pink, his hair a faded
strawberry blond, his beard a graying shade that used to be red.
Though he holds a Harvard Ph.D. and a fancy title at the University of Maryland, he can still repair a tractor and retains, to
this day, a midwestern matter-of-factness. That uncluttered di-
rectness, coupled with his professorial precision (he often talks
in paragraphs, complete with "indeeds"), would make him pe-
dantic if not for what you notice first of all: a jumpy, delighted,
almost pixieish excitability when he talks about ideas. He may
ask you to let him pace while he talks, and then prowls the way
some people gesticulate, as though the movement helped him
form words. The effect is pleasantly gnomish.

The larger world first heard from him in 1965, with the
publication of a short, tightly reasoned book titled *The Logic of
Collective Action,* in which he turned conventional wisdom on its
head. The standard theory was that human beings in general,
and Americans in particular (as Tocqueville, among others, had
said), were natural joiners, combining into groups large and
small. The result was interest-group democracy, in which business interests competed with consumer or labor interests,
animal-rights interests competed with hunting interests, and

sludge-making interests competed with environmental interests, and out of the whole raucous bazaar came a more or less
balanced policy.

Wrong on all counts, said Olson. First of all, forming groups
is not easy, it is hard, and it does not happen naturally. Very
small groups, true, are fairly easy to form, but forming middle-
sized groups is much harder, and very large groups, representing millions of people, literally cannot be formed without using
coercion or offering special rewards for joiners. The reason is
this: the larger the group, the bigger everyone's temptation to
let others do the hard work of joining and organizing.

Suppose that three people in a rural neighborhood share a
private road or driveway. They might easily form a group to
repave their road; each one will pay something, but all will
benefit. If all three chip in, the road is fixed at minimal cost to
each. But now suppose there are a hundred people sharing the
road. Now the temptation becomes strong for each person not
to chip in. Each one thinks, "Someone else can worry about
filling potholes. I'll let other people fix the road, and then I'll be
able to use it for free." If enough people think that way, the road
never gets repaved.

The problem here is an ancient one, namely that people try
to ride for free if they think they might get away with it. It
involves what economists call public goods: goods (or services)
which everyone can enjoy even if only one person takes the
trouble to pay for them. Roads are one classic example; national
defense is another. The classic solution is for a majority to *require* everyone to contribute to road-building and national defense, through taxes. Otherwise, too few roads would be built
and too few soldiers recruited, because too many people would
wait for someone else to do the building and recruiting.

In *The Logic of Collective Action,* Olson showed that the free-
rider problem applies to private collective projects no less than
to government. The bigger the class of people who benefit from
collective action, the weaker the incentive for any *particular* ben-

eficiary to join or organize, and so the less likely that a group will coalesce. "In short," wrote Olson, "the larger the group, the less it will further its common interests."

If that is true, the implications are unsettling. "Since relatively small groups will frequently be able voluntarily to organize and act in support of their common interests," Olson went on, "and since large groups normally will not be able to do so, the outcome of the political struggle among the various groups in society will not be symmetrical." In other words, small, narrow groups have a permanent and inherent advantage, and "often triumph over the numerically superior forces because the former are generally organized and active while the latter are normally unorganized and inactive."

Experience confirms the prediction. A dozen companies making left-handed screwdrivers may organize to get themselves a tax break. If they win a loophole worth $12 million, each earns a cool million, and the investment pays off handsomely. Their tax break comes out of the pockets of everyone else—but the cost is spread out among millions of Americans. And so it would be pointless for someone to try to organize 250 million Americans to win back a fraction of a cent each.

People have tried organizing groups to represent very broad interests, without notable success. The National Taxpayers Union, which lobbies for reductions in what it regards as wasteful government spending, has managed to enlist only about a quarter of a million members. Out of a total pool of 160 million Americans who pay taxes, that is a participation rate (about one in 640) that borders on insignificance. Out of 100 million or so American voters, not one in three hundred is a member of Common Cause, a group that advocates political reforms to reduce the influence of moneyed special interests. By contrast, the American Federation of State, County and Municipal Employees—a group representing a narrower interest—boasts over 1.2 million members, or one of about every six full-time state and local government workers (not counting teachers, who are organized by other unions). Still, the class of state and local government workers is a big group, which is a reason why five of six workers don't join. A *very* narrow interest—say, the three major American auto companies—can produce much higher rates of participation.

Olson's argument became a staple of college political science courses and a pillar of a rising economic literature on what's called "public choice." But Olson wasn't finished. If he was right, what would that mean for a large country like America? He began to think about the ways in which the interest-group dynamic might affect an economy over time. He looked at Europe, and at Japan. The result was his 1982 book *The Rise and Decline of Nations*.

ON A TILT

As Olson pointed out in *The Logic of Collective Action,* organizing a group to seek collective benefits is difficult. Group-forming costs money, takes time, risks failure, and faces an uphill battle against skepticism and apathy. However, one at a time, little by little, over a long period, groups do manage to overcome the obstacles.

Modern trade unions, for instance, didn't appear until almost a century after the Industrial Revolution. Though farmers have plowed the American soil for hundreds of years, farmers' groups didn't appear on a national scale until around World War I, and only in the last fifty years have they really proliferated. Social Security dates back to 1935, but the recipients' main interest group, the American Association of Retired Persons, didn't coalesce until more than twenty years later.

"Organization for collective action takes a good deal of time to emerge," wrote Olson. Having introduced the element of time, he then added another element, that of directionality. Once groups form, they rarely disappear. Rather, "they usually survive until there is a social upheaval or some other form of violence or instability." The two elements combine in a conclusion which Olson italicized: "*Stable societies with unchanged boundaries tend to accumulate more collusions and organizations for collective action over time.*"

In effect, Olson had posited a social field of force. Just as the earth's gravitational field makes it harder to walk uphill than to walk downhill, Olson's directional force points to the emergence of more and more pressure groups in any stable society. Figuratively speaking, society is not on a flat surface, where groups come and go depending only on the politics of the moment; it is on a tilt, so that groups gradually but steadily pile up.

What would be the effect of the piling up of interest groups? To see the answer, you have to look at the economics of what the groups are likely to be doing.

Economic thinkers have recognized for generations that for any one person there are two ways to become wealthier. One is to produce more. The other is to capture more of what others produce. The former is productive activity. The latter is redistributional activity—transfer-seeking, an investment of time or energy in transferring wealth from other people to oneself.

Olson pointed out that no group has much of an incentive to organize with the goal of increasing productivity for the society as a whole. Speaking metaphorically, it pays much better for a group to try to enlarge its share of the pie than to try to make the whole pie bigger. To see why, imagine that you live in a country of a million people. Then imagine a group of a hundred people called the Coalition to Make Ourselves Rich (C-MOR). C-MOR's members make up only one ten-thousandth of the society. If they lobby for a universal job-training program that makes the whole society better off by $1 million, then C-MOR's members will pay the whole cost of their lobbying effort, but they must share their $1 million reward with a million people. Each of C-MOR's members winds up only a dollar better off for his effort—hardly worth the trouble. Now suppose instead that the group organizes for a $1 million tax break focused exclusively on C-MOR itself. This time they split the booty a hundred ways, not a million. That translates into $10,000 per C-MOR member, which is fine boodle. For interest groups, then, the bigger payoff is in redistributing the pie, not growing it.

Suppose people in a group wanted to focus more social resources on themselves. How might they do it? If they were competitors in a market, they might organize a cartel to exclude newcomers and then jack up prices. And, indeed, businesses notoriously do try to do that. However, cartelization is outside the scope of this book, and in any case it has turned out not to be as serious a problem as Americans used to think, partly because the economy has changed. Early in this century, heavy industry called for economies of size, summoning forth corporate giants. Today, flexibility and economies of speed matter more, so that gigantism is often the path to downfall rather than domination. As recently as 1982, International Business Machines Corporation was the target of a massive government antitrust suit, the presumption being that the company's size and power gave it nearly impregnable monopolistic strength. Only ten years later, smaller, nimbler companies were running rings around IBM, and we saw headlines like "IBM Announces Plan to Eliminate 25,000 More Jobs and Shut Some Plants."

Even in a closed market, maintaining a cartel is difficult; bickering and opportunism tend to crack and then destroy cartels in not much time. In today's relatively open world market, which reaches across national boundaries, maintaining a cartel is more difficult still. If cartels organize the domestic market, as some people believed the Big Three automakers were informally doing through the 1970s, their fat profits lure in imports that bust the trust, as Detroit discovered the hard way. In the early 1970s, populists and consumerists regarded General Motors as a domineering titan, a sovereign economic state impervious both to market forces and to the public interest. "If they wanted to wipe out everybody by 1980," one American Motors executive said in 1976, "the only one who could stop them is the government." If so, someone forgot to tell the customers and the Japanese. By 1993, a gasping GM was shutting dozens of plants and laying off workers by the tens of thousands.

There is a second way to organize for redistribution, though. That way is political and substitutes public policy and the strong force of law for private cartels and the weak force of corporate solidarity.

GETTING ORGANIZED

Consider two real-life bicycle couriers in Washington, D.C. Couriers in the District of Columbia are basically independent contractors working for thirty or so little companies—enough competition so it's safe to assume that the couriers' wages are at about the level that the market will bear. That level isn't very high, partly because fax machines are driving messenger services out of business. One courier, who calls himself Suicide, has a plan: organize Washington's messengers and strike for better wages. "If we could have a work stoppage," he told W. Hampton Sides in a *New Republic* article describing couriers' peculiar subculture, "you'd hear it around the world! This city would grind to a halt, man, just completely shut down! They would never fuck with us again." In effect, Suicide's idea is to form a union, or a labor cartel. The collective strike threat would win him and his companions better pay or benefits. On the other hand, courier service would become more expensive, and some customers would switch to fax machines or Federal Express. The end result is likely to be that couriers with jobs will earn higher wages, but fewer new couriers will be hired. Money would be redistributed to the ins at the expense of the outs, with some loss of efficiency along the way. Newcomers lose, Suicide wins.

Unfortunately for him, organizing hundreds or thousands of independent couriers is very difficult, as Mancur Olson showed. Another courier, Scrooge, has a different approach: to raise the prices of the competition and so raise the wages that couriers can command. One way to raise the competition's price, of course, is to get rid of the competition, which is what Scrooge turns out to have in mind. "I'm going to create a [computer] virus that will ruin all the fax machines," he says. "I'm gonna send it out over the phone lines like an epidemic. Then *watch out*. All bike couriers of the world will unite! And we're going to take this country by storm!"

Scrooge's problem is that the mass murder of other people's fax machines is illegal. He will soon figure this out, at which point he may forget about the whole idea. On the other hand, he may not. Rather, he may organize a group, hire a lobbyist, and start a political action committee. For if he can't destroy the fax machines, he can achieve a similar result with a law banning them, or at least restricting their use to long-distance calls, or taxing them heavily, or whatever. Or he can seek a subsidy or tax credit for people who use courier services, diverting business away from fax machines and his other competitors. Or, if he prefers, he can seek a direct subsidy for bicycle couriers, capturing a monopoly claim on a chunk of tax money. All of the above are safe, effective, legal, and as American as apple pie.

In practice, that kind of anticompetitive group action goes on all the time, and has for years. Beginning in 1874, with the introduction of margarine into the United States, the American dairymen found themselves facing a new kind of competition, just as Scrooge has. The dairymen did exactly what Scrooge wants to do. For years, the National Milk Producers Federation made war on margarine, declaring in 1935 that "the oleomargarine problem" was its top priority. The dairymen successfully pressed for taxes on margarine and duties on imported food oils, and for restrictions on the way margarine could be advertised and sold ("Retail packages of oleomargarine must not be over one pound, must bear the words 'oleomargarine' or 'margarine' in type at least as large as any other lettering on the package," and so forth). But that was long ago, you say? In 1991, the dairymen, complaining that milk prices were too low, fought hard but unsuccessfully for a federally enforced, farmer-directed milk cartel. Had they won, a board of dairymen would have been legally empowered to restrict milk supplies and block entry into the dairy business, thus raising milk prices (and hurting consumers, especially poorer ones).

The bicycle couriers or dairymen or whoever may fail at first, but eventually some of them succeed in forming groups and capturing subsidies or anticompetitive rules or other benefits for themselves at the expense of others. True, some groups may seek arrangements that they think benefit society as a whole as well as themselves. Bicycle couriers might argue for road improvements and safety rules. Dairymen might argue for purity standards for milk. But Olson found that, as groups accumulate, they will tend to make society as a whole poorer than it would have been. Remember, the payoff is always higher for a narrow, focused benefit than for a broad, publicly available one. "The great majority of special-interest organizations redistribute income rather than create it, and in ways that reduce social efficiency and output," said Olson. Groups rarely propose "social benefits" that don't also handsomely benefit themselves; I remember fondly how a public-spirited car-alarm manufacturer, concerned about public safety, proposed that alarms be made mandatory in New York City.

As a society becomes more and more dense with networks of interest groups, as the benefits secured by groups accumulate, the economy rigidifies, Olson argued. By locking out competition and locking in subsidies, interest groups capture resources that could be put to better use elsewhere. Entrenched interests tend to slow down the adoption of new technology and ideas by clinging to the status quo, as, for instance, the dairymen did when they fought the advent of margarine. The groups can even slow the pace of innovation: if fax machines are restricted to long-distance service, fax producers will enjoy smaller profits, and their incentives to invest and innovate decline.

Further, as interest groups and their deals pile up, so do laws and regulations and the like, and so, therefore, do the number of people who work the laws and regulations. "When these specialists become significant enough," wrote Olson, "there is even the possibility that the specialists with a vested interest in the complex regulations will collude or lobby against simplification or elimination of the regulation." At last society itself begins to change. "The incentive to produce is diminished; the incentive to seek a larger share of what is produced increases." The very direction of society's evolution may be deflected away from productive activity and toward distributional struggle.

Olson noted one other effect, but only in passing. The accretion of interest groups and the rise of bickering over scarce resources could generate resentment and political turmoil. "The divisiveness of distributional issues," he wrote, "can even make societies ungovernable." Alas, Olson, the economist, left this lead unpursued. It remained a tantalizing hint that government, too, could be a casualty of the process he had described.

DOWN, DOWN, DOWN

Even without venturing into politics, his theory was more than broad enough. Here, if he was right, was a *mechanism* explaining why economies, even whole societies, tend to lose their bloom and then wilt. Instead of relying on ad hoc explanations or clichés, Olson identified a systematic and systemic process which, left unattended, would cause gradual economic sclerosis.

And how far might the process go? Return to the Coalition to Make Ourselves Rich. C-MOR, you recall, represents a ten-thousandth of the population. Now suppose the evidence mounts that C-MOR's small but hard-won tax break makes the society as a whole just a bit poorer. You might suppose that C-MOR would see that its actions were impoverishing the larger society, and would mend its ways. But it probably won't. The reason is that the small group gets all the benefit from its loophole, but it bears only a fraction of the social cost. In fact, if you work out the arithmetic, you discover that it pays for C-MOR to keep seeking perks until the social costs of its goody-hunting are ten thousand times larger than the benefits to the narrow group. The bigger the society, the worse this problem becomes. In a society—like America's—of 250 million people, a group of twenty-five widget makers (a ten-millionth of the population) can continue to earn a profit from new subsidies and benefits until those subsidies and benefits cost society *ten million times* as much as the widget-making group stands to gain.

The arithmetic dictates that groups can hope to reap large gains from their pie-reslicing activity even as that very activity dramatically shrinks the size of the pie. In fact, if a society begins to grow poorer, interest groups may struggle all the more fiercely to expand their own share. The calculus of distributional struggle implies that interest-group activity can, in principle, drive a society to complete destitution, and then keep right on going. At some point, some countervailing force might kick in, but whether that would happen is not at all clear. The Olsonian forces may, in fact, effectively face no natural limit—no point, that is, where interest groups stop being drawn into the benefits-chasing game by visions of profit. Quite possibly, *there is no bottom.*

However, Olson's forces can exert themselves only on one condition: because group-forming is difficult and takes time, the society must be stable enough so that pressure groups have time to form and affix themselves to the body politic. Also, groups need maneuvering room to organize and lobby.

Democracies, of course, guarantee the people's right to form associations and lobby their government. Moreover, democracies tend to be relatively stable. "The logic of the argument," Olson wrote, "implies that countries that have had democratic freedom of organization without upheaval or invasion the longest will suffer the most from growth-repressing organizations and combinations." And so stable democracies are a natural preserve of what Olson pungently called interest-group depredations.

It is not the case that democracies are the only societies that are vulnerable to the Olsonian forces. Stable authoritarian societies also provide happy hunting for pressure groups. In the Philippines, interest groups teamed up with the Marcos regime to rob the country blind; in the Soviet Union, the entrenched industrial barons and state apparatchiks turned the economy into a desert. For that matter, a large private company can turn sclerotic if operating units or management cliques become vested interests—at which point the company either reforms or goes broke and is replaced by a more flexible company. The tendency toward interest-group sclerosis isn't unique to democracy. But, if Olson is right, it is inherent in it.

At last we arrive back at the question that posed itself to Olson during his student days in Europe. Why did Germany thrive economically while Britain wound down? True, Britain was hurt by World War II, but Germany was hurt even more severely. True, a devastated country like Germany should enjoy a spurt of catch-up growth. But that would not explain why the "economic miracle" continued there long after the Germans were fully caught up to their prewar level. Moreover, it seemed unlikely that Germany's boom was a peculiar case, because exactly the same thing had happened a hemisphere away, in Japan.

Perhaps, then, the explanation is this. Occasionally some cataclysmic event—foreign occupation, perhaps, or revolution—might shake a society, sweep away an existing government, and shatter the society's network of interest groups. The old order would be scuttled, and the barnacles would sink with the ship. In the aftermath, the restored economy would be freed from its accumulated burden of protective perks and anticompetitive deals.

Now the theory's darkest implications come into view. "If the argument so far is correct," Olson wrote, "it follows that countries whose distributional coalitions have been emasculated or abolished by totalitarian government or foreign occupation should grow relatively quickly after a free and stable legal order is established." And that is just what happened in Japan and West Germany after the war. In the case of Japan, decades' worth—even centuries' worth—of cozy deals and insider cartels were upset by MacArthur and his occupation forces. As resources were freed from groups that had captured and monopolized them, an "economic miracle" followed. By contrast, Olson noted, Great Britain is "the major nation with the longest immunity from dictatorship, invasion, and revolution." It has also, in this century, "had a lower rate of growth than other large, developed democracies."

Sometimes a slashing fire can rejuvenate a forest by clearing away clots of undergrowth and deadwood. Olson was suggesting that something analogous had happened to Germany and Japan. The fires of cataclysm had cleared away the detritus of stability.

His hypothesis suggested a social cycle. A country emerges from a period of political repression or upheaval into a period of stability and freedom. The country is, at first, relatively unencumbered by interest groups and their anticompetitive deals. If other conditions are favorable, rapid growth ensues. South Korea and Taiwan, both emerging from dictatorship and both growing rapidly, would be in that stage today; China, which grew spectacularly in the 1980s as economic controls were lifted, looks to be next. Gradually, however, interest groups form and attach themselves to the body politic. Each group secures some sort of subsidy or anticompetitive rule. Those benefits accumulate, each jealously defended, and all distorting the economy. Over time, growth slows—as it has done in Japan and Germany in recent years—and anemia sets in.

The idea is difficult to test. Olson and a colleague tried a statistical test comparing forty-eight American states. They looked at the length of time each state had been settled and at each state's rate of economic growth. They found a negative relationship: "the longer a state has been settled and the longer a time it has had to accumulate special-interest groups, the slower its rate of growth." The states of the former Confederacy, which suffered governmental upheaval in the Civil War, enjoyed faster-than-average economic expansion; so did the states of the West, which were comparatively recently settled. The pattern seems to hold also *within* each region; it seems to hold even when other differences between states, even differences in their climates, are taken into account. Among municipalities, the pattern also holds: the most economically troubled cities tend to be the older ones, which often suffer most from fractious interest-group politics, bloated bureaucracies, aging political machines. Think of New York, Philadelphia, Detroit.

Still, such tests are hardly conclusive. Scholars have found more than a few bones to pick with Olson. Too broad, too glib, too fatalistic, too this or too that. And his theory may indeed be all of the above. Like all grand unified theories, his seems to explain rather too much—though, to his credit, Olson has never said that his ideas explain everything that goes on all the time, but only some of what goes on most of the time.

Yet the evidence in his favor—evidence that he is onto something important, even if he isn't entirely right—is becoming harder to wave aside. Twenty years ago, an intelligent observer of politics could have dismissed Olson's ideas, but in today's Washington you need to be a tree frog not to notice hints, traces, even outright demonstrations of Olsonian forces at work. Even more troubling is the evidence of American society itself. Olson's theory coincides eerily well with the most important change in the structure of the American body politic in this century, namely the breathtaking growth of groupism in the last four decades.

3

HYPERPLURALISM

T HERE IS NOTHING even slightly new about groups that form to lobby. In America, the word "lobbyist" goes back to at least the late 1820s. In 1852, the future president James Buchanan wrote that "the host of contractors, speculators, stockjobbers, and lobby members which haunt the halls of Congress . . . are sufficient to alarm every friend of this country." No modern critic of lobbying could do much better than Senator (and, later, Supreme Court Justice) Hugo L. Black, who declared in 1935: "Contrary to tradition, against the public morals, and hostile to good government, the lobby has reached such a position of power that it threatens government itself. Its size, its power, its capacity for evil, its greed, trickery, deception and fraud condemn it to the death it deserves."

Something has changed since Black's day, though. In the old days, if you conjured up an image of a powerful moneyed interest, chances are you would imagine not a group but a man, with a first and last name (the 1850s' most powerful lobbyist was named—really—Thurlow Weed), rather than a five-letter acronym beginning with N and A, for "National Association of." You might imagine a robber-baron industrialist like Cornelius Vanderbilt, who in the mid-1800s led the steamship companies in their fight against the railroads. You might imagine a political kingpin like Tammany Hall's Boss Tweed, whose portly figure is still familiar from Thomas Nast's cartoons. A special interest, back then, was really someone special, someone with great personal power or extraordinary personal connections or an unusual personal following. "Quite simply," the journalist Jeffrey H. Birnbaum has written, "lobbying power resided with people who had personal connections to government."

That was what changed. By the middle of this century, the complexion of lobbying was clearly different, and in a way whose implications we are only now sorting out. In 1950, Representative Frank M. Buchanan of Pennsylvania, who headed a congressional investigation of lobbying, said: "In the 1870s and 1880s, lobbying meant direct, individual solicitation of legislators, with a strong presumption of corruption attached." By contrast, "Modern pressure on legislative bodies is rarely corrupt. . . . It is increasingly indirect, and *largely the product of group rather than individual effort* [italics added]. . . . The printed word is much more extensively used by organizations as a means of pursuing legislative aims than personal contact with legislators by individual lobbyists." The group was displacing the individual, the professional was displacing the amateur, and the groups and professionals were multiplying.

People have noted, and many have bemoaned, the rise of ethnic groupism in America, in which blacks and Hispanics and Asians and women and others separate into groups by gender or skin color or parentage and then demand things. What too many people have missed is that ethnic groupism is merely one part of a much larger pattern. The blacks and Hispanics and Asians and women have just been doing what everyone else has also been doing, namely, organizing into interest groups and making demands. Groupism has exploded, not only along ethnic lines, but along *all* lines.

When people look at the political system and say it works less well than in the past, they naturally assume the reason is that somehow the process has changed. It has. But to focus on process is to troll for the Loch Ness monster with a bamboo rod and a ball of twine. People need to think bigger and deeper. The much more important change is not in the political process but in the American body politic. No society can reorganize itself into benefits-seeking groups and expect to function as it did before. The proliferation and professionalization of interest groups and lobbies over the last three decades—the advocacy explosion, as the political scientist Jeffrey Berry has called it—represents a deep and fundamental change in America's social structure, a change at least rivaling and perhaps surpassing the civil rights revolution in scope and import. Just look at the scale and speed of what has happened.

OUT OF ONE, MANY

In the late 1920s, a congressional investigation found about four hundred lobbies in the Washington phone book; in 1950, Frank Buchanan's congressional commission counted more than two thousand. Though the numbers were small, the growth was impressive. One small milestone was passed in 1920, with the founding of the American Society of Association Executives (motto: "Associations Advance America"). That year, sixty-three associations turned up at the first annual meeting of the new group representing group representatives. A bigger milestone, though unrecognized at the time, came in 1958, with the founding of what is now the largest lobby in America, the American Association of Retired Persons. Starting about then, the growth moved into a higher gear. Only three decades later, a moment arrived when arguably *everyone* had an association in Washington. I refer, of course, to the opening of the Baha'i religion's Washington lobbying office in July 1987, complete with a staff of four and a budget of $400,000—a telling moment, because the Baha'i faith requires its members to abstain from politics. When I peeked through the Baha'is' window one day, the only

Figure 1

GROUPS LISTED IN THE *ENCYCLOPEDIA OF ASSOCIATIONS*

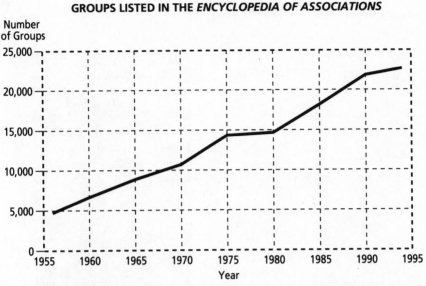

NOTE: Figures prior to 1975 are estimates by the American Society of Association Executives

SOURCES: Gale Research, Inc.; American Society of Association Executives

thing that looked at all remarkable about their Washington office was that it looked exactly like every other Washington office.

Counting groups with any precision is hard, because definitive numbers don't exist, but the numbers of listings in Gale Research Inc.'s *Encyclopedia of Associations* make a good starting point. Those numbers are graphed in Figure 1. In 1956, fewer than five thousand associations were listed. The number had doubled by 1970 and then doubled again by 1990. Over the period 1970 to 1990, an average of about ten new groups were formed every week.

The data suggest a general pattern, though not a universal one. Groups still tended to be relatively sparse until about the time of World War II. Then they started proliferating, and in the 1960s the pace picked up. As a result, a disproportionate number of interest groups arrived on the scene quite recently. For example, a study by Kay Schlozman and John Tierney found that 40 percent of the groups listed in a lobbying direc-

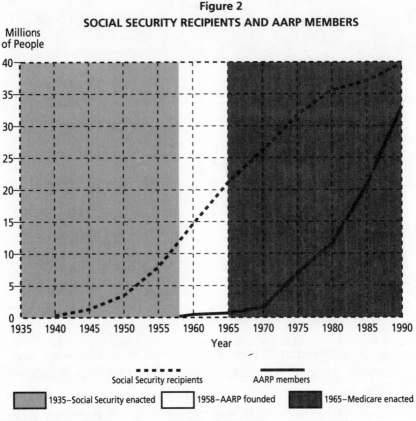

Figure 2
SOCIAL SECURITY RECIPIENTS AND AARP MEMBERS

Millions of People

Year

Social Security recipients   AARP members

1935–Social Security enacted   1958–AARP founded   1965–Medicare enacted

SOURCES: American Association of Retired Persons; Social Security Administration

tory were founded after 1960, and 25 percent after 1970. Those results are typical.

Looking at particular groups serves to confirm the pattern: within particular sectors and interest areas, the big movement toward organizing into groups began about half a century ago and sped up in the last two or three decades. Perhaps most impressive, because of the sheer number of people involved, is the explosion of membership of the American Association of Retired Persons. Figure 2 shows the AARP's membership, along with the total number of Social Security recipients—the AARP's core (though not its sole) constituency. As recently as 1965, the group still had fewer than a million members, which meant that

Figure 3
MEMBERSHIP OF THE AMERICAN FEDERATION
OF STATE, COUNTY AND MUNICIPAL EMPLOYEES

SOURCE: AFSCME

only one in thirty Social Security beneficiaries had actually joined. That was as one would expect: banding together takes time. But once the ball starts rolling, watch out. In the 1970s, the elderly began joining with a vengeance; between 1980 and 1990 alone, the group tripled its membership. By the early 1990s, the AARP's membership accounted for the vast majority of Social Security recipients; the organization's headquarters in Washington had grown so large as to have its own ZIP code, a legislative and policy staff of 125 people, and sixteen registered lobbyists with a $3.5 million budget.

The AARP's story is not special; it is typical. The American Federation of State, County and Municipal Employees was founded in 1936, growing out of the Wisconsin State Employees Association. Its membership, charted in Figure 3, shows the familiar pattern, though the big spurt begins earlier than for

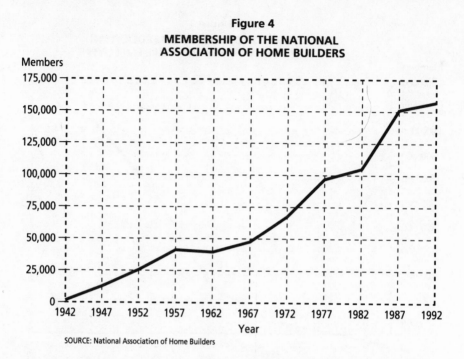

Figure 4
MEMBERSHIP OF THE NATIONAL
ASSOCIATION OF HOME BUILDERS

SOURCE: National Association of Home Builders

some other groups. In 1955, the group had organized only about one in twenty-five of its potential members; by 1975, it had organized more than one in eight.

A business group? Same pattern. Figure 4 shows the membership of the National Association of Home Builders. The group was born in 1942, it grew steadily for twenty years, and then the membership more than tripled from 1967 to 1987.

Or look at the aforementioned American Society of Association Executives, the association of people who run associations. Its membership roster lists individuals rather than groups, and so the numbers don't tell you how many groups there are. But when you look at Figure 5, you won't be surprised by the pattern. Since its founding in 1920, the group grew steadily through the 1960s and then really took off after that, with membership increasing sixfold from 1970 to 1990.

As groups became bigger and more numerous, they also, not surprisingly, started taking up a bigger share of economic

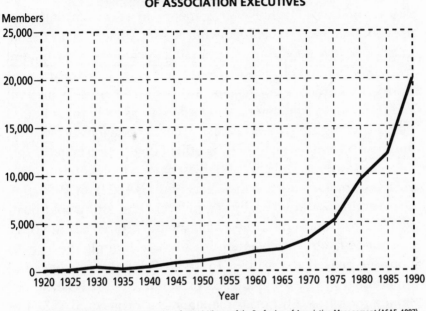

Figure 5
MEMBERSHIP OF THE AMERICAN SOCIETY
OF ASSOCIATION EXECUTIVES

SOURCES: ASAE; Sam Shapiro, *A Coming of Age: A History of the Profession of Association Management* (ASAE, 1987)

space. They became million-dollar businesses. According to membership surveys conducted in selected years by the American Society of Association Executives, in 1946 fewer than 25 percent of groups had budgets of more than $500,000 (in constant 1985 dollars); by 1985, two-thirds of them did.

These groups represent every conceivable collective interest. There is the Association of Old Crows (for veterans of the counterintelligence community); the National Paint Varnish and Lacquer Association; the Possum Growers and Breeders Association; the American Association of Sex Educators, Counselors and Therapists; the Bow Tie Manufacturers Association; the Association of Metropolitan Sewerage Agencies; the association of this and the association of that. They also do every conceivable kind of thing, including, but not limited to, educating, licensing, confabbing, holding contests, setting standards, certifying tournaments, collecting for charities, selling goods and services, wearing silly hats, giving themselves awards. When they start out, they may or may not intend to get involved in politics. Sooner or later, however, someone in a group usually figures out that it would be worthwhile to seek what Mancur Olson calls a collective good: some benefit that the members can obtain from nonmembers by lobbying and agitating as a group.

Agricultural groups began as distributors of information and technology to farmers, and ended up as lobbyists for subsidies. Civil rights groups began by seeking equal justice under the law, and ended up defending affirmative-action benefits for their constituents. In 1967, a hobbyist named Ray Scott founded the Bass Anglers Sportsman Society (yes, "BASS"); by 1990, the membership was approaching a million. The group sold boat owner's insurance, published a magazine, offered fishing tips, sanctioned fishing tournaments. And, sure enough, the lure of lobbying proved irresistible. In 1989, Scott personally (and, apparently, successfully) lobbied President George Bush about money for various fisheries management projects; BASS also lobbies on water-quality issues and files class-action lawsuits against polluters.

For the benefit of offended group members, I'll happily agree that groups do many good things. But that's the subject of some other book. For this book, the main point is that sooner or later every group becomes a pressure group, at least on some issues and some of the time. After all, if you have a rifle, why not hunt? And if you have a membership list and a staff and a budget, why not lobby?

WHOSE INTEREST IS SPECIAL?

As industries and trades and companies organized, reformers and activists and miscellaneous aggrieved citizens inevitably followed suit. What is astonishing is not that public-interest organizations and grass-roots pressure groups formed, but how quickly they did so. With the help of tax breaks and of the general perception that these were good people trying to make society better, public-interest groups have proliferated startlingly in the last twenty-five years or so.

Indeed, in that brief time they transformed the political landscape. A typical study in 1985 found that fully two-thirds of 250 major public-interest groups had been organized since 1968. By the early 1990s, environmental groups alone numbered an estimated seven thousand. Meanwhile, the older public-interest groups grew. For example, from the early 1970s to 1990, the Natural Resources Defense Council's membership tripled; the Environmental Defense Fund's more than quintupled; the Sierra Club's septupled; the National Audubon Society's almost octupled—and so on.

On the surface, public-interest groups may seem to break Olson's paradigm of collective action, in which groups pursue benefits for themselves while paying scant attention to the costs imposed on society as a whole. After all, the whole raison d'être of environmental groups and peace groups and consumer groups and antigovernment groups is to change society as a whole, supposedly for the benefit of all. Ostensibly, public-interest groups are outward-looking, seeking to reform the whole country or even the whole world, rather than inward-looking, seeking to suck in benefits for themselves.

In fact, though, public-interest groups don't break the paradigm; they merely enrich it. For one thing, they do rather well for themselves and have a strong interest in staying in business, just as other groups do. "Many of the so-called Big Ten environmental groups are multimillion-dollar corporations," reports the *National Journal;* the National Wildlife Federation boasted 5.3 million members and $77 million in revenues in 1991, and its president occupied plush headquarters and earned $300,000 in pay and benefits. The people who staff these groups may work for less than they might earn at *Fortune* 500 companies, but they aren't necessarily selfless servants of the public good. They run business enterprises in the interest-group sector.

More fundamentally, these groups are just as dedicated to transferring resources as any other group is. When they lobby, they want society to divert more resources to some activity that they like, and away from some activity that they don't like. They are out to get something they value, and what they want will cost someone else time or money, or they wouldn't need a law to get it. AIDS activists believe that AIDS research is more important than defense spending or low corporate taxes; they, no less than defense contractors and tax lobbyists, seek to redistribute social resources so as to get more of what they value. Environmental groups that advocate preserving spotted owls or old-growth forests value endangered species and ancient trees more than inexpensive timber, a preference which some home-buyers and logging towns might not share. In Tucson not long ago, an advocacy group called the Arizona Center for Law in the Public Interest announced the following antismog agenda: "We're going to take the position that the EPA cut off all funding to any capacity-enhancing roadway project." In its members' minds, this group was a crusader for the public good. But to people who don't share the rather idiosyncratic belief that tying up traffic is a good way to fight smog, the center was a pressure group pursuing its agenda at considerable expense to the general public.

It's completely legitimate for groups to say, and believe, that they serve a broader public interest. The reason we have a political system is to determine whose claim is in the public interest and whose isn't. The point is not that self-styled public-interest groups are necessarily more self-serving than, say, the National Association of Manufacturers or the National Association of Truck Stop Operators—just that they are not necessarily any less so. It all depends on where you sit.

Moreover, the coin flips: the corporate lobbies that pursue profits and the narrow groups that chase subsidies neither admit nor, usually, believe that they're crassly hunting money. Automakers that lobby against environmentalists see themselves as saving jobs threatened by unreasonable demands. Textile companies that seek import barriers see themselves as protecting low-wage workers and strengthening a vital American industry. Pharmaceutical companies lobby to "make us healthier," real-estate interests lobby to "make housing more affordable," agribusiness lobbies to "preserve America's food-production base," and on and on.

Even in principle, the line between public-spiritedness and pursuit of private gain is subjective. One person's public-spirited crusader for environmental sanity or entrepreneurial freedom is another's job-destroying Luddite or selfish tycoon. Garment workers' unions long defended federal regulations forbidding people from doing commercial sewing at home. You could say they were fighting to prevent a resurgence of exploitive sweatshops, or that they were trying to throw their non-union competition out of work. Take your pick.

The fact is that all groups, without exception, claim to be serving some larger good, and almost all believe it. And all groups, without exception, are lobbying for more of whatever it is that their members want, generally at some expense to non-members. By the same token, every single law, regulation, subsidy, and program creates losers as well as winners, and whether you think justice is served depends on who pays when the bill arrives.

Because the point of this book is to look at the game as a whole, and not to cheer for any particular player, I'm going to make an intellectual move that may make some people uncomfortable. Instead of taking any particular viewpoint about justice or fairness, I'm going to treat all interest groups as morally interchangeable players in a giant game. From that point of view, AIDS-research lobbies fit within the same conceptual framework as pharmaceutical lobbies, and gun lobbies are very like environmental lobbies. I like some lobbies, you like others, but never mind. They are all playing by the same rules in the same game. None is really special.

GROUPS "R" US

That's one reason I renounce calling the groups "special interests." Another is that the "special interest" label is three decades out of date. Groups are interested, yes; often narrow, certainly. But the fact is that today seven out of ten Americans belong to at least one association (according to a 1990 survey conducted for the American Society of Association Executives), and one in four Americans belongs to four or more. Further, many of these group members have no illusions about what their own and other people's organizations are doing: in the 1990 survey, half of the respondents said that the main function of most associations is to influence the government. And so we're kidding ourselves if we pretend there is anything special about either interest groups or their members. Almost every American who reads these words is a member of a lobby. "They" are, in fact, us—you and me.

Our groups have overrun Washington, covering it and inhabiting every cranny of it. You can see the result by walking into any office building in the city and reading the directory. I tried this myself, using the highly scientific random-sampling procedure of going into the first building I saw when I walked out the front door. The directory of this modest-sized building boasted:

> Advertising Council
> Affiliated Hotels and Resorts
> Agudath Israel of America
> American Arbitration Association
> American Federation of Clinical Research
> Americans for Economic Renewal
> Center for the Advancement of Health
> Congress of Russian Americans
> Consortium for the Study of Intelligence

And that was just through the Cs; keep reading and you came to such delectables as the Institute of Chemical Waste Management, the Hispanic Association on Corporate Responsibility, the National Coalition to Prevent Impaired Driving, and the U.S. Cane Sugar Refiners' Association.

"It's to the point where there are so many causes organized in this way that there's very little space left," says Senator Richard Lugar, a Republican of Indiana. Day after day, groups stream in and out of his office, all asking to be seen, more and more of them every year. Lugar, scrambling to see them all, compares himself to an overbooked dentist jumping from chair to chair.

"We have developed enormous skills in this country of organizing for the status quo," Lugar said in a 1992 speech. "Anyone who doubts this need only take a look at the people coming into my office on a normal Tuesday and Wednesday. Almost every organization in our society has a national conference. The typical way of handling this is to come in on a Monday, rev up the troops, give them the bill number, and send them up to the Hill on Tuesday. If they can't get in on Tuesday, strike again on Wednesday.

"I have regularly on Tuesday as many as fifteen constituent groups from Indiana, all of whom have been revved up by some skillful person, employed for that purpose in Washington, to cite bills that they don't understand, have never heard of prior to that time, but with a scoresheet to report back to headquarters, whether I am for or against. It is so routine, it is so fierce, it goes on every week every year, that, you know, at some point you [can't be] immune to it. You try to be responsive. These people don't realize what they're doing, how they're being used, or even what the implications are of what they want."

The old era of lobbying by "special interests" is as dead as slavery and Prohibition. Where influence peddling was once the province of the privileged, it is now everyone's game. We Americans have achieved the full democratization of the special-interest deal: influence peddling for the masses.

Why so much groupism, so quickly? Cultural theorists could spin out a dozen plausible theories, and some of those would be at least partially right. Some analysts point to the increasing size and complexity of American society. The country's population has doubled since FDR's first year in office, and perhaps people form groups in order to carve out communities amid growing diversity. Also, new technology breeds new activities and new puzzles, and people band together in response. Genetic-engineering associations didn't exist in 1970, and the reason is obvious.

There are many more explanations of that kind. Yet it's a mistake, when dealing with human beings, to overlook crass, material explanations. Like the bank robber Willie Sutton, Americans look for cash where the money is. If the costs of a certain kind of activity fall over time, and if the potential benefits grow, then you expect more people to engage in it. And that is what has happened with group-forming.

YOU CAN AFFORD ONE

First, the costs. Mancur Olson's work shows that anyone who wants to organize a group not only is likely to be met with apathy from many potential beneficiaries, but also can count on investing some of his own time and money. That's why a group doesn't automatically appear wherever someone thinks it should. However, organizing costs have fallen. In 1920, if you wanted to round up ten thousand people, you had your work cut out for you. You would have needed to print and mail thousands of letters, make hundreds of phone calls at expensive rates, travel hither and yon by car on dirt roads, and gather followers one at a time. Today, if you want to round up ten thousand people you can do a lot of the work from your living room, with a fax machine, a phone, a copier, and a modem. You can travel by air, exchange money in seconds, and join a computer network, all within a modest budget.

More important still, in 1920 you were more or less on your own, making up a strategy as you went along. You had few examples to look at and few neighbors who could advise you. Today you can instantly tap into a whole infrastructure of group-forming know-how. You can hire consultants to run a direct-mail campaign, you can buy mailing lists, you can consult by phone with any of thousands of associations already in the business, you can hire any of thousands of experienced professionals who float from one interest group to another. Liberal public-interest groups can visit the Advocacy Institute, which "provides training in advocacy skills, such as long-range strategy planning, coalition-building, media advocacy, and advocacy uses of new communications technologies to a variety of citizen groups at the local, state, and national levels from around the world." Environmentalists can check in with the Whetstone Project, whose business is "to provide technical assistance to grass-roots organizations and to develop new methods of holding corporations accountable." What should be your group's tax status? How should it advertise? How much should it spend? Should it incorporate? Should it lobby directly? What about direct mail? Is there a market for its cause? What exactly should the cause be? Lawyers, lobbyists, accountants, consultants, market researchers, public-relations people, and many more all stand ready to tell you anything you need to know.

The techniques of lobbying have been codified, boiled down, and made handy for ready reference. You can buy *The Lobbying Handbook,* by John L. Zorack. ("The best way to learn the legislative process is to get a job in the United States Congress." "Helping to raise money for Members of Congress is part of the 'softening-up' process that paves the way for successful lobbying." Yours for only $125.) You can get a copy of Stanley J. Marcuss's *Effective Washington Representation.* If you're a scientist, you can get *Working with Con-*

gress: A Practical Guide for Scientists and Engineers, by William G. Wells, Jr., from the American Association for the Advancement of Science. ("Keep your message simple, focused, and short." "Remember that telephone calls based on 'outrage' and 'demands' don't go over well.") You can buy a thousand other books, magazines, newsletters, software programs, and there are more all the time.

Finally, your job will be a lot easier than it used to be because you usually won't have to start from scratch. Rather, you can stand on the shoulders of existing groups. Compared to organizing individuals into an interest group, organizing groups into an interest group is fairly easy. A 1992 *Wall Street Journal* article told a typical tale. In 1987, a forty-year-old Minnesota farm activist named Mark Ritchie became fascinated with the global trade talks. An experienced activist who had organized food co-ops and a corporate boycott, Ritchie began arguing his case in meetings with environmentalists and foundations, and in 1990 pulled down a $50,000 grant from a Unitarian Church environmental charity. With that money, he hired a veteran environmental organizer, and their Citizen Trade Campaign was launched. Labor groups signed on, followed by populist farm groups, environmental groups, religious groups, and animal-rights groups. Just a few months later, the coalition came within thirty-nine votes of defeating President Bush's request for authority to negotiate a trade pact with Mexico and Canada in 1991. An activist like Mark Ritchie could hardly hope to form a group of thousands of individuals so quickly on his own. Instead, he linked existing interest groups. Other things being equal, then, groups help breed groups.

As information moves more quickly and cheaply, as ever more of it is prepackaged by professionals, as new groups form to serve as networkers and facilitators, the cost of group-forming falls. In some ways, that's good: the bigger America becomes, the more important it is for people to stay in touch with each other and find friends in distant places. But in other ways the change is problematic. "A single person with access to the right mailing lists," writes the journalist Robert Wright, "can send solicitation letters to tens of thousands of Americans and, with the money thus reaped, mold this inchoate group into a force to be reckoned with." An entrepreneur, a mailing list, a computer, a bit of cash—another interest group is up and lobbying.

Today, grass-roots organizing is as sophisticated as any business going. The National Association of Home Builders has put together a political manual explaining how to run a telephone bank and a house-to-house canvassing campaign, how to organize "victory caravans" to transport political volunteers, and so on. When Congress considered raising milk-price supports, it heard from thousands of worried managers of fast-food restaurants who were quickly mobilized by their trade association's "action alert" newsletter. With the help of computers, mobilization is now practically instantaneous. In 1993, for instance, the U.S. Chamber of Commerce set up a computer system that could patch through calls and faxes to members of Congress from a ready pool of about fifty thousand volunteers. ("People on the Hill are getting tired of hearing from old Washington insiders like us," said one Chamber official.) Computer-assisted groups can inundate congressional offices with carefully targeted mail, and do; since the early 1970s, the volume of mail received by the U.S. House of Representatives has roughly quintupled.

Back when lobbying was a game for tycoons and giant companies, you had to have deep pockets to invest. Now, with the electorate sliced, diced, and presorted by ZIP code, it's easy to find an interest group, if one doesn't find you first. Much as mutual funds have offered ordinary people access to almost every kind of productive investment, so interest groups have offered ordinary people access to almost every kind of redistributive investment. Want to invest in rare-metals futures? It's as easy as finding a mutual fund and writing a check. Want to invest in lobbying for government benefits? It's as easy as finding an interest group and writing a check.

What Olson said is still true: you need to put up time and money if you want to organize an interest group or invest in one. But the investment becomes less daunting every year.

TOO SWEET TO RESIST

To the reduced costs that make interest-group activity more accessible, now add the higher benefits that make it more attractive. Never before has organizing groups to lobby for benefits been as potentially lucrative as it is today; never have the sums available been as large or the paths to them as plentiful.

In 1929, the United States government's entire budget occupied 3 percent of the American economy. Even through the 1930s, when the economy was shrinking and the New Deal was in full flower, government still took up only around 10 percent of the economy, on average. This 10 percent was a notable slice of the pie, but you could still ignore it and occupy yourself with the other 90 percent without too much risk. Republicans often charge Franklin Roosevelt with turning government into a swollen monster, but only after FDR was dead did the stakes in Washington become so large that no sensible person could ignore the game.

Many objective measures—the numbers and length of laws, of regulations, of court decisions—suggest that the big jump in the level of federal activism came in the Johnson and Nixon years, around the same time as the rate of group formation took off. Starting in the mid-1960s, government was seeking to do more things for more people and groups than ever before. "In the Progressive Era early in this century," writes Robert C. Clark, the dean of Harvard Law School, "there were five new federal statutes enacted in the area of health and consumer safety; in the New Deal period, there were eleven; during the

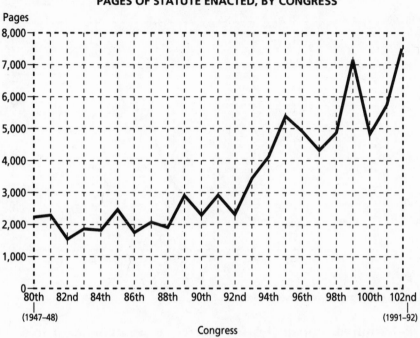

Figure 6
PAGES OF STATUTE ENACTED, BY CONGRESS

SOURCE: Norman J. Ornstein, Thomas E. Mann, and Michael J. Malbin, *Vital Statistics on Congress, 1993–94* (Congressional Quarterly, Inc., 1993)

period from 1964 to 1979 (the 'third wave,' as it might be called), there were sixty-two." He notes that the same pattern holds in other areas of federal activity, such as energy and the environment.

As Figure 6 shows, before the early 1970s the number of pages of bills enacted by each Congress averaged a bit more than two thousand. Then it jumped up to an average of five thousand pages. (And Ronald Reagan's antigovernment presidency didn't change that a bit.) The annual page count of the *Federal Register,* where new regulations are printed, drifted gradually upward from Truman's day until about 1970. Then, in the space of only about five years, it tripled, remaining in the higher range ever since, as Figure 7 shows. Between 1960 and 1985, the page count of new federal court decisions in the West

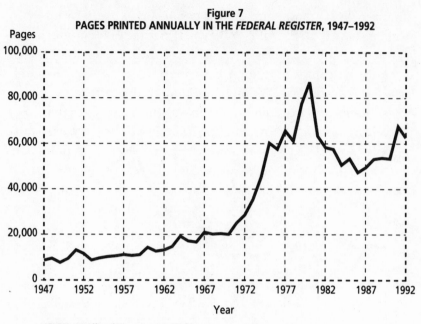

Figure 7
PAGES PRINTED ANNUALLY IN THE *FEDERAL REGISTER*, 1947–1992

SOURCE: U.S. Office of Management and Budget

Publishing Company's case reporters more than quadrupled.
And so forth.

Today, the federal government's budget runs to a sum
equivalent to almost a quarter of the entire American economy.
To the direct spending must be added thousands of laws and
regulations that redirect private money, time, and energy. Regulations now cost Americans, economists estimate, several hundred billion dollars a year, or several thousand dollars per
American household per year.

Whether you think those amounts are too much or too little
depends on how much of the bill you pay and whether you feel
you get your money's worth. But what is not seriously in question is that the sums being moved around in Washington—
through the budget plus regulations—are now much too large
to ignore. They are more than large enough to ensure that
everyone has a major stake in at least breaking even when the
chips are divided in Washington. Everyone needs a vigilant

agent in the capital, and anyone can hope to profit by lobbying well. As one lobbyist told Jeffrey Birnbaum, "The modern government is huge, pervasive, intrusive into everybody's life. If you just let things take their course and don't get in the game, you get trampled on. You ignore it at your peril."

The point is not that government's heightened activism is a bad thing, as such. Government has been doing more because people have called on it to solve their problems, and politicians are eager to help. The point, rather, is that the more actively and ambitiously government moves resources around, the more can be gained by forming a group and lobbying for a bigger share, and so the stronger the incentive to do it. There is no way out of that dilemma; the bad comes with the good. Indeed, a built-in side effect of new government programs is their tendency to summon into being new constituencies— which, in turn, often lobby for yet other new programs, keeping the whole cycle going.

Fifty years ago, the elderly were a demographic category. Today they are a lobby. Why the transformation? As an anti-poverty program for the elderly, Social Security was resoundingly successful, but its side effect—and, later, Medicare's—was to create an irresistible reason for the elderly to form an interest group. Before 1935, the government wasn't giving much to the aged, it wasn't taking much from them, so why lobby? But after Social Security and Medicare were in full swing, the elderly had so much at stake in Washington that they would have been crazy not to have organized, both to protect "their" programs and to agitate for new benefits (long-term care, for instance).

In 1920, four farm groups ran offices in Washington: the National Farmers Council, the National Board of Farm Organizations, the National Grange of Patrons of Husbandry, and the American Farm Bureau Federation. On May 12, 1933, President Roosevelt opened the era of modern farm politics by signing the Agricultural Adjustment Act, which was soon followed by the Agricultural Adjustment Act Amendments of 1935, the

Soil Conservation and Domestic Allotment Act of 1936, and the Agricultural Adjustment Act of 1938. Farmers now had programs to defend. By the late 1950s, groups had sprung up to represent growers of each subsidized crop—the National Cotton Council in 1938, the National Peanut Council in 1941, the National Association of Wheat Growers in 1950, the National Corn Growers Association in 1957, and so forth. Today American agriculture fundamentally *is* a collection of groups, organized around federal programs. By extension, if American society is increasingly organized as a collection of groups, that must be at least partly because American government is organized as a collection of constituency-based programs.

TOO MUCH OF A GOOD THING

The point of all this isn't to argue for or against Medicare or corn subsidies or whatever. Rather, it's to look at the interest-group sector as one might any other industry. If the potential rewards of group-forming increase, and if the average costs of group-forming decrease, you don't have to be Einstein to see that the likely result will be more and bigger groups.

No wonder, then, that the groups have grown and multiplied. The interest-group industry pays rising returns on investment and enjoys falling costs; its potential base of investors includes nearly the whole adult population, creating a practically unlimited pool of capital; its technological base grows ever more sophisticated; it is supported and staffed by an expanding infrastructure of professionals who know the business. From an economic point of view, the American interest-group sector is a classic growth industry, rather like the American automobile industry of half a century ago.

Well, so what? Maybe more groups are better. At a party in Washington not long ago, I ran into a youngish journalist who works for a prominent liberal magazine. We got to talking about the way federal programs tend to be taken over by the people who can hire the slickest lobbyists with the shiniest Gucci shoes. He agreed with me that it's a problem. But when I suggested it's a fundamental problem, he demurred. On the contrary: the way to deal with the plague of corporate lobbyists is to organize more citizens' groups and public-interest groups to fight them, on the model of Ralph Nader's far-flung organization. I suppressed the urge to roll my eyes. "After twenty years of that," I said, "haven't we learned anything? All you get is an escalating spiral where groups breed more groups, and the system gradually chokes."

He saw the postwar explosion of groups as a flowering of citizen activism that helps to perfect democracy. I saw it as a burgeoning of pressure-group entrepreneurship that seeks to exploit democracy. I thought he had his head in the sand. He thought I was a defeatist, or maybe a corporate stooge. In any case, our argument represented a clash between two views of how America is working. He was talking about pluralism. I was talking about hyperpluralism.

In the political science theories of the 1950s and '60s, pluralism dominated. The idea was that in a democracy it's only natural for people to form groups, which will compete and negotiate in order to create a reasonably good approximation of what's good for the whole society. If some group becomes disproportionately powerful, or begins to abuse its power, an opposing group will form, and the system will be tugged back toward balance. More groups will involve more citizens and interests, thus counteracting the influence of narrow groups and powerful insiders. The more groups, the merrier.

In the 1970s, the pluralist model began to fall apart. For one thing, it was empirically wrong: often, countervailing groups did *not* spring up against narrow interests, because, as Olson showed, narrow interests enjoyed stronger incentives to organize and an easier time getting together. There would be no point trying to form a national organization merely to get rid of subsidies for beekeepers.

Moreover, it turns out that not everyone is equally likely to join groups. The educated are much likelier to be joiners than the illiterate, the rich are likelier to join than the poor. A 1990 survey for the American Society of Association Executives found that people with college educations are more than twice as likely as the less-educated to join four or more associations; and the less-educated are twice as likely as the college-educated to join no group at all. Groups, apparently, are skewed toward privilege. Environmental groups' members, for example, tend to have above-average incomes. "Readers of *Sierra,* the magazine of the Sierra Club, have household incomes twice that of the average American," noted Terry L. Anderson in *The New York Times.* "Environmental magazines are more likely to feature Rolex and BMW than Timex and Volkswagen advertisements." When such groups lobby for emissions controls or pesticide rules that raise the prices of cars and groceries, they may be reflecting the preferences of people who buy Volvos and Brie more than the preferences of people who buy used Chevies and hamburger. Moreover, the people at the very bottom—the downtrodden and the excluded—tend to be the hardest of all to organize; people foraging for food in Dumpsters don't write $20 checks to associations in Washington. It wasn't at all clear, then, that group bargaining would produce fair or even representative outcomes.

Most important, there was growing concern about the side effects of groupism itself. Consider an economic analogy.

In economics, inflation is a gradual increase in the level of prices. It's usually a more or less stable rate of increase, so people can plan around it. But if the inflation rate starts to speed up, people start expecting more inflation. They hoard goods and dump cash, driving the inflation still faster. Eventually an invisible threshold is crossed: the inflation now feeds on its own growth and undermines the stability of the whole system. That is hyperinflation, the most dangerous and destabilizing of all economic pathologies. When hyperinflation sets in, the economic system begins to defeat the very purpose for which it exists, namely to provide a stable market where people can trade and invest dependably. The economy enters crisis, confidence in it plummets, capital flees, government itself may collapse.

Suppose something similar happens with groups. More groups demand more benefits, more benefits spawn more groups. As the group-forming process picks up speed, an invisible threshold might be crossed. At some point, there might be so many groups, and so many more groups forming every year, that they would begin to choke the system that bred them, to undermine confidence in politics, even to erode political stability. The system might begin to defeat the purpose for which it exists, namely, to make reasonable social decisions reasonably quickly. That would be what James A. Thurber, a political scientist at the American University, calls hyperpluralism.

In his view, America is now there. "I think we have reached a threshold of so much competition among the groups for scarce resources," he says, "that we've reached a level of deadlock and crisis."

NO RETREAT

Perversely, from today's vantage point the age of the smoke-filled room, when lobbying was a game for the well-heeled and well-connected few, turns out to have had its strong points. In those days, the transfer-seeking game was exclusive, which meant that many people and interests were effectively shut out. But the very fact of its exclusivity meant that it was relatively small; by today's standards, it involved few people and modest sums of money. That game was shady, but at least it was fairly inexpensive. It was controlled by old boys in patent-leather shoes and silk hats, but at least it was under control.

However, there's no point hankering for political bosses and robber barons and smoke-filled rooms. A politics which excludes all but the privileged and the connected is repugnant, and a shady game, however small, is still shady. Say what you like about the corporate lobbies or public-interest groups whose work you find distasteful, they operate more or less in the sunshine according to fairly regular rules, and their combination of openness and inclusiveness (practically everyone is spoken for by somebody) has made American politics among the world's cleanest. Japan has held to the smoke-filled-room model straight through the postwar period, with the result that a parade of corruption scandals has brought down one government after another. In any case, there is no repealing the group proliferation and the enriched stakes which have turned redistributional politics into a popular, rather than an elite, sport. Having changed, American society won't change back and shouldn't.

The trouble is that the change from the smoke-filled room to the mass-membership lobby has created a set of problems which Americans have not even begun to learn how to manage. By the standards of a country more than two centuries old, hyperpluralism is brand-new. Experts in universities, to say nothing of the general public, have only recently begun to take a hard look at what's going on. In Franklin Roosevelt's day or even Lyndon Johnson's, social reformers took the structure of American society more or less as a given, and built groups and programs upon it. Hardly anyone foresaw that the democratization of interest-group politicking might work to transform society itself into a collection of interest groups—and do so at an accelerating rate. Even today, few Americans have reckoned the extent of the change, much less revamped their thinking to accommodate it.

In fact, the standard kind of political thinking makes matters worse, not better. Liberals and conservatives still think they can bring the interest-group spiral under control if they can just beat the groups on the other side. Liberals, like the journalist I met at the party, want to beat corporate lobbyists and the religious right; conservatives want to beat environmental activists and unions. What few on either side have figured out is that they are all trapped together in a self-defeating mind-set. Their mind-set might have made sense fifty or a hundred years ago, when the smoke-filled room was small enough so that you could hope to push your enemies out and slam the door, but it is useless today, when there is no smoke-filled room and there is no door. The more you try to beat the other guy, the more the game expands.

And it does expand. Growing seems to be what it does best. I mentioned that the benefits-hunting industry—the transfer-seeking sector—resembles the auto industry of decades ago. So it does, but with a difference. The automotive industry grows until additional cars become superfluous, at which point profits vanish and investment shifts to other sectors. The transfer-seeking industry appears to be able to generate profits simply by growing. The auto industry grows like bone or muscle. The transfer-seeking industry appears to grow more like cancer. To understand why, it's necessary to look at the curious dynamic of the parasite economy.

4

THE
PARASITE ECONOMY

L IKE MOST OF THE LAWYERS in Washington, Mike LaPlaca
lobbies. Like a few of them, he wishes he didn't. In 1972,
he was a businessman, working in the productive economy. By 1992, when I met him, he was a lobbyist, working in the
parasite economy. It had sucked him in, just as it has sucked in
thousands of other people. His career was, in that respect, a
microcosmic version of America's recent experience.

In 1972, LaPlaca was national sales manager for the Hertz
car-rental company. After the constant traveling gave him
health problems, he decided to leave business. Having picked
up a law degree along the way, he moved back home—to Washington, D.C.—and opened a legal practice, emphasizing, naturally enough, franchise law and car-rental companies. He went
on about his business until 1989. Then a Republican member of
Congress, Lynn Martin (later a secretary of labor), introduced
an obscure piece of legislation involving collision-damage waivers. It changed Mike LaPlaca's life.

A collision-damage waiver, as many car renters know, gets
you off the hook for damage to your rental car. The waivers are
a profit-maker for rental companies and are often convenient
for renters, who no longer need to worry about being stuck with

a big bill if the car crashes. The trouble was that some car-rental companies were pushing collision-damage waivers at customers who, for one reason or another, didn't really need them. Consumer groups, using the sledgehammer logic of political activism, declared that if collision-damage waivers were sometimes being sold misleadingly, then they ought to be banned altogether.

Who, then, would pay for damage to rental cars? That's easy, said the activists: the car-rental company. The consumer rents the car, the business pays for any damage to the car. No customer liability, no problem. The upshot was a bill that said: "No rental company shall . . . hold any authorized driver liable for any damage," except in a few specially defined cases, like drunken driving. Did you drive your rented car into a tree? Did you leave the keys in it so that it got stolen? Not to worry: the rental-car company would have to fix or replace the car. This was a textbook bit of legislative cost-shifting: car-repair costs would be shifted from consumers to businesses.

One obvious result of such a bill would be to make people less careful about their driving. Renters would damage more cars (who cares? The rental company will pay); costs would go up throughout the whole system. But another result was more subtle and interesting, and explained why the two industry giants, Hertz and Avis, both threw their weight behind the liability bill.

A cost increase doesn't necessarily affect all companies the same way. The costs of fixing and replacing damaged cars are relatively easy for a huge company, like Hertz or Avis, to absorb. But small rental companies don't have a lot of cash. To keep afloat, they rely on their cars' coming back safely and then going back out the door. If you're a small operator with only a handful of cars, you're in trouble when you have to write a few checks to replace $16,000 cars.

Suddenly Mike LaPlaca's legal clients were looking at a law that they believed would drive up their relative costs. "What the bill does if it becomes law," LaPlaca said, "is to put enormous pressure on smaller companies to raise their prices." In New York State, where a similar law had passed, dozens of little car-rental companies, with names like Ugly Duckling and No Problem Rent-a-Car, went bust. "Only large companies with thousand-car fleets can absorb such loss expenses," wrote the owner of a Budget Rent-a-Car franchise in California. "We could go out of business with just a few major losses." The fact that the two biggest companies, Hertz and Avis, were strongly supporting the bill only confirmed the smaller companies' belief that they were under attack. A classic distributional struggle—consumer activists and big companies on one side, small and midsized companies on the other—was now under way.

When people believe that their interests are under attack, they band together to form an interest group. In 1989, shortly after the liability bill was first introduced, Mike LaPlaca organized a coalition of car-rental companies to fight the liability bill.

Until 1989, small and midsized car-rental businesses had never maintained much of a presence in Washington, because Washington had never paid the industry much attention. The rental-car business was one of the least regulated transportation industries, and for many decades it functioned well. But by the time I met LaPlaca, things had changed. The Car Rental Coalition and its member companies had spent roughly $1 million retaining five lobbyists or lobbying firms—a figure that did not count time donated by hundreds of executives and workers in the car-rental business (or, of course, the money spent by their opponents).

More: if an interest group wants to enjoy clout with politicians, it has to give them a reason to pay attention. The Car Rental Coalition created such a reason in 1992 by forming a political action committee, or PAC. Like all PACs, theirs invested in friendly politicians rather than in new jobs or factories. "We were making contributions literally minutes before the election," LaPlaca said.

The coalition managed to stave off the liability bill in two Congresses, but it could never know when its enemies would try again. In Washington, if you don't keep your eyes open you can wake up one morning and discover that your livelihood is illegal. So, once you have invested in bringing an interest group to life, you will probably want to keep it alive. And the Car Rental Coalition didn't seem to be leaving anytime soon. "This is a watershed kind of experience for us," LaPlaca said, "and one that ought not to be abandoned."

Feeding a Washington lobby is now a regular cost of doing business in the car-rental industry, even for tiny companies that got along without representation in the past. Rental-car customers pay the price. Only one class unequivocally wins: the lawyering, lobbying, and politicking class of Washington's K Street is several million dollars richer.

Those millions produce nothing. They merely guard against distributive raids, real or expected or imagined. They have been diverted from the productive economy into the parasite economy. So has Mike LaPlaca. The man who was a business executive in 1972 was, in 1992, spending half of his time lobbying.

No doubt because he was new to the world of lobbying and power-politicking, he spoke of his experience with a note of outrage. "I'm an innocent at this, and I can say I was shocked," he said. "I lived fifty-two years without ever having to petition the Congress on behalf of myself or a client. And in many ways I wish I could go back to the fifty-second year."

Shed no tears for Mike LaPlaca. He earns several multiples of the average family income and works in pleasant offices on H Street in Washington. But do wonder, as he himself outspokenly does, whether there isn't something peculiar and insidious about the forces that bent his career. Although we normally think of wealth as money, the real source and meaning of wealth is the career product of a human being's talent and energy. The diversion of a career from the business sector to the lobbying sector affects wealth in the most fundamental sense.

Note, then, the lessons of LaPlaca's story:

One, that everyone involved was doing what made sense for him—looking out for his interests. Consumers were looking out for their interests (as they saw them); so were the little companies; so were the big companies; so were the politicians. And the lawyers and lobbyists were looking out for their clients' interests.

Two, though some of the players may in fact have been acting out of cynicism and opportunism, their actions could also be squared with reasonable viewpoints and decent motives. Take your pick—we'll never know. But it doesn't matter anyway, because either way—

Three: the end result was a new interest group, a new political action committee, and several new lobbying jobs, at a cost in the millions. That is how the parasite economy grows, despite, or because of, the best intentions of all concerned.

MAKING AND TAKING

As a thought experiment, imagine you're the president of Acme Big Flange Company, and you have an additional—"marginal," in econospeak—$1 million to invest. Obviously, you want the highest return possible. You are locked in a stiff competition with, say, mini-flange mills. The question you face is how best to invest your $1 million so as to get the jump on the competition. What are your options?

First, you could buy a new high-speed flange-milling machine or a better inventory-control system. Either of those would improve your company's productivity. However, in a developed economy, where most competitors are technologically up to date, such investments are unlikely to improve your company's productivity dramatically. Rather, the improvement will be incremental. (Remember, this is a *marginal* $1 million. You would have made the most lucrative investments already.)

Over a decade, you might earn an annual return of something like 10 or 15 percent on your investment—maybe $100,000 or $150,000 a year.

Not bad. But there's a second option to consider. For $1 million you could hire one of the best lobbyists in Washington. This fellow is a former staff member of the House Valve and Flange Subcommittee, he knows the legislators, he knows the issues, he is persuasive and ingenious. With his help, you could invest some of your $1 million in campaign contributions to members of the Valve and Flange Subcommittee. Though you can't count on buying anyone's vote, your money would buy you access, which your competitor might not enjoy. Your lobbyist and your PAC might win you a tax break, a subsidy, or, best of all (because least visible to the public), a law or regulation hobbling mini-flange mills. Any such tax break, subsidy, or regulation could easily be worth, say, $10 million a year.

So here is your equation. New machines earn a return of $100,000 or $150,000 a year; a successful lobbyist earns potentially fifty or a hundred times that amount. Which is the better investment?

The example is hypothetical but hardly farfetched. This is from *The New York Times* of October 22, 1992:

> It was an obscure provision buried deep in the arcane language of a 1,000-page trade bill, but Senator Alfonse M. D'Amato was on the case. A handful of sugar refiners, including one with a plant in Brooklyn, stood to gain $365 million in tariff rebates and Mr. D'Amato was all for it.
>
> With his help, the provision squeaked through the Senate in the summer of 1987. That fall, five years before his next race, Mr. D'Amato received $8,500 in campaign contributions from the sugar refiners.

Assuming that the sugar refiners spent about $8,500 for a tariff rebate worth $365 million, this was no ordinary investment.

Never mind 15 percent or 150 percent; the rate of return was better than four *million* percent. You can't earn that kind of money opening a car wash. And, frankly, if you met an investment opportunity that paid $42,941.17 for every dollar you put in, you would be a fool to pass it up.

No wonder, then, that people invest. "If I throw in a million here or a million there, I might get a hundred million back," said one Washington lobbyist (and, yes, former House of Representatives staff member). "And there are probably enough cases like that so they keep throwing money in."

Actually, in any economy, rich or poor, there are always lots of cases like that. You just have to hunt for them. When one person starts hunting, others follow, not wanting to be left behind. When I spoke to the economist Gordon Tullock, whose pioneering work in the late 1960s opened up the academic study of this kind of behavior, he said, "I think it may be that the thing feeds on itself. Every time you have a successful lobbying effort, that advertises the value of lobbying."

This game of trying to capture a larger share of existing wealth is transfer-seeking. Unlike productive investment, it poses a social problem. From any particular individual's point of view, productive investment and transfer-seeking are more or less equivalent. They are both ways of investing your time and energy to make yourself better off. But from a social point of view, the two are very different. Whereas productive investment makes society wealthier, transfer-seeking investment makes society poorer, in two ways.

First, the process of transferring resources from one pocket to another is never perfectly efficient; something is lost along the way. Agents take fees, negotiations take time. Conflict further adds to the cost: if I don't want you to get what I have, I'll do everything possible to make the transfer expensive and difficult.

Second, and what's much more profound, the game destroys wealth relative to the proper baseline for comparison, which is the wealth that *would* have been created if people weren't busy trying to grab pieces of each other. Every bit of energy we spend fighting over existing wealth is that much less energy spent producing more wealth. The negative sums of transfer-seeking, then, are the sums that would have been produced but are not: the inventions not developed, the crops not planted, the equipment not bought, the employees not hired, and, in all other forms, the investments forgone.

And how large might the negative sums be? Consider a second thought experiment.

Suppose you have $100. Suppose I want $100. In principle, how much might I be willing to spend to get your $100? The answer is: up to $99, because if I invested that much and captured your $100, I would come out a dollar ahead. And, again in principle, how much might you be willing to spend to keep your $100, once you realize I'm after it? Answer: $99 again.

If you add the numbers, you quickly see a startling result. In principle, the two of us can rationally consume almost $200 fighting over an existing $100. Yet no wealth would have been produced.

In practice, it would be rare for two people to spend $19,999 fighting over a $10,000 car. If, for instance, the chances that any particular car will be stolen are only one in ten, you might spend only about $1,000 guarding your car. However, the broad point holds: an investment in capturing wealth from someone else is likely to summon forth a roughly equal and opposite defensive investment, and the sums involved can get very large.

But doesn't transfer-seeking create jobs? After all, if I hire a lobbyist to win a tax break, that money doesn't disappear into a black hole. Rather, it hires secretaries, rents office space, buys a Xerox machine, and so on.

True, but from an economic point of view, paying people to capture more of other people's money is like hiring people to steal cars. If I hire workers to build cars, the result is new jobs *and* new cars. But if I hire someone to steal existing cars, I have merely moved a job out of the productive sector and into the car-theft sector. My employees will buy screwdrivers and crowbars and wire cutters, thus creating business for hardware stores—but meanwhile a car owner (or insurance company) will be several thousand dollars poorer, and will have that much less to spend or invest. Similarly, I can create jobs in the roof-repair industry—and also in the roof-guarding industry—by going around punching holes in people's roofs. But no one would think those jobs were making society as a whole better off. They create activity, but they destroy wealth.

Actually, the example of someone who drills holes in roofs is not as whimsical as it may sound. It brings us within eyeshot of the central peculiarity of transfer-seeking—the peculiarity which earns it the distinctive adjective "parasitic."

PAY THEM OR ELSE

If someone climbs on your roof with a hatchet, he puts you in a difficult position. You're going to have to respond, or else you're going to be out the price of a new roof. He may protest that he is doing the morally right thing, helping humanity, taking what is rightfully his, or whatever. You don't much care. If you let him alone, your roof is a goner. (And don't be surprised when he offers to do the repair work.)

In the economy, as in nature, a parasite is set apart from a mere freeloader by its ability to force its target to fend it off. This is the sense in which transfer-seekers are, not so loosely speaking, parasitic: they are not only unproductive themselves, *they also force other people to be unproductive.*

Is that really so unusual? What about corporate takeover artists? Wall Street financiers and brokers who just move money around? Freeloaders who ask for handouts? Aren't they parasites, in some sense?

In some sense, maybe. But not in the particular sense at issue here. None of those people really fits the bill, because none has the power to make you engage in a distributional struggle.

A corporate takeover artist certainly does command the attention of entrenched company managers, who resent the intrusion. But takeover artists merely offer money for a company; it's up to the stockholders to take the deal or not. Managers may feel obliged to fight the takeover in order to save their jobs. They are in the position of a caretaker who doesn't want the house sold: he'll try to block the sale or keep his job, maybe by promising to fix up the property. (Corporate takeover threats are often productive: they can make managers perform better, so that the stockholders are less willing to sell.) But the would-be buyer of the house isn't a parasite; he's a purchaser.

By the same token, financiers and brokers and other such middlemen are also not really parasites. You hire them because they know, or are supposed to know, how to move money around and where to put it. Using old resources more productively creates new wealth. That's why bankers, who borrow money and lend it out again, are not only productive but essential. Similarly, a Wall Street trader who sees an underpriced stock may buy low, sell higher, and make a killing—but in the process he is moving capital away from an overpriced company and toward an investment that is more productive. That kind of middleman is like a professional librarian who offers, for a price, to catalog a big book collection. You hire him to make your assets more productive.

And what about the guy with his hand out on the street, or the guy selling pet rocks, or the inept stockbroker? Is he a parasite? Again, he flunks the basic test: he is not forcing anyone else to fend him off. You can brush off the beggar, you can leave the store without the pet rock, and you can dump the stockbroker and go it alone. A bad stockbroker or a pesky real-estate agent can take your money if you do hire him, but only a transfer-seeker can take your money if you *don't* hire him.

In America, only a few classes of people have the power to

take your money if you don't fend them off. One is the criminal class. People who break into your car or rob your house (or punch holes in your roof) are members of the parasite economy in the classic sense: they take your wealth if you don't actively fight them off. Such people are costly to society, not only for what they take, but for the high cost of fending them off. They make us buy locks, alarms, iron gates, security guards, policemen, insurance, and on and on. David N. Laband and John P. Sophocleus, economists who have studied transfer-seeking, have estimated that, in 1985 alone, American criminals invested at least $324 billion in "illegal wealth transfers." Recall how two people can spend $200 fighting over an existing $100, and you won't be surprised to learn that, according to Laband and Sophocleus, American individuals and companies spent about $340 billion that same year trying to fend off thieves (we spent almost $10 billion just for locks).

Criminals, however, aren't the only ones who play the distributive game. Legal, noncriminal transfer-seeking is perfectly possible—on one condition. You need the law's help. That is, you need to persuade politicians or courts to intervene on your behalf.

Remember Scrooge, the bicycle messenger from Chapter 2. If he spreads a computer virus that shuts down fax machines, he's a criminal. But if he wins a law that taxes fax machines or that subsidizes couriers, he's a Republican. Or a Democrat. Similarly, businesses seek tariffs, unions seek minimum-wage laws and laws against hiring permanent replacements for strikers, farmers seek subsidies, consumers seek lemon laws, environmentalists seek regulations on industry, plaintiffs seek damages, postal workers seek bans on competition, car-rental companies seek liability legislation that hobbles their competition, and so on, and on, and on.

These groups all think they are doing society a favor, and no doubt some of them are. Many redistributive laws and regulations are worth having, though many also are not. For now, however, focus not on the value of particular laws or benefits but on the dynamics of the game as a whole. As each group seeks transfers, other groups respond. And that is the magical talent of the parasite economy. To fend off a politician, lobbyist, or lawyer, you need to hire *another* politician, lobbyist, or lawyer, whether you want to or not. If your business competitor starts to move legislation that costs you money, you would be stupid not to hire a lobbyist of your own to block it. If your competitor opens a political action committee to donate to a key politician, you could lose your shirt if you don't do the same. Similarly, when you get sued, you don't have the option of ignoring the lawsuit; for months or even years, you are going to spend a lot of time and money on lawyers.

Fending off transfer-seekers isn't cheap, as anyone knows who has ever been sued. In 1993, a Texas jury needed less than four hours to exonerate American Airlines in a predatory-pricing suit brought by American's competitors, but American was stuck with a $20 million legal bill nonetheless. Lawyers can cost $200 an hour, lobbyists $10,000 a month, and politicians whatever the market will bear. And the energy and money you spend on them will be diverted from investments that would have been more productive for you.

What is peculiar about the parasite economy, then, is its ability to suck in resources that people would rather invest elsewhere. Activism on one side draws counteractivism on another; motion begets more motion. "For example," write the political scientists Allan J. Cigler and Burdett A. Loomis, "the National Association of Manufacturers . . . originally was created to further the expansion of business opportunities in foreign trade, but it became a more powerful organization largely in response to the rise of organized labor. Mobilization of business interests since the 1960s often has resulted from threats posed by consumer advocates and environmentalists." Mike LaPlaca was sucked into the parasite economy because it was attacking his clients. That is how the parasite economy grows, even if society as a whole would be better off if it shrank.

PAVED WITH GOOD INTENTIONS

Who are these evil parasitic people, and why don't they just mend their wicked ways?

Meet Milt Brown. He is gentle and genial, a retired consultant who now lives in Phoenix. His wife, Catherine, is a woman whose graciousness and sincerity serve her well in a business—real-estate agentry—which could do with more of both qualities.

They don't like being taken advantage of, though. Mail from a group in Washington told the Browns that Milt was a "notch baby," one of a group of Social Security recipients who believe (wrongly, but that's another story) that they are entitled to more in benefits than they receive. Milt got mad and began paying the group $10 a year to get his fair share. He kept investing for four years, until he realized that the benefits increase he might receive would be only about $10 a month instead of the $50 he had first supposed—not worth the trouble, he figured.

"When someone tells me, 'Gee, you should get another fifty dollars a month,' " he later said, "I'm going to do what I can to get it." Remind Milt Brown that any additional Social Security money he received would have come out of someone else's pocket, and he would remind you that he was not seeking anything he wasn't entitled to. He just wanted his fair share.

So is Milt Brown a seeker after justice? Or is he a vulture-eyed predator?

Inevitably, the first reaction when I talk about the parasite economy is: Who, me? People point their fingers at lawyers and lobbyists and politicians—*they* are the problem, yes? Yes—and no. They are the professional *agents* of legal transfer-seeking. They don't go fishing for goodies without the enthusiastic support of the people who hire them. Those clients are transfer-seeking *investors*, because they invest their money or their votes, or both, to get and keep benefits and subsidies. Put together investor and agent, and the parasite economy is in business. Of course, the two sides can get together more easily if someone takes the initiative to form an interest group, round up members, and hire lobbyists or file lawsuits. People who do that are transfer-seeking *entrepreneurs*. Often, the agents act as entrepreneurs, imagining new benefits or legal claims and then rounding up clients to seek them.

"Well, surely you don't mean *me*—I'm one of the good guys." After they're finished blaming lawyers and lobbyists, as though lawyers didn't have clients and lobbyists didn't serve interest groups, that's what people always say. Public-interest advocates are especially indignant if you suggest that they, too, are playing the transfer-seeking game. When I talked about transfer-seeking with a liberal environmental activist I know, he said: "I don't hear you making distinctions between different kinds of parasites. I would suggest there's a distinction between people who do what they do because they believe it's in the public interest [i.e., himself] and people who do it purely for financial gain [i.e., his corporate enemies]." Then when I talked with an antitax activist who works for a conservative public-interest group, he said of lobbying and lawyering, "It's an evil thing that happens on the left—and it's a necessity on the right. As long as there are criminals [i.e., his liberal enemies], you need to have policemen [i.e., himself]." He loathes the environmentalist. The environmentalist loathes him. Each is valiantly protecting the country from the depredations of the other. Each is, therefore, the selfless public servant.

In Washington you soon discover that everybody is a selfless public servant. Not only does everybody say so, almost everybody believes it. One of the transfer-seeking game's most wickedly ingenious defenses is that it allows every individual player to think that he is serving the greater good while everyone else is evil. The conceptual breakthrough comes when you realize that the parasite economy doesn't care whether the people feeding it are vicious opportunists or high-thinking moralists; it thrives just as well either way. In the transfer-seeking game, *motive doesn't matter.* That is another peculiarity of the parasite economy. Whether the people engaging each other in distributive struggles are idealistic or cynical, the economic outcome is the same: people devote scarce reserves of time, energy, and money fighting back and forth over existing wealth.

Indeed, idealistic activists can be much more expensive than cynical opportunists. A man who wants to take your car just for the money can often be warded off by an alarm, which may make the effort not worth the trouble. But the man who believes he is entitled to your car can be much more persistent. "Dammit," he thinks, "that's *my* car, and no bastard is going to keep it from me." The merely greedy give up when they stop seeing dollar signs, but the outraged don't stop lobbying or suing till they get their rights. In fact, someone who is morally outraged is easily capable of spending *more* than $10,000 to get your $10,000 car: even if he suffers a financial loss, he makes his point and makes you miserable. He might even destroy the car if he fails to get it; better to ruin the car than allow you to enjoy it.

A tapeworm doesn't hate you and isn't out to get you. It is just trying to get what it thinks is its fair share. Similarly, the investors in the transfer-seeking economy aren't out to wreck the economy. They are just trying to get what they think is their fair share.

Or, rather, *we* are just trying to get *our* fair share. If you seek or receive any sort of benefit from Washington (or the state capitals), you are in on the game. It is safe to say, indeed, that every American is implicated in transfer-seeking. If you think otherwise, look at the table on the next page showing, by income class, who receives direct entitlement subsidies from the federal government. Benefits flow to all income groups, roughly in proportion to their share of the population. Rich, poor, and middle—all are enjoying benefits and feeling entitled. America is the land of the free and the home of the subsidized.

**DISTRIBUTION OF FEDERAL DIRECT ENTITLEMENT SPENDING,
BY INCOME GROUP**

Taxable Income	Percent Share of Population	Percent Share of All Benefits
Below $10,000	21.9	23.4
$10,000–$20,000	20.4	22.3
$20,000–$30,000	16.3	16.3
$30,000–$40,000	12.1	11.4
$40,000–$50,000	9.0	8.0
$50,000–$75,000	12.2	10.5
$75,000–$100,000	4.2	3.6
$100,000–$200,000	2.8	3.1
Over $200,000	1.1	1.5

SOURCE: Progressive Policy Institute

CHESSBOARDS AND SLOT MACHINES

You may be wondering why I keep referring to transfer-seeking as a game. It certainly isn't a game in the sense of being childish or inconsequential. In the sense I mean, a game is a social system with a set of rules and players and an inner dynamic of its own, such that no individual player can predict who will win. To find out who wins, you have to play.

Some games are closed and self-limiting—chess, for instance, where someone wins (or the game stalemates) and that's that. Other games are open-ended and can become all-consuming—playing the slot machines, for instance; the insidious dynamic ("My next coin might win, and I've invested so much already") can trap you until you've lost all your money.

Transfer-seeking appears to be a classic open-ended game. If you look at its implicit logic, you see a potential spiral:

1. Someone can always make a bundle investing in legal transfer-seeking, so someone will always do it. But whatever one person wins, someone else must lose.
2. Therefore, when someone enters the game or expands his position, he effectively forces someone else also to enter the

game or expand *his* position. Every new player drags in other new players.

3. The more people and groups play, the more money there is to be made or lost in the game. As the stakes rise, you risk more if you ignore the game and you gain more if you play it well. Therefore, more is invested. Return to Step 1 and repeat.

On paper, this logic looks like an ideal engine for an open-ended, self-perpetuating game, the sort of game that can keep going and even expanding until it bumps into some outside constraint. In reality, is that happening? To find out, you have to get a handle on the size of the parasite economy.

A PARASITE CENSUS

Unfortunately, the Commerce Department's national accounts don't include a line for transfer-seeking, and the Labor Department's employment figures don't have a "wealth-sucking parasites" category. Even in principle, it is impossible to know just how much transfer-seeking goes on, because economists, true to form, disagree on what exactly counts as transfer-seeking.

Still, there are things you can count. If you don't know the amount of construction activity in your city, but if you do know that the number of contractors and architects has doubled over the years while the population stayed the same, you can make some reasonable, albeit imperfect, inferences. Similarly, if you don't know how much transfer-seeking goes on in America, but if you do know that the number of transfer-seeking professionals has increased relative to the economy and the population, you can infer that Americans are probably investing more in transfer-seeking. Since most transfer-seeking professionals are lawyers or lobbyists, we have a clue where to begin.

Since 1955, the number of law degrees granted annually in the United States has more than quadrupled, even though the

Lawyers

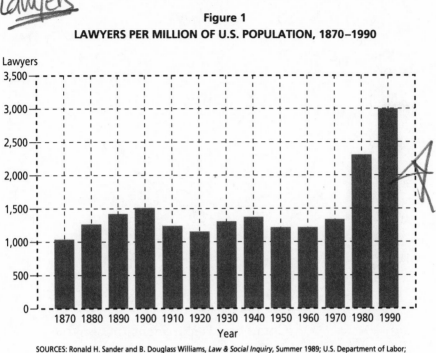

Figure 1
LAWYERS PER MILLION OF U.S. POPULATION, 1870–1990

SOURCES: Ronald H. Sander and B. Douglass Williams, *Law & Social Inquiry*, Summer 1989; U.S. Department of Labor; U.S. Census Bureau

population grew by only about 50 percent over the same period. In effect, a larger and larger share of American talent has been going into the legal business. The result appears in Figure 1, which shows the number of lawyers per million of U.S. population, going all the way back to 1870. For a hundred years, the proportion of lawyers stayed about the same; then, since 1970, it has more than doubled. The number of lawyers in Washington, D.C., grew even faster, quadrupling just between 1972 and 1987.

Not surprisingly, you find a parallel pattern if you count lawsuits, as Figure 2 shows. The number of filings in the federal courts drifted mildly upward from 1950 to the mid-1960s; but then it took off, nearly quadrupling by the mid-1980s. "Comparable figures for the state courts are not available," writes the legal scholar Marc Galanter, "but a sense of the growth of state judicial activity can be gathered from the increase in lawyers

Figure 2
PRIVATE CIVIL SUITS FILED IN THE FEDERAL COURTS, 1950–1992

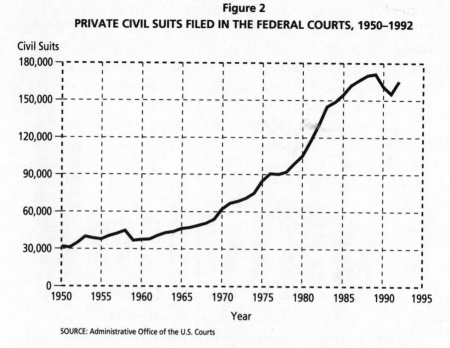

SOURCE: Administrative Office of the U.S. Courts

employed by state courts, from 7,581 in 1960 to 18,674 in 1985."
When I asked Brian J. Ostrom, of the National Center for State
Courts, about state lawsuits, he said, "The amount of litigation
in state courts grows every year. It's always increasing—by an
amount in excess of population growth. The process of people
making mutually acceptable bargains among themselves seems
to be breaking down."

The increase in lawyers and litigation probably has several
causes. One might be, as Ostrom says, an increase in people's
contentiousness. Another cause might be lawyers themselves.
To some extent, they can act as transfer-seeking entrepreneurs.
Long before science had any real idea whether electromagnetic
fields from power lines caused cancer, lawyers were lining up
clients and preparing to sue power companies. One enterprising lawyer, reported *The Wall Street Journal,* carved out a niche
as "the leader of a nationwide group of law firms eager to turn
EMF [electromagnetic fields] into a legal battleground." An-

other lawyer said, "All it's going to take is one or two good hits [i.e., big judgments against power companies] and the sharks will start circling." Lawyers' constant scouring of the law for new claims and claimants, and then for new defenses against those new claims and claimants, can and most likely does feed litigation and distributional struggle.

Almost certainly, however, the biggest cause of more lawyers and more litigation is more laws. To take just one example, in 1990 Congress passed, and the president signed, the Americans with Disabilities Act. The act was billed as a civil rights measure, but it was also a broad new economic entitlement, transferring resources from society generally to the disabled. As such, it was a good example of how transfer-seeking can be driven equally well by idealism (advocates for the disabled wanted their rights) and by pecuniary interests (activists for the disabled wanted more social spending)—indeed, the two are hard, or even downright impossible, to tell apart.

The idea was to widen handicapped people's access to all kinds of jobs and to buildings, transit systems, and so on. In an attempt to fit the law to a complex world, Congress wrote the disabilities act vaguely, requiring, for instance, "readily achievable" measures and "reasonable accommodations." But what did that mean? Thrashing out what the law required would keep a legion of lawyers busy. Responding to those lawyers' lawsuits and petitions would keep another legion of lawyers busy. "Most major law firms," *The Washington Post* reported in 1992, "are well aware that the law . . . will open up a vast new area of discrimination law and, potentially, a lot of business." Already, said the report, many law firms were holding seminars on the act, as were disability-rights groups and businesses, "searching for answers to such questions as, how does a ski resort get a paraplegic up a mountain?"

From one point of view, the disabilities act was a civil rights measure seeking to expand justice for the handicapped. But from another point of view, it was a public-works jobs program

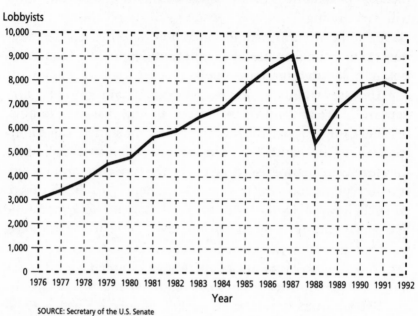

Figure 3
ACTIVE LOBBYISTS REGISTERED WITH THE SENATE, 1976–1992

SOURCE: Secretary of the U.S. Senate

for lawyers—and a new battleground for distributional warfare in general. Which view was right? Both. As the number of laws and claims escalates, as issues become more complex, as the law struggles with ever finer distinctions, more lawyers become necessary. For better and for worse, legal entitlements and lawyers come together as a package deal.

Lawyers do a lot of things besides litigate back and forth over existing wealth, and to blame the lawyers is in many instances to confuse the symptom with the illness. Lobbyists, by contrast, are wholly creatures of the transfer-seeking economy. That makes them an even better thing to count than lawyers or lawsuits.

There are, alas, only estimates, because we don't require lobbying licenses and many people lobby who aren't full-time lobbyists. One measure is the number of people who register with the Senate as actively lobbying on Capitol Hill, though that is only a small fraction of all lobbyists. As Figure 3 shows, the number tripled in the decade after 1976 (the year when the records begin); it dropped in 1988, but then bounced back up.

Various other counts show increases. *Congressional Quarterly* reports that the number of people lobbying in Washington at least doubled and may have quadrupled between the mid-1970s and mid-1980s. (State capitals, by the way, also show healthy increases.) Between 1961 and 1982, the number of corporations with Washington offices increased tenfold. "The chief beneficiaries of this trend," write the political scientists Cigler and Loomis, "are Washington-based lawyers, lobbyists, and public-relations firms." Meanwhile, many companies that already maintained lobbying and public-affairs offices expanded them; one study found that almost two-thirds of companies surveyed had increased their public-affairs staffs between 1975 and 1980. The Washington office of General Motors employed three people in 1968 and twenty-eight in 1978, though no cars were built in the District of Columbia. By 1992, roughly 92,000 people worked in Washington for groups and firms seeking to influence policy, according to a count by the political scientist James A. Thurber.

Another indication of whether the transfer-seeking economy is growing is political spending. If the amount that people are investing in, say, the computer business triples over some period, you can assume that the sector is growing and that it has earned favorable returns over the period. The same inference holds for politics: if the investment in political campaigns grew from 1968 to 1992, you can assume that more people were spotting politics—ergo, transfer-seeking—as a sound investment.

And, indeed, political spending has grown dramatically, far outstripping inflation (and also increasing, though less dramatically, relative to the size of the economy). Figure 4 is from data compiled by Herbert E. Alexander of the University of Southern California and Monica Bauer of Western

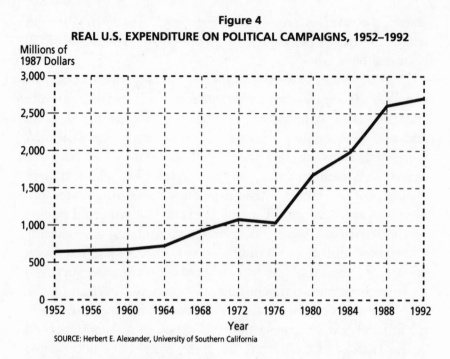

Figure 4
REAL U.S. EXPENDITURE ON POLITICAL CAMPAIGNS, 1952–1992

SOURCE: Herbert E. Alexander, University of Southern California

New England College. It shows, in constant 1987 dollars, the estimated total spending on political campaigns—federal, state, and local—in each major election cycle since 1952. The data fit the usual pattern: upward creep until the mid-1960s, and then an upward zoom. In 1988 alone the investment in politics increased by 30 percent over the level of 1984, though fortunately the pace slowed in 1992. Like any other rewarding investment, politics was attracting venture capital.

Perhaps you could wave aside an increase in the number of lawyers *or* of lobbyists *or* of political contributions *or* of interest groups. But, as far as I can see, there is only one way to read the fact that *all* of those numbers rose sharply beginning in the 1960s and early 1970s, and continued to rise through the Reagan-Bush 1980s. America was a society increasingly structured for, and so dedicated to, transfer-seeking.

PERPETUAL MOTION

In time, a curious thing happens. As the parasite economy thrives, transfer-seeking agents become wealthy and numerous. They become a powerful interest group in their own right. On the one side, they develop and pursue claims on the behalf of their clients. On the other side, they act as an interest group to keep the game going. When there are enough of them, they may begin using their access to government to draw more resources into lobbying. At that stage, the parasite economy may take on the peculiar ability to grow entrepreneurially. In effect, it goes into business for itself.

Most Americans are aware of the power of business interests to influence politics with money. Few are aware, however, of the extent to which the influence business now *is* a business interest. In 1990, notes the Center for Responsive Politics, a watchdog group that monitors money in politics, fully 10 percent of all business-sector contributions to congressional campaigns came from lawyers and lobbyists. In 1992, the center examined more than $240 million in political contributions of $200 or more. Then it broke down the contributions by industry. Insurance gave almost $10 million, as did oil and gas; the securities and investment industry gave more than $11 million. But at the top of the list, with almost $13 million in political contributions, were none other than lawyers and lobbyists. They gave more than $2 million to George Bush and well over half again that much to Bill Clinton.

When the parasite economy reaches this peculiar self-referential stage, one can no longer be certain whether association professionals and lobbyists work for their group members or the members are worked by the association professionals and lobbyists—or whether there is even a difference. Lobbyists conceive tax breaks and build coalitions of businesses which become clients who pay the lobbyists to seek the tax breaks from politicians who seek contributions from the lobbyists who deliver subsidies to clients who make contributions to politicians. The agents excite the clients and the clients excite the agents and the agents excite each other and thereby excite the clients. The transfer-seeking economy begins to look like a swarm of bees exciting itself into a state of perpetual frenzy.

Government itself becomes a marketable resource and a profit center for an expanding group of career-minded professionals, many of whom use government jobs as stepping-stones to lucrative careers lobbying government. According to *CongressDaily/A.M.*, fully 40 percent of the House of Representatives members who left office in January 1993 went to work as lobbyists. Though no one can prove that politicians and Capitol Hill staff members gin up laws and programs and regulations to create jobs for themselves with interest groups and lobbying firms, everyone suspects that it happens, a fact which is itself corrosive of democracy.

These resource-shuffling professionals have a weird incentive: any kind of distributional struggle benefits them. The more transfer-seeking battles they manage to spark, the better off they will be. Every new legislative fight, every new lawsuit, every new regulatory struggle means new fees for politicians and lawyers and lobbyists, at least in the short and medium term. They win, as a class, no matter who else loses.

Most of what happens in Washington is driven by ideological passion, the desire to do good, or the fear of being harmed. Lobbyists and politicians are typically not cynical people. They are doing their job. But that is the whole problem: transfer-seekers' job is to seek transfers. A lobbyist is paid to stay alert to new opportunities or, when possible, to create them. His job is to call a potential client and say, "If you hire me, I think we can get the subcommittee chairman to insert a provision letting us depreciate Luxembourg." A politician's job is to keep himself in office by giving things to people who want things. Everyone wants to keep the gaming tables busy. One House member, on hearing that the Car Rental Coalition wanted to stop a bill, told

Mike LaPlaca to substitute a bill of his own. When LaPlaca replied that no bill was necessary, the member retorted, "Don't you know why we're here? We're here to pass laws."

Want to raise campaign money? Nothing better than to get a seat on the House Energy and Commerce Committee, whose jurisdiction includes railroads, trucking, broadcasting, environmental rules, health care, and telecommunications. "A seat on the committee," reports Chuck Alston in *Congressional Quarterly*, "makes raising campaign money as easy as licking the stamps for invitations to fund-raisers." In an article bluntly headlined "As Clean-Air Bill Took Off, So Did PAC Donations," the magazine noted that in 1989, when the big 1990 Clean Air Act began moving, donations to committee members from the big political action committees—surprise!—increased sharply. Representative Edward J. Markey, a Democrat of Massachusetts, began his political career as an anticorporate liberal, but by the time he became chairman of the Energy and Commerce Committee's subcommittee on telecommunications and finance, he had learned the value of business money. "He has used his subcommittee slot to raise substantial sums from individuals with a stake in the panel's activities," wrote Paul Starobin in the *National Journal*. At one of his fund-raisers, 125 lobbyists paid $500 each to hobnob with him. "Everybody's here," said a telecommunications consultant. "Bullshit walks and money talks. You gotta be here."

Professionals in the interest-group business have their own reasons to stir the pot. These are not underpaid people. In 1991, according to a *National Journal* survey, the average salary of trade and professional associations' top officers was $211,000 (not counting benefits and perks). The top people at unions earned $163,000; at issue-oriented interest groups, $110,000. Like anyone else in business, these people want to build their organizations and earn rising paychecks, which means generating new demands that bring home more benefits for the membership. "Washington has become a major marketing center," writes Jeffrey Birnbaum, "in which issues are created by interest groups and then sold like toothpaste to voters from Portland, Maine, to Portland, Oregon."

The combination of ideological agendas, group demands, and agents' appetite for fees is more than potent enough to ensure that the transfer-seeking game keeps itself constantly energized. The more motion, the better. Bill Clinton rode to Washington on a promise to take America back from the special interests by breaking "gridlock"—that is, by trying to pass lots of laws. Actually, plenty of laws had been passing already, but now the lobbyists and interest-group professionals were ecstatic. "The one thing everyone agrees on," Tom Watson, a lawyer with the firm of Crowell & Moring in Washington, told *Legal Times* shortly after the election, "is that the government will now be more interested in regulating business. We are all expecting about a 33 percent increase in fees." Lawyering-lobbying firms went straight to work loading up on former government officials and Capitol Hill staff members. At firms with good Democratic connections, reported *Legal Times,* "the jubilation was palpable." But Republicans would make out just fine, too. "This Congress and the promises that Clinton made," said Tom Korologos, a high-powered Washington lobbyist, "means an almost automatic defensiveness from the corporate community on most issues it faces." Translation: money for lobbying. Parasite heaven.

The mere possibility of government action pulls resources into the whirlpool. Figure 5 shows the number of health-care groups in Washington from 1979 to 1991. Over little more than a decade, the number more than sextupled. Why? From 1960 to 1990, the proportion of health care paid for by the government doubled, to two-fifths. Add the talk of health-care reform, and you had Washington staging a show that no one could afford to miss. In July 1991, the American Hospital Association moved its top officers to Washington, believing that they "should be closer to the action." In March 1992, the American Nurses Association

Figure 5

NUMBER OF HEALTH GROUPS IN WASHINGTON, 1979–1991

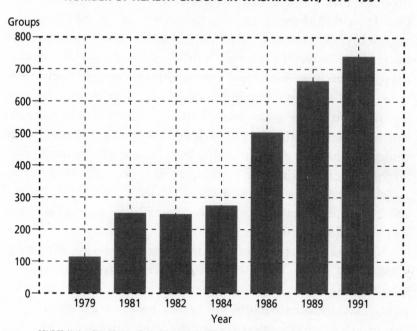

SOURCE: National Health Council, *Health Groups in Washington*, various editions

moved its headquarters—and half a million pounds of office furniture and equipment—to Washington, after twenty years in Kansas City. "We have nursing's agenda for health-care reform," they said. And so it goes. In 1971, 19 percent of trade and professional associations were headquartered in Washington; by 1990, 32 percent, and counting. That is Mike LaPlaca's story, writ large.

Ross Perot was fond of saying, in the 1992 presidential campaign, that the giant sucking noise you heard was the sound of jobs being vacuumed up by low-wage countries south of the border. He was wrong. The giant sucking noise was the sound of the whirlpool in Washington, sucking up investment capital, talent, energy.

In their ability to attract resources merely by being active, politicians and, to a lesser extent, lobbyists and lawyers resemble the man standing in the center of a trampoline, who can draw objects on the edge toward him just by bouncing up and down. One House staff member, who has worked on the Hill for two decades, said, "The power of a member to call a hearing or get his chairman to call a hearing, and therefore shake the tree, is very, very real, and it bothers me a lot. And members can play it even if they're not playing it." That last observation was interesting. When I asked what it meant, he replied that well-meaning activity stirs the pot no less than cynical activity. Never mind the motives; if a politician holds a hearing or submits a bill, all the affected industries juice up their troops and make campaign contributions. Even if there's only a one-in-ten chance that a bill will actually pass, no one can take the risk of failing to put a few dollars into the machine.

Significant bills revising the tax code passed in 1981, 1982, 1983, 1984, 1986, 1988, 1989, 1990—"more frequent and detailed changes in taxes than ever before in American history," wrote David E. Rosenbaum in *The New York Times*, adding that a presidential veto stopped yet another new tax law in 1992. Investment and saving incentives were expanded and then withdrawn, a Medicare surtax on the elderly was adopted and then repealed, real-estate loopholes came and then went and then came again, corporate taxes went down and then up, excise taxes fell while payroll taxes rose. In the 1960s, the tax code and related rules filled two volumes, whereas they now fill eight; just in the five years after the 1986 tax reform passed, Congress made about 5,400 changes to the tax law through twenty-seven different pieces of legislation. Constant rewriting of the rules acted as a subsidy for tax lawyers and accountants, but it made life miserable for people trying to invest and plan. "Changes in the law," noted Rosenbaum, "forced people to alter the way they saved and spent and invested their money." Hank Barnette, the chairman of Bethlehem Steel, told *The Wall Street Journal* in 1993, "It makes long-term financial planning very difficult."

Yet—wasn't this odd?—the overall tax burden did not change significantly over the whole period, despite the record budget deficits. "And despite all the turmoil," says Rosenbaum, "politicians seem to feel just as strongly today that the tax system needs to be revamped as they did in 1980." They went right to work on it in 1993, and chances are they're at it again as you read these words.

Wherefore all the activity? Why, during the period of putative "gridlock," was a new record set for tax-law churning, leaving people apparently as unhappy as ever? There were lots of reasons. One was that as a million groups clamor for a million tax breaks every year, they are bound to pull the tax code hither and yon in a random walk. Imagine many people pulling on a circular fire net, each trying to drag it his own way, and you see why the tax code wanders all over the place. Another possible reason is hinted at by the fact that in 1985, as the Reagan Administration's tax-reform effort got under way, contributions to the House tax-writing committee doubled from the level of 1983, the previous nonelection year. As the House moved to pass the reform bill in December 1985, reported *Congressional Quarterly*, "One Democrat was overheard suggesting to another that the party prevent a final vote so the bill would remain in limbo for a few more months. 'Why kill the goose that laid the golden egg?' he asked."

In 1992, after rioters and looters sacked much of South Central Los Angeles, what began as an urban-relief bill turned into—surprise again!—a tax bill. There would be new tax breaks for small savers, college bowl games, insurance agents, bingo players, yacht owners, tuxedo renters, users of reloaded shotgun shells, etc., etc. There would be higher taxes for securities dealers, people who move, people who join clubs for business reasons, etc., etc. What fun. Fun, at least, if you were a politician counting the receipts, or a lobbyist counting the fees, as affected interest groups circled past the tollbooth.

The real beauts were the temporary tax credits. Some of those credits mattered, especially the credit for research and development. Temporary credits need to be renewed every year or six months, creating a Chinese fire drill for politicians and lobbyists, and business for both. "It's a degrading process," said one lobbyist. "Law firms and lobbyists are always the gainers."

As citizens, the lobbyists and lawyers and politicians and interest-group professionals want to solve many problems while minimizing fuss; yet, as transfer-seeking professionals, they soon learn that their paychecks and campaign coffers reward them for solving few problems while maximizing fuss. As citizens, they wish society had less need of people like themselves; yet, as professionals, they are adept at creating jobs for one another by prospecting for transfer-seeking opportunities. They believe that they serve the public, or at least provide a necessary service. Yet the public despises them.

To the public, Washington looks more and more like a public-works jobs program for lawyers and lobbyists, a profit center for professionals who are in business for themselves. From the public's point of view, the lobbying business is self-serving, elitist, and corrupt. But the public is only half right.

THE TRAP, AGAIN

That the parasite economy is self-serving is true. But the transfer-seeking industry is no more self-serving than any other business. Lobbyists and group organizers and transfer-seeking entrepreneurs are working stiffs and capitalists, like anybody else. They see opportunities and they take them. It's just that they work in a sector that tends to destroy wealth.

That lobbies are elitist is true only in the limited sense that they are disproportionately run by elites. You'll find plenty of people with high-class law degrees working in interest groups, lobbying firms, and government itself. In fact, of the eighteen jobs in the Clinton Administration's first cabinet, fourteen were occupied by lawyers—an ironic accomplishment for an administration that prided itself on its diversity.

Despite the often-stated contention that Washington is run by corporate moneybags, however, in no sense do lobbies *represent* only an elite. They represent groups, which include practically everybody. Ultimately, the lobbying sector keeps producing jobs because Americans keep organizing to lobby. The parasite economy thrives because America's countless and diverse groups are, if anything, represented too well.

That lobbies are corrupt is hardly true at all. Corruption implies secrecy and money under the table. The parasite economy, by contrast, is like a New York Stock Exchange on which government benefits are sought and traded openly and (for the most part) honestly. Anyone can join a group and invest in lobbying government—and everyone does. It's worth remembering, too, that virtually all of those investors, far from being "corrupt," conceive of themselves as doing worthy or useful things: aiding cutting-edge industries, or giving veterans their fair share, or supporting small businesses, or helping the elderly afford health care.

If the parasite economy were the product of a few evil elites and corrupt Washington insiders, it would be comparatively easy to control. The whole problem is that it isn't.

In the first chapter, I mentioned that politics seemed caught in a kind of trap. Government tried to do more, yet people were less satisfied; politicians railed against special interests, yet special interests proliferated. Now the nature of that trap emerges. From the individual's point of view, it always makes sense to hire a lobbyist, or vote for a politician, who can bring you a subsidy or use public resources to solve what you believe are pressing problems. But if everybody follows this seemingly sensible logic, everybody spends more and more time chasing everybody else's money and protecting his own. That logic, ultimately, is why the game is not self-limiting. The lobbying and political classes can stir the pot, and they do, but the fire beneath it is the deceptive logic of transfer-seeking.

"The greatest goodies for the greatest number" is how a wag once described the time-honored principle underlying American politics. In 1936, Senator Richard B. Russell, finding himself in a tough primary race, made his case plain. "The farmers are awake to the fact that my opponent is promising them nothing except to cut off their checks," he declared, mincing no words, "while I stand for larger benefit checks." He buried his opponent. Today the amounts changing hands are much bigger, and the brokers are far more numerous and sophisticated, but the same logic applies. When Senator Arlen Specter, a Republican of Pennsylvania, had some trouble in 1992, he responded by touting his seniority, which he dedicated "to using every bit of influence I can." "On the campaign trail," reported *The Economist,* "Mr. Specter has something for everyone. He fights as hard as the best Democrat for import quotas on steel. Roads? He has brought back $1.28 for every tax dollar sent to Washington." That was the logic of transfer-seeking. Senator Alfonse D'Amato, the New York Republican, "makes the clearest, rawest pitch in politics," reported *The Washington Post* in 1992: "Look what I done for you lately," D'Amato said. "If you put the pie out, don't blame me for wanting a slice of the pie for my people—who've gotta eat also." That, too, was the logic of transfer-seeking.

I'll spare you a wheeze about public greed and the decline of civic virtue. As I hope the preceding pages make clear, people invest in transfer-seeking because it seems to make good economic sense or because they believe it's good for society, not because they want to rob each other blind. I'll also spare you a diatribe against "corruption" or "elite lobbies" in Washington that are out of touch with "the people." That whole way of talking misses the point. I'll argue that the main reason to worry about the growth of the transfer-seeking economy, and about trying to control it, is simply this: it is expensive.

Expensive in two fashions. The political cost is the toll on government, which, as Chapter 6 argues, is demosclerosis. The economic cost is less ruinous but more insidious, payable in cash and paid in a thousand almost invisible ways.

5

HIDDEN COSTS

I 'VE MENTIONED THAT THIS BOOK is about side effects. Before talking about the costs of devoting more and more resources to lobbying and other forms of transfer-seeking, I want to emphasize that point again.

To say that medicines have side effects is not to say that medicines are worthless and should be abolished. It is to say that you have to be careful and selective. Taking higher and higher doses of more and more medicines, in hopes of curing more and more diseases, will cripple or kill you. The same goes for government benefits. Every program does some good for somebody, or else it wouldn't exist. Many programs—unemployment insurance, say, and space exploration and veterans' benefits— deliver real benefits to society. But if you neglect to be selective or forget to keep track of the costs, many individual programs that seem worthwhile on their own merits may add up, collectively, to a wildly incoherent and expensive jumble that nourishes thousands of ravenous lobbies and breeds more of them every month.

With medicines, it's fairly easy to be careful. If you take too much or too many, you get sick. But federal programs are different from medicines in this respect: the benefits flow to the recipient, but the side effects are borne by society as a whole. If medicines made their users feel better while making *non*users sick, you would expect a lot of people to be using too many medicines. Something like that seems to have happened in the universe of federal transfer programs.

The very first bill that President Bill Clinton signed into law required businesses to grant workers time off for family needs. "Only Scrooge, it seems, could oppose the Family and Medical Leave Act of 1993," wrote James V. DeLong in *The New Republic*. Yet the fact is that this new middle-class entitlement, like countless others that it was piled on top of, wasn't free. Any business manager can tell you that holding a job open for up to twelve weeks per year per employee is a headache. Businesses would have to maintain workers' health coverage during leaves; a three-month leave might cost the employer well over $1,000. Workers might not come back after the leave, DeLong noted, "so any worker who leaves a job within a year of the birth of a child, or for any health-related reason, can get three extra months of health insurance coverage quite easily."

The benefits of mandated family leave were obvious—so obvious that only sourpuss economists and annoyed business groups objected. But the costs were obscure. To pay for family leave, consumers would pay slightly higher prices and employees would be paid slightly lower wages. Some employers would try to avoid hiring young women or others who seem likely to use family leave. Other employers would substitute part-timers, who weren't covered by the act. There would be new lawsuits, new paperwork, new rules, new kinks in the labor market.

Was the family leave act worth the cost? Maybe, maybe not. The problem, however, was that few voters were willing to believe that there *was* a cost. They believed they had received a free gift from their politicians, when in fact they had merely cadged from each other. Later they might pout and rage at the price, cursing government and demanding still more benefits to salve their pain.

Here is a key to the transfer-seeking economy's ability to grow even when society would be better off if it shrank. Benefits from lobbying—subsidy checks, tax breaks, favorable regulations, court awards, and so on—are highly visible; but the costs—the waste, the inefficiency, the rigidities, the complexities, the policy incoherence as subsidies and deals redistribute money in every direction at once—are diffuse and often invisible. Maritime interests are only too well aware of the large subsidies they receive ($112,000 per job, at costs to consumers running into the billions each year): in 1990, they paid almost $4 million in political contributions. But are you aware of the higher shipping costs you pay? Of the investment forgone because of the tidy lump of money that the maritime lobby has captured? And even if you were, would you care enough to tackle this determined and well-funded lobby, for the sake of the productivity of the economy as a whole?

This chapter makes no attempt to assess the worth of particular government programs. I'll operate on the assumption that readers will make up their own minds about whether arts subsidies or farm subsidies are worthwhile. Instead, the point is to look at *systemic* costs: costs arising from the accumulation and interaction of programs as lobbies weave an ever denser web of programs and benefits and subsidies and anticompetitive rules.

Rather than try to cover all the bases, I will focus on costs of three orders. First, the cost of direct investment in the transfer-seeking economy. Second, the cost of defensive maneuvering against potential transfer-seekers. Third, and largest, the cost of the subsidies and rules that transfer-seekers put in place.

FIRST-ORDER COST: PARASITE FOOD

How much do we feed the parasite economy and its professionals? It's hard to know, but some of the components give a sense of the magnitude.

We have a rough idea what we feed lawyers, though lawyers do a lot besides transfer-seeking. "A conservative estimate is that legal services now account for 2 percent of the economy's output," writes the economics columnist Robert J. Samuelson in *The Washington Post.* "In 1991, law firms collected an estimated $100 billion in revenues, up from $10.9 billion in 1972. That's double the growth rate of the total economy." By no means did all of the increase disappear into a black hole. Some of it was productive. But some of it came because legal costs escalated as more litigants fought over existing wealth.

When combatants drag each other back and forth, the frictional costs are bound to be high. A RAND study looked at nationwide tort litigation in 1985 and found that the costs of the litigation process itself—mostly lawyers' fees—"consumed about half of the $29 billion to $36 billion that were spent on litigation," leaving only the other half for actual compensation and damages. A dollar in legal costs for every dollar paid to a wronged plaintiff is a lot of friction. This is probably not a very productive way to spend $15 billion or more every year.

Agents' fees also include payments to lobbyists and politicians. How much lobbyists earn in aggregate, we don't know. The economists David N. Laband and John P. Sophocleus have estimated that about $4.6 billion was spent on state and federal lobbying in 1985. Today, of course, it would be more. As for politicians, in 1992 the direct investment in them ran to more than $3 billion, according to Herbert E. Alexander of the University of Southern California. Harder to count are indirect investments in politics, which tend not to be reported. Executives travel back and forth to Washington to lobby for tax credits; insurance companies treat politicians to junkets in Barbados. "Regulated Industries Were Eager to Bankroll Presidential Galas," headlined *The Washington Post* in the wake of the Clinton inaugural. You could call that sleazy, and it was, but no regulated business can afford to be on Washington's bad side. If you're a company or group with a stake in public policy, then baseball tickets and honoraria for politicians are investments you had best not neglect.

Still harder to count are the amounts spent as Americans struggle to stay up to speed on the transfer-seeking game. If you're a lobbyist or group organizer, you'll need magazines, books, electronic-information services, databases, seminars, who's-who directories, consultants, and more. Those materials don't come cheap—a fact which is itself further evidence of the high return on transfer-seeking investment. A subscription to the *National Journal,* a weekly on government and politics which is required reading for parasites (and for which I'm a contributing editor), costs more than $800 a year.

If you lobby and know what's good for you, you'd better buy this stuff, as the publishers and seminar organizers will be happy to remind you. "Keep track of the political influences that affect your bottom line—before it's too late," a promotional mailing for *State Legislatures* magazine says ominously. In the transfer-seeking game, what goes into one person's pocket comes out of someone else's, so don't be the slowpoke who gets taken to the cleaners. Why buy the National Conference of State Legislatures' books on annual state tax and spending actions? Because, says a mailing, "Whatever your business, you have a serious stake in state taxes and spending. . . . *Isn't a $70 investment worth the potential impact on your bottom line?*" Italics in the original, and well deserved. Wouldn't it be a shame if you were slammed with a $7 million tax surcharge, all because you forgot to feed $70 to the parasite economy?

Add up the costs of paying for transfer-seeking professionals and paraphernalia, and you have a sum somewhere in the tens of billions. A surprising aspect of that sum is how small it is—in the range of 1 percent of the gross national product. Remember, however, that much of this money comes out of the pool of investment capital, which runs to less than $300 billion (on a net basis). Diverting precious capital from productive investment is not a very good idea.

In 1992, American steel companies filed six dozen lawsuits alleging unfair competition from foreign producers. "A financial windfall for Washington's trade bar," was the way the *National Journal* described the legal action. The initial filing involved more than two million pages of allegations in 650 boxes; several major law firms each reported having the equivalent of a dozen full-time lawyers on the cases; each foreign defendant company hired its own battalion of lawyers, as did each country named in a suit; and all concerned acknowledged that the legal fees would run into the tens of millions of dollars. One lawyer joked, "It's an enormous contribution to the services balance of trade." Ha, ha. The American steel industry suffered for decades from chronic underinvestment, and swaths of it remain technologically laggard. Do we really want to see heavy industry investing its scarce capital in lawsuits? And remember how the game grows: foreign companies must defend themselves, diverting still more capital from steelmaking to lawyering. "In anticipation of the U.S. filings, two Mexican companies filed antidumping suits against seven U.S. flat-rolled producers," the Commerce Department reported. "Canadian producers indicated that they too were preparing antidumping suits against U.S. steelmakers." To pay the lawyers, steel prices must go up, making refrigerators and cars more expensive. Yet, when the returns on investing in lawsuits become higher than the returns on investing in machinery, what do you expect?

SECOND-ORDER COST: DEFENSIVE MANEUVERING

If you stopped there, you could safely conclude that the parasite economy isn't all that expensive to support. However, the direct costs of paying transfer agents are only the tip of the proverbial iceberg. To bring more above the surface, move to another hidden cost, one which is even harder to trace with any precision but is probably an order of magnitude more expensive.

That is the cost of defensiveness and uncertainty generated

by the very existence of the transfer-seeking economy. On a block where burglaries are common, people spend heavily on alarms and guards and outdoor lights, even if they never wind up being burglarized. Something a bit like that happens in a society where transfer-seeking is common.

Although defensive maneuvering is an important factor in lobbying (everyone needs a lobbyist because everyone else has one), its effects probably show up most clearly in the area of litigation. If you want to give someone benefits or help him solve his problems, one way is with a direct subsidy or a regulation requiring others to help him. Another way, however, is to give him a legal claim against someone else. Once he has the right to sue, he can go to court seeking compensation or damages. As always, important social goals are served this way. Again, though, there are side effects, which become more noticeable as new laws create more grounds for lawsuits.

David Meglathery is the principal at a public elementary school in Wilton, Connecticut. He has worked in education since 1968, and has seen many changes—including one he doesn't much like. These days, it's not uncommon for parents to threaten a lawsuit when they're unhappy. When Meglathery caught a child stealing pencils from the dispensary, he suspended him for one morning, and the father threatened to sue. "It has become a part of the frustrated parent's repertoire," Meglathery says. Plus, Meglathery has been named as a defendant in an employment suit. Plus, "there's no such thing as an accident any longer," and so the playground seesaw is gone, as is the merry-go-round, as is the jungle gym. "Basically," he says, "playgrounds have been stripped of their equipment." Playgrounds are probably safer, but that isn't an unalloyed blessing. "It has eliminated a few risks that were there, but it has also eliminated a lot of opportunities for kids to cooperate and do some imaginative and creative things." And today's safer playground equipment is so expensive that "most school budgets do not contain the money for them"—including his own budget.

School principals are in the trouble business. "You're dealing with people and you're constantly being bombarded by crisis situations," Meglathery says. Nowadays, he says, he's always looking over his shoulder. "It just isn't worth getting involved in a lawsuit, even though you know you're right. It restricts my ability to be as effective as I could be, because of caution, because of anxiety. You live with it day and night. You wonder: am I going to find a letter in my mailbox that's going to summon me to a situation where I'll have to testify?"

Steve Lichtman owns a smallish plumbing-supply company in Michigan City, Indiana. His family has been in the business since the 1930s, and he prides himself on knowing his customers and his business. He also knows the joy of being sued. His wife got into a low-speed fender-bender and he was sued for a sum in the low six figures. The other driver reported being fine at the scene but showed up at the deposition in a wheelchair.

"The lawyers told us that if it went before a jury it could go into boxcar numbers," he said. "So we just settled."

At work, his liability-insurance costs have risen smartly. That's less money, he says, for new workers, which he could use. To jockey for advantage, customers send lawyer-letters and drop hints about suing. You never know when a lawsuit might strike from out of the blue. "It always seems like you've got to look over your shoulder," Lichtman says.

Welcome to the high-claims world, where there are lots of laws allowing people with complaints to attach themselves to other people with money or insurance. Because those claims bring some benefits, you cannot assume the high-claims system is terrible and should be junked. But it is important to see that you also can't assume that more claims equals more justice, more efficiency, or anything else. Claims against schools may mean that fewer kids break bones on playgrounds, but they may also deprive many kids of jungle gyms and merry-go-rounds. Is that fair? Is it progress? It's not obvious.

Rather, the high-claims system constitutes a more or less

blind gamble. Lawsuits undoubtedly deter some bad behavior, enforce some contracts, spread some existing risks, and punish some wrongdoers. But they also undoubtedly deter some beneficial enterprise, open loopholes in some contracts, create some new risks, and terrorize some innocents. And we have no way of knowing whether the balance sheet comes up positive or negative.

To see why, imagine that you decide to reduce fire injuries by holding firefighters liable for fire damage. "Now," you think, "they'll be darn sure to put out every fire." Maybe, but maybe not. Chances are that litigation will drive up the cost of firefighting. The city may cut back on the fire department, or cut child nutrition or education. Both actions are plausible, when you consider that, for instance, in the space of a single decade (1976 to 1986) Washington State's legal costs rose ninefold as it faced ever more lawsuits; and that in 1985 there were more than 54,000 claims pending against the federal government, demanding more than $140 billion. New Jersey, plagued by claims against its transit systems, staged a bogus bus accident in 1993. "Video cameras inside the bus and outside filmed seventeen people scrambling onto the bus before the police arrived," reported *The New York Times*. "All later claimed to be injured in the accident. Another two who were never even on the bus also filed claims." In 1992, New York City spent nearly $200 million satisfying jury verdicts and settlements—money diverted from other city needs. "New York City," writes Saul B. Shapiro, a lawyer, "is subject to trial by jury virtually every time someone trips on a crack in the sidewalk, slips on ice, or drives into a pothole."

Moreover, once the inevitable horror story gets around about a firefighter who was taken to court and stripped of all his worldly possessions, people may start fleeing or avoiding the business. In New York State, where a third of all obstetricians have been sued four or more times, one out of every six had stopped delivering babies by early 1993. In 1986, according to

Peter Huber of the Manhattan Institute, a new claim was being filed against the makers of whooping-cough vaccine every week; "one former manufacturer faced one hundred suits demanding more than $2 billion in compensation, or two hundred times the total annual sale revenues of the vaccine." Manufacturers retreated from the business, and by 1986 only two major companies were investing heavily in vaccine research. "In America," notes *The Economist,* "fear of litigation and of political fallout has encouraged some companies to abandon contraceptive development. This restricts the contraceptive options open to American women—IUDs are virtually unobtainable, and all the compounds used in chemical contraceptives in the United States today were available in the 1960s." From 1977 to 1985, the manufacturers of small airplanes saw their liability-claim payments rise ninefold. The result, as they retreated from the business, was to keep older, less safe planes on the market, even though, notes Huber, "the new models kept off the market were notably safer than the old ones people went on using instead." One study of small manufacturers of farm equipment in California found that 22 percent had dropped product lines out of fear of liability litigation. And so on.

In just the same way, litigation against firefighters may result in more fire damage rather than less. Now, the key word here is "may." The point isn't that litigation necessarily makes matters worse on net, but that there is no a priori reason to suppose it makes matters better. We don't know.

And what about the victims of fire? At least they will be compensated for their losses, because there will be someone to seek compensation from—yes? Alas, that isn't clear, either. Because litigation is expensive and often traumatic, very few people who suffer personal injuries ever sue—about 2 percent, according to RAND research. Those who do sue may receive awards out of all proportion to the losses they suffered, or they may receive nothing. And the process will take months.

The litigation system does, of course, compensate some people, albeit almost arbitrarily. But its very arbitrariness creates negative elements on the other side of the equation: defensiveness and fear. You might at any moment be sued, but you might not. One consequence is business uncertainty, which can cloud the investment climate, complicate decision-making, introduce ever more lawyers and paperwork into deal-making. Everyone hires more lawyers and buys more liability insurance, even though most people won't actually have to pay a claim (just as everyone buys locks, even if most people aren't actually robbed). Insurance, of course, is expensive. For instance, in the 1980s, doctors' liability premiums rose by about 15 percent a year; much of that cost was passed on to patients.

Moreover, many people become more careful than they need to be, and that's harmful too. Playgrounds banish jungle gyms, even though most schools might never actually be sued. In 1989 alone, according to the Council of Economic Advisers, defensive medicine—medical procedures protecting doctors from lawsuits, rather than patients from disease—cost at least $20 billion, or more than a sixth of total physician expenditures.

And there is that other consequence, anxiety. You never know when a transfer-seeker will come to get you. Maybe he has a good case or maybe not, but either way, you'll pay the lawyers—just as you'll pay the lobbyists if your competitor goes after you on Capitol Hill. This problem can become worse as transfer agents—lawyers, in this case—learn how to churn the system to get the most out of it. "Some kinds of claim," writes the legal scholar Dan Dobbs,

> offer potential recoveries so great that many people may be induced to assert them, even though the win-rate is very low. But if one out of every ten plaintiffs is able to win such a claim, that means nine out of ten defendants must pay attorney fees and other expenses of suit even though they are entirely innocent. The innocent nine

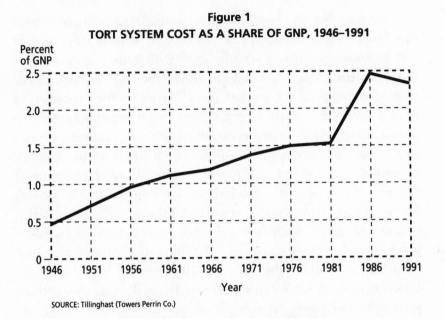

Figure 1
TORT SYSTEM COST AS A SHARE OF GNP, 1946–1991

Percent of GNP

SOURCE: Tillinghast (Towers Perrin Co.)

are hostages for the liability of the tenth. The costs to them in money and in life disruption may far exceed the gains to the one plaintiff. I count this a very high cost indeed.

I think the only fair conclusion today is that we have no idea whether the high-claims legal system is making us better off or worse off on net. Indeed, about the litigation system there is little that we do know. Among those nuggets of uncontested knowledge is that the system handsomely benefits the professionals who work it. When Arista Records became the target of an enterprising class-action suit, on the grounds that the company's pop duo Milli Vanilli didn't do their own singing, Arista settled. Eighty thousand or so alert fans could send in for $1 refunds on singles, $2 on cassettes, and $3 on compact disks. That might have made the fans feel a little better. But the lawyers felt a lot better, because they walked away with considerably more than $3 each.

Figure 1 gives some clearer idea what we're talking about.

It was compiled by the Tillinghast consulting company from insurance-company data, and shows the annual costs of the tort system (just one part of the civil-litigation system) as a share of the gross national product since 1946. The curve rises smartly over the period. In 1991, insurance companies paid $132 billion in damages, claims, legal expenses, and administrative costs. That accounted for more than 2 percent of the national economic output—twice the level of 1966. A remarkable thing was how much money did *not* go to injured parties. "If viewed as a mechanism for compensating victims for their economic losses," reported Tillinghast, "the tort system is extremely inefficient, returning less than 25 cents on the dollar for that purpose." If you add compensation for pain and suffering, the injured still received less than half. Lawyers and administrators, especially the former, wound up with the remainder. It was yet another confirmation of the law of the parasite economy: no matter who else loses, lawyers and lobbyists win.

(In the context of transfer-seeking, litigation is a cousin of lobbying. In both kinds of activity, the system is supposed to provide fair compensation or serve society's larger interests, but it necessarily also creates opportunities for redistributive entrepreneurism and profit-hunting) in both, the parties on all sides wind up feeding middlemen and hiring expensive professional agents; and in both, the very existence of the transfer-seeking activity leads to defensive maneuvering—companies maintain huge legal staffs, for instance, or they open more Washington offices—which may itself feed the cycle. But there are, of course, some important differences. For one, relatively few Americans actually litigate, whereas most Americans lobby, if not personally then through their interest groups. More important, a lawsuit seeks a direct transfer from a particular person or company, whereas lobbying usually seeks transfers from the economy at large—from taxpayers or consumers as a class. Which brings us to the next kind of cost.

THIRD-ORDER COST: SUBSIDY MADNESS

This cost is the steepest of all. It is the cost of the goodies themselves: damage done as industrious transfer-seekers weave distortions and inefficiencies into the economy.

If you could maintain just a limited portfolio of carefully selected subsidy programs, chosen to work together, this wouldn't be a serious problem. Markets are not perfect, and every society needs laws and programs to soften life's sharpest edges. By picking a group of core programs and then holding the line, you might be able to meet the most important social needs—a safety net for the elderly, say, and unemployment insurance and a space program or whatever—without drawing new lobbies out of the woodwork to seek ever more benefits. The problem comes because subsidies, once enacted, are fiercely defended and rarely go away. As they pile up, they begin to do to the economy something like what might happen to a patient who used a hundred drugs simultaneously.

To see why, go back to Scrooge the bicycle messenger. Suppose he succeeds in his campaign to restrict fax machines to long-distance use. He now captures local business that otherwise would have traveled by fax. But the reason people were using fax machines instead of bicycle messengers was that faxing was cheaper. Forced to use a more expensive option, people find that communications costs have increased. What used to cost two or three dollars now costs five or six. Less is left over to be spent on other things. That is what economists call a deadweight loss: people pay more, but they don't get more. Wealth is destroyed. Meanwhile, the fax-machine business becomes less profitable, and so fax-machine makers invest less in research and development. At the same time, the coddled messenger business becomes less competitive, and so couriers invest less in making themselves faster and cheaper. Communications technology improves more slowly than it would have. Again, a deadweight loss.

If the story ended there, you could say, "Well, protecting Scrooge's job costs some money, but it's worth it." Unfortunately, the story doesn't end there. Far from it: subsidies and protective rules breed other subsidies and protective rules, in a chain reaction that never really ends.

Thanks to Scrooge, fax makers are outraged and financially pinched. They want redress. Since they couldn't stop Scrooge's fax ban from passing, their lobbyist advises them to ask the government for a tax break. Supposing that they get it, the tax code is now artificially encouraging faxing, but the regulatory code is artificially discouraging faxing. The policy has become incoherent, doing two opposite things at once. More inefficiency.

Meanwhile, suppose, not implausibly, that the government pays for its tax break for faxers by raising the tax on telephones. Now phone calls are more expensive, and resources are diverted from *that* sector. People begin using electronic mail when a phone call would otherwise have been cheaper and more efficient. Again, they are paying more to do effectively the same thing: another deadweight loss.

The phone company, in turn, covers its losses by lobbying regulators to raise prices on mobile-phone service. But—oops—Scrooge depends on his mobile phone to find out where his next delivery is. So the same system that subsidizes him is also raising his costs. He is collecting in one pocket but paying from another. More incoherence.

The chain goes on and on, around and around. Pretty soon the plumbing system of tax breaks and subsidies and regulatory favors is a tangled mass moving resources in every direction at once. It is incoherent and at war with itself. You install pipes to divert water from my sink to your bathtub; someone else diverts this same water from your bathtub to his toilet; and I divert this same water yet again back to my sink. Before long, everyone is rerouting everyone's water and pipes are running in and out of every door and window, all in a mad jumble. The result is the net impoverishment of all classes but one, namely the class of plumbers and pipefitters, of whom there are more every year, getting rich laying ever more convoluted networks of pipe.

Eventually, as everyone seeks subsidies and everyone pays for everyone else's subsidies, the economic distortions become too numerous to count. Money flies in every direction simultaneously. Increasingly, people make their investment decisions so as to maximize subsidies rather than productivity. For investment advice, they buy books like *Tax Guide for Residential Real Estate.* ("Home ownership and real estate renting are among the best tax shelters—*if* you know how to put the tax breaks to work for you," advises the book's publicity kit.) The economy loses efficiency. It either grows less quickly than it would have, which is certainly the case in today's America, or it goes into subsidy shock and stagnates or even shrinks, as happened in many Third World and socialist economies. The one consistent exception is the sector that makes its living by buying and selling subsidies. That sector grows.

The chain I've just described is unrealistic only in that it makes the mess seem less messy than it really is. Here is how American farm policy works today.

Though fewer than 2 percent of Americans now live on farms, agricultural interests make up a powerful political bloc, well represented in every state and well organized in Washington. They are expert at farming the tax code and cultivating Capitol Hill. So they demand and receive massive subsidies— enough, as the writer James Bovard has pointed out, to buy each full-time American farmer a new Mercedes-Benz every year. Those subsidies to farmers pump capital into farming and drain capital from other sectors. The inevitable result is that farmers produce more food than the market will buy. To stop them from doing that, the government, having paid them to grow crops, also pays (or requires) them *not* to grow crops. The policy is incoherent, just as if you were stepping on the gas pedal and the brake at the same time. Accordingly, the waste is large. You can see it in small costs which are tangible and in astronomical costs which can only be estimated.

For instance, billions and billions of pounds of perfectly good fruit have been destroyed year after year by government order. This was the result of the federal marketing-order program, an anticompetitive goody belonging chiefly to California fruit interests and dating back to the 1930s. To raise the prices enjoyed by farmers, the program closely regulated the amount of fruit that growers could sell, thereby stiffing consumers, especially poor ones. The federal navel-orange cartel, for instance, forced growers to withhold hundreds of millions of pounds of navel oranges from the market every year. One grower was actually prosecuted for selling undersized peaches and nectarines to residents of inner-city Los Angeles at reduced cost. Billions of pounds of unsold fruit simply rotted. "They lie rotting in the California desert, piled fifteen feet high over areas the size of football fields," reported *The Economist* in 1992. "Every year something like two billion juicy oranges and millions of lemons have been banned by federal decree from American shops." Yet, through higher prices, consumers effectively paid for the fruit they could not eat: a classic deadweight loss.

Little programs like citrus marketing orders occupy just the tiniest corner of agricultural policy. Multiply them a thousand-fold and you begin to get the picture. And what a picture! In the developed nations, all of which run expensive agricultural programs working at cross-purposes with themselves and each other, farm subsidies cost consumers and taxpayers the staggering sum of $350 billion *a year*, according to estimates by the Organization for Economic Cooperation and Development. Some of that money makes its way to farmers, but much of it evaporates in the form of higher farmland prices, and much is simply wasted because of the economic distortions and counterdistortions it causes. A 1988 Purdue University study found that for every farm job saved by subsidies, the American economy paid $107,000 in lost nonfarm output, $80,000 in federal spending, and $14,000 in higher food prices. (Think how many jobs all that money could have created, had farm interests not monopolized it.) When two Australian economists, Kym Anderson and Rod Tyers, looked at farm subsidies and protection among developed nations, they found that the cost came to about $1,400 a year for each nonfarm household in 1990. Worse, for every dollar of farm subsidies reaching producers, thirty-seven cents were wasted.

And that is just agriculture, itself just one small corner of the universe of subsidies and counter-subsidies and counter-counter-subsidies. In America, the tax bill of 1981 handed out giant tax breaks to the politically powerful real-estate industry. The result was to shift resources artificially into office buildings and away from, say, commercial research and factories. That, in turn, contributed to the massive overbuilding that brought down the savings-and-loan industry, at a cost of hundreds of billions.

Or again: one of the main reasons American health-care costs have run out of control is that health benefits have been exempted from the income tax. If your boss were to give you an extra $1,000 in cash, you would pay a chunk of it in taxes; but if he gave you the same amount in added health benefits, you would pay no additional taxes. Of necessity, such a policy amounted to a big subsidy for health-care consumption. It artificially diverted resources into health care and out of other sectors, feeding health-care inflation and sapping the rest of the economy.

Or again: when the sellers of smaller and cheaper kinds of mobile phones needed radio frequencies, the existing frequency users moved in Congress to prevent the government from granting them. The result of such maneuvering was to delay the introduction of new technology and raise its cost.

Or again: over the 1980s, almost all states curtailed employers' ability to fire workers at will. That seems harmless enough, but the picture isn't complete until you also look at the costs. When firing becomes riskier for employers, hiring necessarily also becomes riskier, and employers look for ways to avoid doing it. A 1992 RAND study found that the result was a loss of total U.S. employment in the range of 2 percent to 5 percent, a cost which the think tank dryly described as "quite large."

One can go on and on in this way. The vast majority of subsidies and anticompetitive deals distort resource flows and slow the economy's ability to adapt. In today's globalized economy, that problem may be even more serious than it was in the 1950s or 1960s. Robert J. Shapiro of the Progressive Policy Institute, a think tank in Washington, argues that a global market "puts an enormous premium on flexibility and innovation," because companies need to innovate and mobilize quickly to meet needs of disparate local markets. "In economic life, the only force I know that drives innovation is competition," says Shapiro. "This is the fatal flaw of subsidy policies. They insulate sectors from the full force of competition, and insulate them from the need to be innovative in order to be more productive." As subsidized sectors fall behind, growth slows. "Then the demand for subsidies increases as people try to protect their rate of return," says Shapiro. "It's a vicious cycle."

The reason the cycle is so hard to break is that the costs of economic distortion and rigidity are so hard to see. They are marbled all through the economy and embedded deeply within it. When you go to the store, the labels don't tell you how much marketing orders or farm subsidies raise the prices of bread and fruit. To make matters worse, lobbies work hard to hide the costs of their benefits. Interest groups, Mancur Olson has written, "have an incentive to seek [subsidies] that are the least straightforward or the least conspicuous, not those that have the lowest social cost." Given a choice between a direct cash payment from the Treasury or a rule raising prices, business lobbies almost always choose the latter, because it's harder for irate taxpayers to notice.

Yet, though the costs of economic goody-hunting are hard to see, we know that they exist, that they are large, that they twist economies in ways large and small. The economists David Laband, Frank Mixon, and Robert Ekelund, Jr., illustrated the bending of economies in a particularly amusing way. When they compared state capitals with similar noncapital cities (and controlled for extraneous factors), they found that the capital cities boasted a disproportionate number of golf courses and fancy restaurants. They reasoned that this was because golf courses and fancy restaurants are favorite business venues of lobbyists. Moreover, the larger the state government's share of state income, the more fancy restaurants in the capital. The more the swirl of subsidies expands, the better the parasite professionals eat. Like the plumbers we hire to divert each other's water, they win no matter who else loses.

GRAND TOTAL

Now suppose you want to add up the bill.

Scholars who do this kind of work, according to Robert D. Tollison, an economist who specializes in transfer-seeking, come up with a range of cost estimates, all of them necessarily squishy. About the lowest is 3 percent of the gross national product a year. At the other end of the range, David Laband and John Sophocleus figured that Americans—including criminals as well as legal transfer-seekers—invested about $1 trillion in transfer activity in 1985, which would have been about a quarter of the GNP that year.

However, most estimates cluster in the range of 5 percent to 12 percent of GNP every year. In 1993, that would be $300 billion to $700 billion. If those estimates are in the ballpark, then by hunting for redistributive goodies Americans make themselves about 5 percent to 12 percent poorer than they otherwise

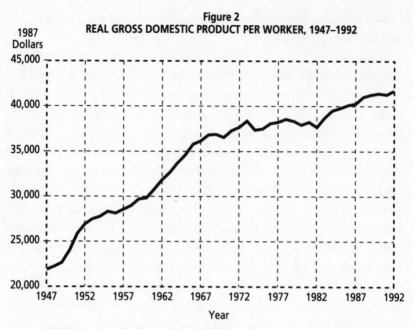

Figure 2
REAL GROSS DOMESTIC PRODUCT PER WORKER, 1947–1992

1987
Dollars

SOURCES: U.S. Department of Commerce; U.S. Department of Labor

would be. When I asked Tollison whether 5 percent to 12 percent seemed like a lot, he said, "Even the smallest number, 3 percent, is a lot of wealth to be pissing away, if you can help it." For instance, 3 percent of GNP, if it became available for investment, would increase the amount of gross private investment by something like a fourth; if it were saved, it could roughly double the American pool of personal savings.

And now I want to show why you should care. Figure 2 is one of the most basic of all economic charts. It shows, in inflation-adjusted dollars, the amount of output produced per worker in the economy since 1947. It also shows the most important single economic phenomenon of the postwar era. Around 1973, something happened. The economy's productivity growth rate shifted to a slower track. If real output per worker had continued to rise after 1973 at the same average rate as it did before, it would have been almost 40 percent higher than it actually is. In other words, Americans would be almost 40 percent richer.

Economists don't know all the reasons; when they use every explanation they can think of, they still only explain half of the productivity slowdown. But the effect is clear: a marked sluggishness in the rise of living standards. After 1973, real compensation per worker rose at only a fifth of the previous rate. More tellingly, the median family income, which doubled from 1947 to 1973, turned almost stagnant—partly because families themselves were changing, but also because the engine of wealth, namely productivity, was turning so slowly. Before the early 1970s, rising family income had seemed an American birthright; afterward, it seemed a struggle.

You may have noticed that the productivity curve in Figure 2 looks a little bit like the growth curves for groups and lawyers and political contributions and so on—except upside down. The period of hyperpluralism and the period of slow growth roughly coincide. That may be, literally, a coincidence. We don't know. Transfer-seeking is certainly not the sole culprit—probably not even the main culprit—in the post-1973 economic sea change. On the other hand, it is very likely that the substitution of transfer-seeking for productive investment is at least one of the factors behind slow long-term growth. "I don't think we have good measures," says the economist Gordon Tullock, "but I'm sure the costs are very large."

"We're in an era of low growth," says Robert Tollison. "We're in an era when all kinds of policy ideas are popping up to improve growth." At such a time, Americans need to consider the possibility that one of the problems that ails their economy is their own growing investment in lobbying and lawyering to get at each other's money. A surging parasite economy is certainly a burden, even if the cost can't be exactly quantified. When you already have anemia, a bellyful of parasites is the last thing you need.

If Americans are serious about improving long-term growth and productivity—undoubtedly the most important economic need of our time—then we are going to have to get more serious than we have been about the problem of parasites. We need to think about ways to interrupt, or at least contain, the cycle by which transfer-seeking grows.

Today it is painfully clear that Americans have no handle on the cannibalistic forces unleashed by the revolution of groups and claims and activists and lobbyists and lawyers. In our desire to solve problems, we created a government with vast power to reassign resources, while in our desire to look out for ourselves we created countless new groups. What we did not create—still don't know how to create—was a way to control the chain reaction set off when activist government and proliferating groups began interacting with each other. Worse, instead of demanding less, we keep demanding more. Groups and activists doggedly, often hysterically, deny that their incessant invention of demands feeds distributive warfare and exacts an economic toll. So they reinforce the public's own denial.

All of that needs to change. Just now, the transfer-seeking game appears to have control of us, rather than we of it.

NOT FATAL, BUT ...

Despite everything, the parasite economy is not about to bankrupt America. The United States is a rich country with a resilient and resourceful economy. Companies are clever at adapting. Foreign competition helps curtail the worst excesses. I've been careful not to talk about an economic "crisis," because there isn't one. Transfer-seeking activity is a constant drag on the economy, but not a killer—at least not in the foreseeable future. That isn't a reason to stop worrying. In fact, it may be a reason to worry all the more, since the transfer-seeking mentality is so insidious, and its costs so well hidden. Still, the economic costs appear to be bearable, at least so far.

There is, however, that second kind of cost. Granted, lobbies and groups probably can't wreck the economy. But what if they can wreck the government?

6

DEMOSCLEROSIS

A PRIL 10, 1992. Four U.S. senators, two Democrats and two Republicans, have marched to the Senate floor with a brave and foolhardy proposal. They are going to take a stab at curtailing federal entitlement spending.

Entitlements are the huge check-writing programs whose benefits are guaranteed ("mandatory") by law: Social Security, Medicare, farm subsidies, veterans' payments, welfare, student aid, many more. Most of these are not little "special-interest" programs benefiting the few at the expense of the broad public. Rather, they are among the most popular programs the government runs, distributing Washington's bounty to millions of Americans and accounting for roughly a sixth of all personal income.

The middle class loves entitlement programs, which is precisely why they are so difficult to control. For the last twenty years or so they have been eating the federal government alive. Entitlements account for fully three-quarters of all federal domestic spending, and the proportion is steadily rising. Senator Pete Domenici of New Mexico, one of the Senate foursome, is clearly right when he tells the Senate this day, "If we do not do anything to control the

121

mandatory expenditures, the deficit will continue skyrocketing."

What the gang of four have in mind is an overall limit on the growth of entitlement spending. Bowing to the inevitable, they have exempted Social Security, which is viewed as too popular to touch. Other entitlement programs will collectively grow under their plan, but not as rapidly as in the past. "We do not seek to end entitlements, or even to reduce them," Virginia Democrat Charles Robb tells the Senate. "We do, however, believe that it is necessary to restrain their growth. That is, first and foremost, what this amendment does."

Actually, that's not all it does. It also lights up the civil-defense network of every lobby in Washington. Indeed, well before the proposal reaches the Senate floor, the interest groups are sounding klaxons and manning battle stations. Within two hours of the four senators' first detailed discussion of their proposal, their offices are receiving telegrams, Domenici says, "from all over the country, saying that this is going to hurt a veterans' group, this is going to hurt people on welfare, this is going to hurt seniors on Medicare." Bill Hoagland, an aide to Domenici, later recalls, "We were inundated. Just about every interest group you can think of was strongly opposed. It was very dramatic, how quickly they all came to the defense."

The American Association of Retired Persons calls the proposal a "direct attack." The National Council of Senior Citizens calls it "outrageous." Children's Defense Fund: "unacceptable." Committee for Educational Funding: "unconscionable." Food Research and Action Center: "devastating." American Federation of Government Employees: "unfair and unconscionable." Veterans of Foreign Wars of the United States: "totally unjust." Disabled American Veterans: "unconscionable." American Legion: "incredible." Paralyzed Veterans of America: "inherently unfair." The National Cotton Council of America, the U.S. Rice Producers' Group, the National Farmers Organization: "unfair." American Postal Workers Union: "irresponsible, simple-minded." And so on.

On the Senate floor, opponents of the spending cap move to exempt disabled veterans. This is a way to kill the cap without actually voting to kill it: once disabled veterans are exempted, there will be votes to exempt farmers, children, Medicare recipients, nannies with overbites, and everybody else. Each such vote will allow senators to go home and boast about "saving" a program; and each will allow another clutch of interest-group professionals to tell its membership, "See how badly you need us!" Perversely, the end result of this string of votes will be to entrench the very programs which the four senators—Robb, Domenici, Sam Nunn of Georgia, and Warren Rudman of New Hampshire—are trying to restrain.

The veterans' exemption passes overwhelmingly; the game is over. The senators withdraw their proposal. It is dead. In fact, it never had a chance.

Maybe the senators' plan deserved to die, maybe it didn't. Either way, it served a purpose. It provided a stark demonstration of the forces that are petrifying government.

The key words are "are petrifying"—not "have petrified." Demosclerosis—government's progressive loss of the ability to adapt—is a gradual but continuing process. It is not like an acute fever, which attacks in a sudden crisis and galvanizes one's immune system to respond with an all-out, decisive counter-attack. It is more like hardening of the arteries, which builds up stealthily over many years. Like arteriosclerosis, it can be stopped only by a long-term change in behavior: a disciplined regimen of self-reform. Also like arteriosclerosis, demosclerosis gets worse if it is ignored.

To understand it, one needs to begin with the right question. That question is not "Why does nothing get done in Washington?" Things always get done in Washington, today no less than ever. To frame the issue as a matter of whether "things get done" is to set off in the wrong direction and wind up hunting for ways to "speed up the process" and so on, which is almost entirely beside the point. The crucial question, rather, is this: Why is it that what Washington does is less and less effective at solving problems?

OUT OF KILTER

In the American system, it's *supposed* to be hard to change things. If the founders had wanted government to move quickly and easily, they wouldn't have bothered with competing power centers and a Bill of Rights. They wanted action to be deliberate, in every sense of the word. And they were right. An institution as powerful and as abusable as government ought to move carefully and, where possible, tactfully. Just making change easier (for instance, switching to a parliamentary government, in which a single party controls the whole government) might not solve the problem. In fact, it might make the problem worse, by removing some of the checks and balances that stop interest groups from grabbing goodies at will.

Demosclerosis happens, not because change is difficult, but because change is easier in one direction than in another. The problem, in other words, is asymmetry—a long-term imbalance of forces. Mancur Olson pointed out one such asymmetry: new interest groups form faster than old ones go away. Now here is another, which the founders could not have foreseen and which few people understand even today: in an interest-group democracy, all kinds of action are difficult, but they are not *equally* difficult.

Imagine a rocket ship headed for Jupiter on three thrusters. And now imagine that the thrusters are slightly out of balance. At first, you might not notice. After a little while, though, the rocket would be a little off course, and then a lot off course, and then it would be hurtling aimlessly into deep space. To prevent this from happening, you would have to spend energy just working to keep the rocket pointed straight. If you let it slip off course, you would have to struggle all the harder to bring it back. Control could become difficult, or even, eventually, impossible. You might run out of fuel long before you reached Jupiter. In any case, you could never relax for long. You might need to exert yourself constantly just to keep control.

An interest-group democracy turns out to face a similar problem. To create a new subsidy or anticompetitive deal is hard, but to reduce a subsidy that already exists is much harder. And to completely eliminate a subsidy or an anticompetitive arrangement is hardest of all.

Consider that as few as three or four well-placed congressmen (sometimes even one or two) can create a new subsidy program, if they're careful not to step on the wrong toes. After all, when you add a new program—assuming you're fairly clever about it—few interest groups or politicians complain, and the beneficiaries stand up and cheer. But once a subsidy program or an anticompetitive deal is in place, three or four congressmen can almost *never* get rid of it, because the people enjoying the subsidy can always line up ten or twenty congressmen to defend it.

When you try to trim programs, interest groups complain bitterly and fight hard, as the four kamikaze senators discovered. But woe unto him, above all, who makes bold to grab a subsidy or a special deal by the roots and pull it out entirely. Try doing that, and the affected group flies at you with the fury of the desperate or the damned. It recruits powerful congressmen to block you, it floods your office with mail, it finances your political opponents, it does whatever else it needs to do. Unless you want to be shot, stabbed, and set on fire, the cardinal rule in Washington is: never challenge someone's sinecure.

Ask Ed Derwinski. He is an affable former congressman who landed in 1989 as the secretary of veterans affairs, overseeing a massive health-care system with more than 170 hospitals, twice that many clinics, and a quarter of a million employees. Most veterans' hospitals opened decades ago, when America was a very different place. "What you've got," Derwinski says, "is a structure that, if you invented it today, 50 percent of the facilities would be located elsewhere. I felt the system needed shaking up. But I had been in government a long time, and I realized you couldn't shake it up." Derwinski knew better than to propose closing any hospitals, even if doing so would help improve service in the system as a whole. The veterans' lobbies would scream, the bureaucracy would resist, the mayors would raise Cain, the local congressmen would throw a fit, and the White House would panic. He did propose some consolidation—turning duplicative hospitals into, say, specialty clinics or nursing homes—but in the end was able to do very little even of that.

Then he committed the cardinal sin. Ever so gingerly, he threatened a monopoly franchise. Derwinski and the secretary of health and human services proposed letting nonveterans use a VA hospital.

In the poor town of Tuskegee, Alabama, the only private hospital within a thirty-five-mile radius had shut down; meanwhile, the large VA hospital there had plenty of extra space. Local residents were driving miles for medical care, even though there were empty hospital beds in their backyard. And so Derwinski proposed opening the VA hospital to needy local patients, for a three-year trial period. He did not propose to turn away any veterans: only spare space was to be used, veterans would receive priority over nonveterans, and the VA wouldn't pay an extra cent.

The veterans' groups rose up in fury. Although representing only a minority of all veterans, they were tightly focused, politically savvy, well financed, and well connected to sympathetic politicians at every level of government and in every city, county, and state. Derwinski liked to call them "professional veterans." In their opinion, the veterans' health care system belonged to veterans, and *only* to veterans. With his rural-health proposal, Derwinski was challenging their franchise.

"This is a ridiculous idea," said the head of the American Legion. "Just the tip of the iceberg," said the head of Veterans of Foreign Wars. The VA health-care system "must meet the needs of those it was designed for—veterans," said the head of the Disabled American Veterans. If there are empty hospital beds, said the veterans' lobbies, then extend medical benefits to more veterans and their families.

The strafing began. "Our members have deluged congressional offices, the White House, and the VA with letters and telephone calls to object to this proposal," said the Legion. The VFW called on its posts to "send a telegraph [*sic*] to President Bush demanding an end to the Rural Health Care Initiative and also (if you agree) *demanding* that Secretary of Veteran [*sic*] Affairs Ed Derwinski be fired!" In the Senate, Alabama's own senator, Richard C. Shelby, rose to proclaim that "veterans' hospitals are the exclusive domain of veterans and their qualified dependents."

The Senate voted ninety-one to three to kill the test program, whereupon Derwinski retired it, whereupon the veterans' lobby retired him. In the 1992 campaign, President Bush, seeking the support of veterans' groups, gave them Derwinski's head. Bill Clinton, taking the hint, promised in his campaign to "be a good president for the nation's veterans," endorsed a bundle of new benefits for them, and, upon winning, appointed a professional veterans' lobbyist to head the VA. That appointee immediately journeyed to the Tuskegee hospital and "there he made it clear [reported the *Chicago Tribune*] that he still opposed allowing nonveterans in the VA system."

Game, set, and match.

Nothing that happened to Ed Derwinski was unusual. You want to update the sadly archaic banking laws? In 1991, the Bush Administration sent Congress a banking-reform package. Under ancient statutes dating back to the early years of the New Deal, banks were barred from a variety of money-making activities. They could not underwrite securities, operate mutual funds, sell insurance, or open branches across state lines. Yet their modern competitors—mutual funds, for instance, which didn't exist when the banking laws were written—could perform many such functions with impunity. And so banks were placed at an artificial disadvantage, which restricted their ability to find profits. Weak banks, in turn, weakened the whole financial system.

What happened? "Bank reform succumbed to a frenzied attack by lobbyists," said *The New York Times*. "Small bankers, fearing competition, tore away interstate banking. Insurance firms, fearing competition, tore away insurance underwriting. Securities firms, fearing competition, tore away the proposal to let banks sell stocks and bonds." In the end, the *National Journal* reported, "every administration proposal for permitting banks to widen their business horizons—every single one—was picked off in the carnage." After Bush left, the Clinton people, having received the message, showed little interest in updating the banking laws. The end result was surely one of the most bizarre policies of our time: as the twenty-first century approached, the country limped along with financial rules written in the age of gramophones and green eyeshades.

You want to reform an agriculture program? You may be able to trim a subsidy a little, if you work very hard, but suppose you want to withdraw someone's monopoly claim completely. Take the sugar program, a classic anticompetitive arrangement that subsidizes growers by artificially pushing up sugar prices and restricting imports. The program costs Americans $1.4 billion a year in higher grocery bills, according to the General Accounting Office. The benefits are very highly concentrated; almost half of them flow to 1 percent of the sugar farms. In 1991, more than $30 million flowed to a single giant farm. Sugar parasites are voracious.

Senator Richard Lugar of Indiana tried to whack them. "As we tried to reform the farm budget," he said in a speech in 1992, "I made a specific motion to abolish the sugar program. The administration wanted to cut the support price from eighteen cents to sixteen. Well, my motion to abolish got two votes, Slade Gorton of Washington and my own. I'm ranking [Republican] member of the Agriculture Committee, and I could only get two votes. Five votes out of twenty to cut the support price from eighteen to sixteen. No change in the tobacco program, no change in peanuts, no change in wool, no change in honey or mohair or any of the rest of it."

You want to reform the schools? Another classic anticompetitive franchise protects public-school employees, who enjoy a monopoly claim on tax dollars for education. (By contrast, people spend their Medicare money at any hospital and their food stamps at any grocery store. No provider enjoys a monopoly claim.) What happens when you try to nibble at that franchise? The Bush people timidly tried in 1991. They wanted to finance 535 "break the mold" schools, both public and private, to be chosen competitively in Washington and funded directly from there. They also proposed some mild incentives for localities to try school voucher plans, which let parents spend public money at private schools. In both cases, the idea was to stimulate innovation by bypassing the entrenched establishment of public-school employees and administrators.

Under intense opposition from those groups, the voucher measure was demolished. "Break the mold" schools turned mostly into block grants for state education agencies and local school districts: more money for the entrenched providers. There would be no going around them to finance new competitors. Later on, the Clinton Administration, needing support from the public employees' unions, carefully avoided reopening the issue.

I multiply examples to make a point. Digging out an interest group and its favorable deal is like digging out a splinter embedded deeply in your foot: so painful that you'd rather just limp.

TRY, TRY AGAIN

All right; so it's harder to get rid of subsidies and perks than to create them. So what? How does that asymmetry erode government's ability to adapt?

The crucial element—the nub of the whole argument—is trial and error.

We tend to think of trial and error as a small and sterile idea, a mere commonplace ("If at first you don't succeed . . ."). The method of trial and error certainly seems unglamorous by comparison with, for example, the method of large-scale planning. It's tempting to think that lowly trial and error merely roots out mistakes, whereas planning builds cathedrals. To take such a view, however, is to sadly underestimate the power of trial and error. It is the key to successful adaptation and problem-solving in large, complex systems.

In the large, complex system of biological evolution, species undergo mutations. Mutations themselves aren't evolution. Evolution occurs when a mutant proves better adapted to its environment than its predecessors or its competitors. The critical trick is to find the *useful* mutation, and you never know in advance which mutation will be useful. The vast majority will fail. A few, however, succeed brilliantly. Those high achievers then proliferate by outcompeting their rivals. That is how life adapts to changing environments. And if you replicate the trial-and-error process throughout billions of species over billions of years, you get a thriving biosphere whose nearly infinite complexity and diversity and flexibility put any cathedral—or any other planned and static structure—to shame.

The genius of a capitalist economy is that it uses the same kind of evolutionary strategy. Stalin was able to build state-of-the-art factories in the 1930s and 1940s; what he could not do was keep the factories up to date. His economy could not adapt. Capitalism, by contrast, is good at adapting, and the key to its adaptability is that it makes many mistakes but corrects them quickly. Then it makes many more mistakes, and corrects those. Hopeful entrepreneurs open businesses and corporate executives try new marketing strategies; most fail, but every so often someone hits on a brilliant innovation. You never know ahead of time which innovation will turn out to be brilliant. But the point of the method of trial and error is that you don't need to know. The successful innovations proliferate by outcompeting their rivals. Capitalism, like the biosphere, adapts through trial and error.

Similarly with another complex social system, science. No one knows in advance which idea will turn out to be right. Most new ideas, in fact, are wrong. The key to science's success is that it tries out a million hypotheses every day and abandons most of them. The survivors are our knowledge base. And so the knowledge base adapts through trial and error.

To see the full implications of demosclerosis, it's necessary to apply the same kind of evolutionary thinking to government. In a bafflingly complex world, you can no more know in advance which government programs will work than you can know in advance which mutations will succeed or which new products will be profitable. The only way to find out is to try and see. Moreover, in a world that changes fast, today's successful program is tomorrow's anachronistic failure. The only way to stay abreast is to keep trying new programs and let the successful ones outcompete their rivals. In other words, the way for governments to learn what works in a protean world is by trial and error.

However, something has gone badly wrong.

THE LIVING DEAD

The Reagan Administration believed in killing domestic programs, mostly because its conservative officials disliked government. Ronald Reagan, a popular president who effectively controlled Congress in the critical early portion of his first term, made a fetish of trying to eliminate federal programs. But during his eight years in office, a grand total of four major programs—general revenue sharing, urban development action grants, the synthetic-fuels program, and the Clinch River breeder reactor—actually got killed.

President Bush had no better luck. For fiscal 1993 alone, the Bush Administration proposed ending 246 federal programs. Unlike Reagan, Bush wasn't trying to spear any big (or controversial) fish; if all 246 had been eliminated, the budgetary savings would have come to only $3.5 billion, or a quarter of 1 percent of federal spending. You might think that clearing the waters of such small fry would be fairly easy. But you would be wrong. Out of 246, a not very grand total of eight programs actually disappeared, including the commission on the Constitution's bicentennial (which had occurred in 1987) and a NASA asteroid flyby. The total savings came to an even less grand total of $58 million. In a budget of $1.5 trillion and thousands of programs, that was all the president could get rid of.

It is scarcely an exaggeration to say that, in Washington, *every program lasts forever.* When you stop to think about it, this is an astonishing fact—indeed, almost incredible. How—why—can it be?

Go back to the world of hyperpluralism described in Chapter 3. Remember that one sure way to get an interest group started is to set up a redistributive program. Soon after the program begins, the people who depend on it—both the program's direct beneficiaries and its administrators and employees—organize to defend it. They become an entrenched lobby. They have money, votes, and passion. They have professional lobbyists and rapid-response "action alert" systems. They are slick and sophisticated. When necessary, they scream and yell. At any given moment, it's always safer to placate them than to defy them.

Suppose, then, that you want to get rid of the Rural Electrification Administration, as the Reagan and Bush administrations wanted to do. The REA started as a New Deal relief program in 1935, when only 10 percent of American farms had electricity. A few decades later, its mission was accomplished. Not only did the vast majority of farms have electricity and telephone service (99 percent had power and 96 percent had phones in 1990), they were actually more likely to have such service than the average American household. In fact, the rural electrical subsidies often flowed to the nonpoor and even the nonrural. A lot of people began wondering whether the country really needed the REA.

Those people faced a formidable obstacle. In 1942, hard on the heels of the rural electrification program, the National Rural Electric Cooperative Association arrived on the scene. Today the association represents a thousand farflung rural electrical cooperatives; the cooperatives boast ten thousand local directors and six times that many employees; those people are well connected, politically active, and regularly in touch with members of Congress and each other. If anyone makes a move to abolish the REA or its subsidies, those people—as well as several other lobbying groups—swarm out of the woodwork. "There were so many," recalled one former government official who opposed the program, "they had support everywhere. It was hopeless." To back them up, the association's political action committee raised more than $1 million in the 1991–92 campaign cycle and donated more than $700,000 to almost four hundred congressional candidates. And the association, with its imposing building near Dupont Circle in Washington, wasn't going away. Interest groups almost never go away. Like everyone else, they want to keep their jobs.

These people have more than just the power of a strong grass-roots lobbying network. They also have the power of conviction. They believe in the rightness of their cause and bolster their belief with two appealing arguments—need and fairness.

The need argument says, "We need federal money because, having relied on it for all these years, we can't get along without it." When I asked Bob Bergland, a former secretary of agriculture who went on to become head of the electric-cooperative association, why his members still needed subsidies, he replied: "There's a level at which some of these marginal [rural electric] systems simply won't be able to pass on the costs." (However, he also conceded that rates would go up "not much" without the subsidies.)

The fairness argument says, "Our competitors are subsidized, so it's only fair to subsidize us." Bergland made this argument, too, accurately pointing out that municipal and private utilities enjoy various kinds of tax breaks and indirect subsidies. It would hardly be fair to punish the rural cooperatives while leaving their competitors untouched.

Now, to understand why programs never die, it's essential to see that both of those arguments—need and fairness—are available to *every lobby in Washington*. Because groups that receive subsidies (or other kinds of benefits) soon rely on them, *every* reduction creates some genuine hardship cases. And because nowadays everyone is subsidized one way or another, *every* reduction hurts some people relative to others. Even in principle, there is no patently "unneeded" program or "fair" reduction. Turn over every stone in Washington, but you will never find one. That's another reason lobbies don't go away: they are all defending something which is economically vital and morally urgent for somebody.

Can't you at least get rid of the programs that fail? In principle, maybe, but not in practice. One problem is that people disagree about which programs have failed, and even about what "failing" means. Evolutionary systems get around this problem simply by forcing all businesses, ideas, and species to compete. "Success" isn't argued about; it's whatever wins. If the federal government worked on a trial-and-error basis, it could try many rival programs to solve any particular problem, and then abandon all but the one that worked best. It might start with a dozen competing welfare systems, and close all but one of them—and then close *that* system when a better one came along. The trouble, though, is that in today's world each program instantly generates an interest group, and each interest group lobbies to keep its own program open, drumming up campaign contributions and producing stacks of studies "proving" the program's success. In the end, we get stuck with all twelve programs instead of finding the best one, and before long they're working at cross-purposes and shutting out any new rivals.

So why don't all these lobbies cancel each other out? After all, they compete for the government's money and attention. And, to some extent, that helps. As a rule, though, lobbies work hard to avoid head-on confrontations with other lobbies, for exactly the same reason that politicians work hard to avoid confrontations with lobbies: challenge someone's sinecure, and you get his fist in your face. If farmers tell the government, "We want you to kill the ranchers' subsidies and give us the money," they can count on a bruising fight with the cattlemen's association. On the other hand, if they say, "The ranchers are getting land-use subsidies, so please raise our price supports," they avoid antagonizing any powerful group directly. The choice is obvious, which is why you can't rely on competition between lobbies to control lobbying.

Thus, when I asked Bob Bergland of the National Rural Electric Cooperative Association whether he would favor cutting his own *and* his competitors' subsidies, he demurred. "We think a good argument can be made for support on all sides," he said. In other words, subsidize our competitors *and* us. Which is exactly what usually happens. Other things being equal, lobbies and subsidies tend to reinforce each other, rather than killing each other off. And now we're back where we started: since everybody is subsidized, to cut any particular group's subsidy is "unfair." The circle closes.

The end result is that, with rare exceptions, *we are stuck with everything the government ever tries,* including some rather bizarre things. Today in America, you need a government license to grow peanuts. This is because commodity markets were turbulent in 1934. "The chaotic agricultural and economic conditions that caused the Congress to establish the peanut program fifty-eight years ago no longer exist," noted the General Accounting Office in 1993. "Most peanuts in the United States today are produced by large agribusinesses rather than by the small family farms that dominated agriculture in the 1930s." Has the peanut program ended, now that it protects big agribusinesses that employ slick lobbyists? On the contrary. Today a fifth of the peanut growers control more than four-fifths of the peanut licenses, which they can sell or rent for anywhere from $50,000 to $6 million. Of the third to half a billion dollars that the peanut program costs American consumers every year, as much as a fourth is deadweight loss: wealth that is simply destroyed.

By way of long-lived wacko anachronisms, it would be hard to beat the federal subsidy for wool and mohair. The program was set up in 1955, when wool was a vital strategic commodity for military uniforms. (Mohair growers, who sell the fleece of Angora goats, snuck into the program and came along for the ride. Don't ask what an Angora goat is. The main thing is that there are a lot of them in Texas, which is robustly represented on the House and Senate agriculture committees.) The program failed: wool production went down, not up, because market forces overwhelmed the subsidies. But even if the program had succeeded, its main rationale disappeared years ago. Synthetic fabrics came along, and the Pentagon struck wool from its strategic-commodities list. That was in 1960. In 1992, the wool and mohair program spent a tidy $191 million. Why did Bill Clinton inherit Dwight Eisenhower's failed strategic-fabrics policy? Because it was ably defended by the small but devoted group of people who benefited from it, in some cases richly (several dozen farmers routinely drew subsidy checks of more than $100,000).

If you asked the wool growers or the American Sheep Industry Association why their program was still necessary in the

1990s, they said, predictably, that wool farmers needed the money and that their competitors were subsidized too. When I asked the same question of a professional lobbyist who used to work for the wool growers, he chuckled and gave a plainer answer. "There's nothing more permanent in this town," he said, "than a temporary program."

LIFE IN THE FROZEN LANE

Not only are programs virtually impossible to kill, once put in place they are also hard to change. Every wrinkle in the law, every grant formula and tax loophole, produces a winner who resists subsequent reform, unless "reform" happens to mean more money or benefits for the lobbies concerned. That's why in the 1990s the United States still operated under an anachronistic banking law from the 1930s. Scholars understood years ago that some aspects of the welfare program actually deepened poverty by encouraging fathers to leave home, yet the old policy kept on going almost as though no one knew any better. As of the beginning of the Clinton Administration (which promised to rebuild the system, at long last), only one significant reform had been made to the federal welfare law since it was first enacted in 1935, and that change, the 1988 Family Support Act, was a modest reform affecting only a minority of welfare recipients. If a complicated program takes fifty years to update, it can hardly be expected to adapt to changing real-world problems.

But surely you can change an outmoded funding formula, at least? Don't count on it. In 1989, Pete Perry, an acting head of the federal Economic Development Administration, decided it was time to change the way regional economic-planning districts were funded. There were almost three hundred of those districts all over the country, drawing an average of about $50,000 of federal money every year. Perry had a sensible reason to change the formula: the formula was that there wasn't any formula. Rather, each district received more or less what it had received in earlier years, with an occasional cost-of-living adjustment. By the late 1980s, after two decades when some regions thrived and others decayed, funding bore no relationship to need or anything else. Some of the least needy districts were receiving some of the largest amounts. Moreover, funding wasn't related to districts' performance. And so Perry decided to try a new system. Grants for each district would be based on such factors as local population, income levels, unemployment, geographic area, and the planners' past performance. If a district had gotten richer, some of its money would be rerouted to a needier district.

"That," he says, "hit the fan." The people who run the planning districts enjoy robust support from local bigwigs. They also maintain a pressure group: the National Association of Development Organizations, or NADO, which was founded shortly after the Economic Development Administration was established. When I paid a visit to NADO's executive director, Aliceann Wohlbruck, she agreed that planning-district funding made little sense. "There's no great logic here," she said. "We really agree there are things in the programs that need to be changed. We want to work to improve the program." But her idea of improvement did not include reducing or eliminating funding for any existing district. "I think you've got to have a hold-harmless," she said. "If you've had the same level of funding for twenty-five years, how do you tell people you're going to cut it?"

Not the way Pete Perry told them, apparently. His proposal drew an action memo—URGENT, all capitals, bright pink paper—from Wohlbruck to NADO's constituents. They dropped a blizzard of mail and phone calls on members of Congress, who complained to the secretary of commerce. By the time the dust had settled, Perry's new formula was dead and Congress had raised the minimum level of funding for all the planning districts. End of reform.

To make government work under such conditions is a task

only for the masochistic or the criminally insane. Americans love to dump on government workers and managers. "Waste, fraud, and abuse," they grouse. What Americans overlook, or do not understand, is that their own organization into tens of thousands of permanent interest groups is making public servants' jobs impossible.

Imagine that you are appointed to be head of a bankrupt corporation. Your mission is to straighten out the company's finances and bring its equipment and product lines up to date. "Okay," you say, "let's get to work." But there's a catch. You're told that you cannot drop a single product, close a single factory, or get rid of any old equipment. Sure, you can develop new products. But you also have to keep the old ones on the market. You can manufacture the latest ergonomic office chair, but not drop your line of 1950s-style Naugahyde dinette furniture. You can open a new factory, but not close any old ones. At most, if you concentrate your energy on a few intense battles, in any given year you can drop one or two products and streamline one or two plants.

"Impossible!" you say. "No one could revitalize a corporation under such conditions!" You quit. And you're right.

Talk to anyone who has managed a federal government agency in the age of hyperpluralism, and you soon find that this imaginary situation isn't so imaginary. Orson Swindle, for instance, ran the Economic Development Administration for a few years during the Reagan Administration. He wanted to reform the EDA's University Center program, which gave each of fifty or so universities about $100,000 a year to help plan local development projects. The trouble—as he saw it—was not with the concept itself, which he supported, but that once a center was set up, it kept receiving funds forever. "If the program has merit," Swindle said, "then why don't we wean some of the centers that had been on it for twenty years?" The better centers could stand on their own two feet—selling their services and raising local contributions, for instance. And as money was freed up from existing centers, the EDA would spend it to start new ones. In fact, that was how the program was originally supposed to work when it was set up in the 1960s. "We would never have to ask for any more funds," Swindle said, "and we'd have more and more centers."

Unfortunately, that trick never works. The existing centers and their interest group, NAMTAC (the National Association of Management and Technical Assistance Centers), didn't care for the idea that "their" funding would be diverted to establish new rivals. "Very violently opposed" is how the centers' reaction was described by NAMTAC's Washington representative.

"The people that are in NAMTAC," observed Hugh Farmer, a retired civil servant who had worked at the EDA practically since its doors first opened, "are major universities from across the country, and they have quite a lobbying effort with Congress. They make their living by doing this." They went riding up to Capitol Hill, guns blazing, and without much trouble obtained a law barring any reductions in existing centers' funding. Swindle's attempt to make the program more flexible had instead locked it in place. The program had become a kind of permanent entitlement for a few dozen lucky universities.

So much for innovative management. A disillusioned Orson Swindle wound up as a senior adviser in Ross Perot's 1992 presidential campaign. Hugh Farmer, too, left the EDA with a bitter taste in his mouth. "I was frustrated by the fact that we couldn't change anything, we couldn't try new things," he said. "I think EDA is in a position where it's not being effective because it's too inflexible and it's too set in its ways. It's frozen and inflexible. Or it's semifrozen. It's kind of slushed. You're allowed to move a little to the left or right, but you can't move very far."

In 1991, President Bush appointed Diane Ravitch, a Democrat, to be assistant secretary of education in charge of educational research. She had plans and ideas. She got nowhere. She soon discovered that all but 5 to 10 percent of her department's research budget was preassigned, by law, to entrenched recipients. "There's a little bit of discretion," she told me, "but the vast bulk is frozen solid."

A handful of established regional laboratories virtually monopolized a key chunk of the research budget. They maintained a lobbying group, which was run by a former aide to a key member of the House Appropriations Committee. Another grantee, a center for civics education, was run by a man whose lobbyist had previously worked for the chairman of the House committee overseeing education. (You may sense a pattern. Recall that many politicians, Capitol Hill staff members, and government officials later go to work as lobbyists or interest-group professionals. That is probably another reason that programs are hard to get rid of: policymakers would just as soon not offend their future employers.) I asked Ravitch whether she tried to get rid of the civics program. "There was no point trying to get rid of it; he [the lobbyist] was close to all the guys on the Hill," she replied. "You can't get rid of those things. They don't do it." In the end, she managed to kill one program, called Leadership in Educational Administration. "Amazing," she said. That tiny program spent only $7 million or $8 million at its peak.

She couldn't kill, therefore she couldn't create. She had hoped to create videos for parents and a computerized information network for educators. "But there was no interest group for that." In the end, she found, there were only two ways to do the job. One way, the popular method, was to shovel money out the door to the entrenched lobbies. The other way, always contentious, was to reexamine priorities and fight trench warfare against the beneficiaries of existing programs. The former approach was politically painless but unsatisfying; the latter was politically painful and almost always unsuccessful.

"At first," she said of her days in Washington, "I thought it was about people really solving problems. But what it's really all about is people protecting their districts and the organizations they're close to. If you don't get the interest groups' support, you can't change anything, but if you change anything, you don't get their support. That's the conundrum.

"At the beginning, I thought I could shape the agency. But I couldn't do that. That was already done. My priorities were irrelevant. And that, for me, was a devastating discovery."

HOW BIG IS TOO BIG?

How would a giant, complicated social system look if it couldn't get rid of its failures and overhaul its anachronisms, or couldn't do so quickly enough? Imagine an economy in which every important business enterprise was kept alive by a politically connected coalition of enterprise managers and government officials. Over time, the world would change, but the universe of businesses wouldn't. Obsolescent companies would gobble up resources, crowding out new companies. The economy would cease to adapt.

That was what happened to the Soviet economy. Which collapsed.

In principle, the United States government's situation is like the Soviet economy's, though the U.S. government doesn't seem likely to collapse. In both, the method of trial and error reached the point of critical failure.

In Washington, old programs and policies cannot be gotten rid of, and yet they continue to suck up money and energy. As a result, there is less and less money or energy for new programs and policies. Every time a peanut-subsidy program from the 1930s or an EDA university-center program from the 1960s becomes entrenched, it occupies a spot where an experiment might have been performed or a start-up might have been tried. The old crowds out the new.

A second consequence, which is at least as important, is that when every program is permanent, the price of failure becomes extravagant. The key to experimenting successfully is knowing that you can correct your mistakes and try again. But what if you have only one chance? What if you are stuck with your mistakes forever, or at least for decades? Then experimentation becomes extremely risky. In fact, an experiment which you can try only once and then are stuck with is not really an experiment at all. In a one-shot environment, the very possibility of experimentation, which by nature is a trial-and-error process, breaks down.

To make this point clearer, let me invoke the physicist Freeman Dyson. In many of his writings, Dyson has argued that size matters. But he doesn't mean size just in the physical sense. Rather, if you want to know whether a machine is worth building or a program is worth undertaking, you have to scale it to make sure it's flexible enough to adapt to a changing world. "Never sacrifice economies of speed to achieve economies of scale," says Dyson. "And never let ourselves get stuck with facilities which take ten years to turn on or off." Otherwise, projects are out of date by the time they open for business. He writes:

> Judging by the experience of the last fifty years, it seems that major changes come roughly once in a decade. In this situation it makes an enormous difference whether we are able to react to change in three years or in twelve. An industry which is able to react in three years will find the game stimulating and enjoyable, and the people who do the work will experience the pleasant sensation of being able to cope. An industry which takes twelve years to react will be perpetually too late, and the people running the industry will experience sensations of paralysis and demoralization.

The American automakers in Detroit learned the hard way that a car which takes five years to bring to market is a very different product from a car which takes two or three years to bring to market, even though they might be physically identical. Slow-to-market cars from General Motors were always behind the market. Quick-to-market cars from Toyota were on top of the market. Quick is beautiful.

Moreover, Dyson argues, not only should a project or institution be quick enough, it should also avoid one-shot operations, which don't allow you to fail and try again. Among human beings, it's axiomatic that hardly anything ever goes right the first time. Any reformer who depends on hitting the bull's-eye with his first arrow is doomed. When locked in place, first-try "solutions" soon cause more problems than they solve.

In the mid-1980s, several years before the big and very costly Hubble Space Telescope was launched and then discovered to have been an optical botch, Dyson prophesied the fiasco. The Hubble, he noted, was a one-shot operation that had to go right the first time. "It is heresy or treason for a scientist to express misgivings about the Hubble Telescope," Dyson wrote. "But I have to say in all honesty, the Hubble Telescope is a basket with too many eggs riding in it. It would have been much better for astronomy if we had had several 1-meter space telescopes to try out the instrumentation and see how the sky looks at a tenth-of-a-second-of-arc resolution, instead of being stuck with a single one-shot 2.4-meter telescope for the rest of the century." Repairing the Hubble—which, luckily, turned out to be possible—was difficult and dangerous and extravagantly expensive (almost half as much as the telescope had cost in the first place). But scientists had no choice except to save their single basket of astronomical eggs. They couldn't afford to let the Hubble fail.

"The right size," says Dyson, "means the size at which you can afford to take a gamble." If a project is so big that you're stuck with it even if it fails, don't do it. In other words, the right size for any program or institution is no larger than the biggest size which still lets you correct your mistakes in time. Larger, and you either fail to solve problems or you cause more problems than you solve. And by those standards, government today is scaled incorrectly.

THE END OF ADAPTATION

Flexibility

The size of government is the great ideological divide in American politics. Liberals want government to do more, conservatives want it to do less. But big versus small is not, in itself, the best place to draw the distinction. The more important question is not how big government is, but how *flexible*.

Flexibility depends, not just on size of government, but on the society in which government is embedded. In a society with few lobbies, government can be large yet still quite flexible. A few decades ago, when fewer lobbying groups were around to defend everything, the government could be more experimental and so was better able to solve problems. But as Americans increasingly organized themselves into transfer-seeking lobbies, they eroded their government's flexibility, and so, in effect, made themselves harder to govern. Today, the federal government is swimming in molasses instead of water. It can't correct its mistakes in time. Therefore it has a very hard time solving problems. And, of course, more lobbies form every day.

People often look at Franklin Roosevelt's period of governmental experimentation and say, "If we could do it then, we should certainly be able to do it now." But they miss the point, which is that the society has changed. In a society dense with professional lobbies, FDR's brand of experimental central government *cannot exist*.

Roosevelt was able to experiment in ways that are inconceivable today, not only because his government was smaller and more manageable, but also partly because there were far fewer organized lobbies around to gum up the works. He was able to move programs into place quickly. On the seventeenth day of his administration, he proposed the Civilian Conservation Corps; three weeks later, it was law. On November 2, 1933, he was given a proposal for a Civil Works Administration employing people to repair streets and dig sewers; by November 23, the program employed 800,000 people; five weeks later, it employed 4.25 million people, or 8 percent (!) of the American workforce. Just as important, Roosevelt was able to get rid of programs. He ordered the Civil Works Administration shut down at winter's end; its total lifespan was only a few months. Similarly, the Civilian Conservation Corps went away in 1942, once the war effort made it superfluous. In those days, the government had some capacity to move programs on line quickly, try them out, and then get rid of them when their time had passed. It could declare a problem solved and then move on to the next thing, and it could correct its errors, if not perfectly, then far more easily than it can today. And this error-correcting capacity—which is the capacity to solve problems—has steadily diminished ever since.

Today, we must expect that anything the government tries this year will still be with us fifty years from now. What's dangerous about this is that even the most promising policies and programs cannot be made to work when you lack the flexibility to fail, adjust, and try again. By eroding the capacity for error elimination, demosclerosis has changed the very parameters of the doable.

A good example is industrial policy, which seeks to use targeted subsidies to support industries deemed to have special strategic or economic value. The only way such a policy could ever work is through constant experimentation and tinkering. First you might subsidize steel, but if that didn't work you could switch to research support for computer chips, and then if that failed or became unnecessary you could tinker with patent rules for biotech. You would constantly move your resources around, hunting for approaches that work. Ira Magaziner, a business consultant and industrial-policy proponent who went to work for the Clinton Administration, has said: "What you could loosely call industrial policies are, by their nature, trial-and-error policies, similarly as they would be in companies." In FDR's day, industrial policy might have been possible. (In fact, something like it was tried and rejected.) But in the age of demosclerosis, each industry runs a sophisticated lobby and can capture and then cling to any resources you throw in its direction. Industrial policy soon turns into an encrusted mass of subsidies for anachronistic industries with high-priced lobbyists. It blocks, rather than advances, useful change.

Or again, suppose you think a national system of high-technology trains is a good idea. In a nonsclerotic world, the government can help develop such a system and, if it fails, adjust it or go on to the next thing. But in a demosclerotic world, the case is very different. You begin setting up a system of, say, magnetic levitation trains this year. With luck, it's mostly ready ten years hence. Long before then, however, the National Association of Maglev Development Authorities ("NAMDA") boasts thousands of influential members around the country and runs a half-million-dollar political action committee. NAMDA's job is to make sure that the existing high-tech train systems (translation: its members' jobs) are funded forever. End result: twenty years hence, the country is stuck with an obsolete train system that actually blocks other advances in transportation.

This is what happens in real life. In 1992, the House of Representatives tried to kill an enormous atom smasher in Texas called the Superconducting Super Collider, or SSC. Reasonable people disagreed on whether the project was worth the many billions of dollars that it would cost. Never mind: the logic that applied was the logic of demosclerosis, not of science. The effort to kill the SSC ran smack into—surprise!—the National Association for the SSC, a lobbying group of companies with contracts to build or operate the Super Collider. "This is a knife fight now," said the head of that group. "And we're going to win it." And on that occasion, with the help of the Texas congressional delegation, they did.

The point isn't that defended programs never die; now and then, they do. (In 1993, the House again tried to kill the Super Collider, and this time it succeeded.) The point is that killing or getting rid of anything is such a slow, agonizing process that the rate of calcification outstrips the rate of adaptation. In fact, in a demosclerotic environment the government may find itself trapped in a cycle in which, over time, its attempts to solve problems actually diminish its problem-solving capacity. With enormous effort, it may succeed in reforming, say, the health-care system. But a decade later a thousand lobbies will have nailed the reforms in place, including the ones that failed. The government may be stuck in the 2000s with the aging reforms of the 1990s. The very process of reform may thus be hijacked by the forces of reaction and turned against itself.

"Medicare is a state-of-the-art 1965 benefits package," Willis D. Gradison, the head of the Health Insurance Association of America, said one day, by way of illustration. "It's a good program. It just wouldn't be done that way today. And if you look at the changes we've made in Medicare, it's amazing how narrow they are." Medicare was a shining reform in its day. But then it got stuck. Decentralized private plans evolved new ways to deliver care; by the early 1990s, insurance companies were funneling their customers into health-maintenance organizations, almost half of which the insurers themselves owned. Medicare did no such thing. It failed to evolve.

Eventually, caught in an impossible bind, the whole system may begin to go critical. Driven by the demands of a changing world, the government has no choice but to pass new programs. Yet at the same time, driven by the demands of the organized lobbies, the government struggles desperately to keep doing everything it ever tried for every group it ever aided. And so, lacking any better option, Washington just piles new programs on top of old programs. Laws are passed, policies adopted, programs added or expanded—things "get done"; but, as layer is dropped upon layer, the whole accumulated mass becomes gradually less rational and less flexible. To form a mental picture, imagine that you were forced to build every new house on top of its predecessor. That could work for a while, but eventually you'd have a teetering, dysfunctional mess. Similarly, accumulated programs and policies work to every end at once and often block each other, sometimes creating new problems, which may create the need for still other programs, leading to still more interest groups and locking-up. Bit by bit, program by program, the government turns dysfunctional.

As Americans heap ever more tasks on their government, while simultaneously organizing themselves into ever more lobbies, is it any wonder that government fails to meet expectations? And as government disappoints, is it any wonder that Americans despise it? By the 1990s, when polls showed that public confidence in the federal government had fallen to record lows, government and the public had become like the ill-tempered farmer and the arthritic nag. The farmer loads more and more on the nag, the nag becomes weaker and weaker, the angry farmer beats and whips the nag, the battered nag becomes weaker still.

In the period beginning with the New Deal and peaking with Lyndon Johnson's Great Society, Washington seemed one of America's most adaptive and progressive forces—which, at the time, it was. What Roosevelt's and Johnson's visionaries did not foresee was that every program would generate an entrenched lobby which would never go away. The same programs that made government a progressive force from the 1930s through the 1960s also spawned swarms of dependent interest groups, whose collective lobbying turned government rigid and brittle in the 1990s.

Demosclerosis has thus turned progressivism into its own worst enemy. Yesterday's innovations have become today's prisons. One of the main paradoxes of demosclerosis, and one of its nastiest surprises, is that the rise of government activism has immobilized activist government.

No one starting anew today would think to subsidize peanut farmers, banish banks from the mutual-fund business, forbid United Parcel Service to deliver letters, grant massive tax breaks for borrowing. Countless policies are on the books, not because they make sense today, but merely because they cannot be gotten rid of. They are like dinosaurs that will not die, anachronisms whose refusal to go away prevents newer, better-adapted rivals from thriving. In a Darwinian sense, the collectivity of federal policies is ceasing to evolve.

A STRICKEN GIANT

As the disease advances, it causes a weird and pathetic symptom: bogus national poverty. In Washington today, conventional wisdom says that programs and ambitions which were once affordable are now "too expensive." In the 1940s, America could "afford" the Marshall Plan to set Europe back on her feet; in the 1990s, America could not "afford" any remotely comparable effort to help Russia and her former satellites find political and economic stability. In the 1960s, America could "afford" a program to send astronauts to the moon; in the 1990s, America writhed and flailed to "afford" even a modest orbiting space station.

Subjectively, in the world of feeling, the government is poor, or in any case much poorer than in the fat years of Kennedy and Johnson. But objectively, in the world of fact, this is absurd.

The United States is now wealthier than any other country in human history, including its prior self. Per capita disposable income, adjusted for inflation, is twice as high as in 1960, when the federal government could "afford" almost anything. Real wealth per capita and real economic output per capita are both 75 percent higher than in 1960. To speak of the American economy as though it were "poor" or unable to buy what was once affordable is, by this standard, ludicrous.

Likewise, the federal government is not poor, either in absolute terms or relative to its postwar heyday. The government's income, after adjusting for inflation, is more than twice its income in John F. Kennedy's day; government spending, also adjusted for inflation, is considerably higher than in 1945, the peak of the mighty mobilization for World War II. The notion that taxes have been slashed to unusually low levels is simply wrong: measured as a share of the economy, the government's receipts in the 1980s and early '90s have been well in line with the postwar norm, and slightly *above* the level of the "wealthy" 1950s and 1960s. Objectively speaking, the federal government today is better able to "afford" initiatives than ever before in peacetime history.

So here is another paradox of demosclerosis: as the nation grows objectively richer, it feels subjectively poorer. Why? If government today is "poor," if it is unable to "afford" things, that is because of its inability to unlock resources from entrenched claimants and reallocate them for new needs. It can let go of nothing. And so government is not poor, it is paralyzed. It is not malnourished, it is maladaptive. It is trapped in its own past, held there like Gulliver in Lilliput by a thousand ancient commitments and ten thousand committed lobbies.

EATING THE CHILDREN

Yet the world doesn't stand still. Unavoidably, every year the country faces urgent new needs: an emergency bailout for savings and loans, a war or a peacekeeping action, new roads and bridges, hurricane relief, a replacement space shuttle. Every year there are things that *must* be done.

When an irresistible force meets an immovable object, something has to give. Unable to break through the encrusted mass of lobbies which shield all existing programs, yet unable to deny funds to worthy new claimants, politicians grope for money. In their desperation, they break out of the present and pilfer from generations yet unborn. Perhaps the saddest aspect of demosclerosis is that its victims live disproportionately in the future.

Figure 1 shows the average federal budget deficit, mea-

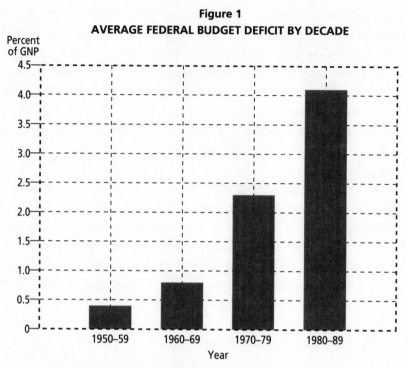

Figure 1
AVERAGE FEDERAL BUDGET DEFICIT BY DECADE

SOURCE: U.S. Office of Management and Budget

sured as a percentage of the gross national product, for each of four decades starting with the 1950s. In the Eisenhower years, federal deficits were close to negligible; by the 1980s, they were running over 4 percent of GNP. Never in peacetime had the federal government behaved so profligately.

It may have occurred to you that Figure 1 has roughly the same shape as the various curves, charted in Chapter 3, which show the numbers of group members, lobbies, and so on. Hyperpluralism and deficit spending roughly coincide.

Deficits have many causes: demographic change, health-care costs, new social problems, and so on. But that the lobbying explosion is connected to the fiscal crisis is indubitable. As groups and subsidies proliferate, total demands on government grow. But revenues can't increase boundlessly; taxpayers won't put up with it. Faced with implicit limits on tax revenues, and unable to pry resources from existing groups, needy politicians and lobbies look to transfer money from a group that won't organize to defend itself.

The young and the unborn are the ultimate unorganized interest group. Children don't organize and lobby. That's undoubtedly one reason why, for instance, real federal spending on them declined from 1978 to 1987, while spending on the elderly grew by more than half. The elderly vote; the children don't.

If one way to take from the young is to reduce spending on them, another way is to pile up debts that they'll have to pay. Imagine yourself in the shoes of a politician facing demands from a swarm of noisy lobbies. Every time you hand out a subsidy check or a tax break, some group says "Thank you" and rewards you with votes or campaign contributions or both. To pay for the subsidy, you can raise taxes, but that's politically risky. Why not put it on credit? No group screams at you if you do that, because many of the people who will pay don't yet exist.

Budget deficits help hungry lobbies accumulate, by letting them draw resources from the future when money gets scarce in the present. Returning the favor, hungry lobbies help budget deficits accumulate, by adding to the fiscal demands on politicians and so creating pressure to write IOUs. In that way, deficits and demosclerosis go hand in hand—and in another way, too: demosclerosis makes getting rid of a deficit, once one exists, practically impossible. Balancing the budget would be easy if the government had the flexibility to shut down programs and move resources around—but, of course, that flexibility is exactly what government does not have. Unable to scrub programs and afraid to raise taxes, politicians have only one other choice: learn to live with deficits.

What does a budget deficit mean? Not economic collapse or calamity. Rather, incremental but inexorable diminution of future wealth. The federal government finances its deficit by bor-

Deficit

rowing from the nation's pool of savings. That pool—which is surprisingly small to begin with—is what we rely on to finance long-term investment: the future. Work by the Organization for Economic Cooperation and Development, among others, has found a clear relationship between countries' saving rates and the growth of their labor productivity, which, in turn, crucially influences future living standards. In the 1950s and much of the 1960s, federal deficits absorbed only a negligible share of the country's savings; by the 1980s, they were absorbing *more than half*. By sucking up scarce capital and spending it on current consumption, government burns up the money available for productive investment and so destroys wealth in the future. It is robbing the unborn.

If government were running deficits to finance productive investment—roads and bridges, say—this wouldn't be a problem. But the deficits haven't financed investment. Since the early 1960s, federal long-term investments (excluding defense) have run at about 2 percent of the gross national product; but short-term benefits, as defined by the government itself, rose from 6 percent of GNP in the early 1960s to more than double that percentage in 1992. So the worst is really true: budget deficits are being used exclusively to finance consumption. Out of the mouths of babes, and into the mouths of the interest groups.

The government's burning up of scarce investment capital was not the only reason for America's disappointing economic performance in recent years, but it was surely one of the reasons. Disappointing economic performance fueled the public's determination to keep its subsidies and perks—and, for that matter, to demand new subsidies and perks ("help for the embattled middle class," in the political jargon). The cycle can go on indefinitely. In all likelihood, there will be no economic crash, just a steady denudation of the future. Thus does demosclerosis, like alcoholism, finally manifest itself as degeneracy.

economy
public
wants
which
makes
economy
worse.

HERE, THERE, EVERYWHERE

In America, demosclerosis is furthest advanced within the federal government. That isn't surprising; as a general rule, the bigger and more centralized a government and the more redistributive power it commands, the more it is beset by parasites and gold diggers and professional favor-brokers. But the disease is in no sense unique to the federal government.

Look, for example, at California, the largest state government. Dan Walters, a *Sacramento Bee* columnist who has been covering California state government for years, observes, "The process has slowed and slowed and slowed. In terms of major policy stuff, absolutely nothing gets done." On education, health, tort reform, and other major issues which energize interest groups, there are "no major policy decisions whatever. This is a total lock-up situation."

Barry Keene, a Democrat representing the northern coast, was the state Senate majority leader when he quit in disgust in 1992. "I came to the Senate to make policy, and the legislative body stopped doing that," he says. "It was like glue in the engine. It just gradually started slowing and slowing and then came to a virtual stop." After leaving, he became president of an interest group (what else?) called the Association for California Tort Reform. He acknowledges that he has joined the problem, but what can he do? The interest groups in California, like the ones in Washington, know that they're choking the system, but none can stop lobbying until all the others do. "There is a general recognition among the interest groups that the thing is not working very well," says Dan Walters, "but as long as it is the way it is, they're going to protect whatever interest they've got." Just like Washington.

Many Californians, like Washingtonians, blame demosclerosis on divided control of the government: Republicans in the governor's mansion, Democrats in the statehouse. But that can't be the whole story. In California, divided control has been common for decades, yet sclerosis has become steadily worse in recent years. Others point to California's sagging economy, which reduced the flow of taxes in the early 1990s, making legislators' jobs nastier and more contentious. But, again, demosclerosis had become glaring well before the economy sank. So something else must be going on.

Take a look at California's official biennial directory of full-time lobbyists. What you find is that, between the mid-1970s and the early 1990s, the number of companies and groups employing lobbyists more than doubled. "Our directories have been getting bigger every year we publish them," says David Hulse, a political reform specialist in the California secretary of state's office. In 1989, that office registered 783 full-time lobbyists (all of whom are required by law to register); only four years later, there were 1,024, an increase of 30 percent. Over the same four-year period, the number of groups hiring outside lobbyists grew by almost half; the number of companies hiring in-house lobbyists increased by more than a fourth. In the past, California lobbyists mainly worked for interest groups and deep-pocketed companies. Today many are in business for themselves, free-floating entrepreneurs. "Now you have lobbyists coming in without a client," Hulse says; career-minded entrepreneurs register as lobbyists and then go hunting for work. And they find it. According to the independent California Commission on Campaign Financing, the amount spent lobbying the California government, after adjusting for inflation, more than doubled from 1980 to 1992.

In fact, the day before I talked to Barry Keene, a brand-new interest group—one representing occupational therapists—had paid a call on him. They wanted to know how to lobby legislators. "It's a growing process," Keene told me. "The people who represented interest groups in Sacramento became more professional, they made more money, you had more contract lobbyists, as opposed to in-house lobbyists. You saw law firms opening offices in Sacramento providing lobbying services and appearances before administrative agencies. And that process is still evolving. You had television, you had targeted computer mail, you had phone banks, and you had the introduction of high-paid hired guns, people who knew how to manipulate these things."

Familiar stuff, all of that: the standard paraphernalia of professional parasitism in its high-growth mode. But then came something unexpected. As the legislative process died, the initiative process came alive. In theory, initiatives allow voters to pass their own laws. In practice, interest groups can use initiatives, too. "The initiative process is not truly a public process anymore," Keene says. "So when I say people do things on their own, I don't truly mean the general public, I mean the people who finance initiatives. They began circumventing the legislature. In doing so, they created a body of law that began putting a straitjacket on the setting of priorities by the legislature and the governor." In 1978, antitax activists used Proposition 13 to pass a property-tax cut for themselves, and—a classic anticompetitive maneuver—they did it in a way that favored existing property holders (themselves) at the expense of newcomers. Then came the environmentalists. Then came the California teachers' union, which passed an initiative requiring that about 40 percent of the state budget go to education every year.

What with initiatives, federal mandates, court orders, and legally guaranteed entitlement benefits, by the early 1990s 85 percent or more of the state's giant budget was locked in place, according to the state department of finance. Busy lobbies were working to lock in still more. The government of California was becoming a solid, calcified mass.

In New York City, thanks to the political clout of vested taxicab companies, the number of taxi licenses has been frozen since *1937*. The schools of New York spend more per student than all but a few other big-city districts, yet produce dismal results. Only a third of each education dollar goes to teachers and classroom instruction; hiring a new security guard can take five layers of bureaucracy. "A Soviet-style bureaucracy has enveloped the school system," reports *The Economist,* "and powerful, obstinate unions prevent reforms from happening at anything more than a snail's pace."

Sclerotic local governments like New York's possess a perverse advantage: their residents can flee and their credit ratings can sink—and then they're forced to reform, at least a bit. After Philadelphia hit the fiscal wall in 1990, it renegotiated its labor contracts, thinned its workforce, and contracted out a few lines of work—for instance, the city print shop. Even so, Philadelphia's leaders couldn't bring themselves to close offices or end old programs. "What they wound up doing was proposing to close one small library in a leased building, and one stable for the mounted police," Ronald G. Henry, the executive director of the Pennsylvania Intergovernmental Cooperation Authority, says. "They really have to do much more to try to make some fundamental structural changes."

If reforming Philadelphia is hard, imagine how much harder reforming Washington may be. The United States government can't go bankrupt and its citizens aren't about to flee. There is no wall for it to hit, at least in the foreseeable future. And so its slide toward stagnation is that much harder to check.

So here we are. For conservatives, demosclerosis means that there is no significant hope of scraping away outmoded or counterproductive liberal policies, because nothing old can be jettisoned. For liberals, it means that there is no significant hope of using government as a progressive problem-solving tool, because the method of trial and error has broken down.

The federal government is rotting. The only hope of arresting the process is to attack the Olsonian forces themselves.

7

DEALING WITH IT

EMOSCLEROSIS ISN'T A PROBLEM you solve. It's a problem you manage.

The government-friendly environment of mid-century is gone forever. There is no repealing the technologies that have made lobbying so cheap, so accessible, so fast. There is no dismantling the infrastructure of professional subsidy brokers and group organizers and lobbies, now that it's here. Banning lobbies is, of course, out of the question in a free country, where the right to petition government is fundamental. If you were foolish enough to abolish lobbying, you would only drive it underground, where it would be far more abusive and corrupting than it is in the open.

Demosclerosis is a natural by-product of government's power to solve problems by reassigning resources: interest groups accumulate because government offers them opportunities to get things. In the final analysis, you can't decisively "solve" demosclerosis without rendering government impotent. The trick, rather, is to manage demosclerosis by preserving as much of government's problem-solving capacity as possible.

In that sense, demosclerosis is like aging (except, as I'll argue later, it's not necessarily fatal). It has undesirable effects and you can't make it run in reverse, but you may be able to slow down its effects, mitigate its ravages, learn to cope with it.

What measures, then, might be available? The suggestions that follow—in roughly ascending order of importance—aren't meant to be exhaustive. More thought by more people will generate more and, with luck, better ideas. The suggestions also aren't mutually exclusive; in fact, they tend to reinforce one another, much as exercise, diet, and drugs do to fight heart disease. As with arteriosclerosis, however, there is no one-shot cure. Managing demosclerosis requires a standing regimen of discipline. The regimen needn't be all that painful, if you stay with it. But you had better not declare yourself cured one morning and stop fighting, because the demosclerotic forces never go away.

FIXING THE PROCESS

For many people, it's almost an article of faith that political reform is the key to revitalizing government and reducing the power of "special interests." The idea is that if Americans can't stop each other from forming interest groups, then at least we can reform the political process to reduce our groups' influence on our government. We would isolate government from lobbies, as the body might wall off a tumor. The three kinds of reform most talked about are tighter limits on lobbying, reform of the campaign-finance system, and limits on the amount of time that politicians can serve in office.

I don't want to pour cold water on these ideas entirely. Some of them are certainly worth trying or improving. Nonetheless, expectations for process reforms are generally too high, and, indeed, tend to miss the point. The process isn't the problem; the problem is the problem.

Consider, first, lobbying restrictions. Disclosure rules have been leaky and should be tightened. But impose actual limits on lobbying, and you tread on the First Amendment's explicit guarantee of the right "to petition the government for a redress of grievances." Reduce that right in any fundamental way, and you compromise the openness of democracy itself.

Anyway, as long as seeking government transfers is a lucrative business, people will invest in it. When your business is at stake in Washington, you *must* find a way to influence the government. You can no more ignore government than you can ignore a fire in your basement. Reforms of the lobbying process may force you to use more devious channels, or more open ones. But the millions of ingenious lobbyists and groups whose livelihoods are at stake will always be many steps ahead of reform bills that Congress passes once every ten or twenty years. The more sophisticated and professional the lobbyist, the more ingeniously he can find ways to cope with any limits that you set in front of him. That's his job.

Though campaign-finance reform is a more promising route than suppressing lobbying, it faces analogous problems. "I don't think that would affect me one iota," an anonymous but frank "veteran Washington lobbyist" told the *National Journal* when he was asked about President Clinton's campaign reform plan. "You can't eliminate the total costs of campaigns for candidates, and there will always be people who want to give. All I need to do is figure out how to get those two together." The more skillful this man is at defeating the campaign-finance limits, the more he'll be paid.

Many clean-up proposals focus on limiting (as opposed to rechanneling) political spending, on the theory that the money corrupts the system. It's a weak theory. The truth is that politics is inherently expensive: reaching 100 million voters can't be cheap. "In a vast and heterogeneous society like the United States," writes Norman J. Ornstein, a prominent scholar of Congress, "elections are expensive, and have to be." If you clamp down on the supply of money without reducing the demand, you just force politicians to search more frantically for cash. In fact, that has been the effect of reforms since the 1970s, which, by making money harder to get, have made candidates more obsessed with raising it.

More fundamentally: political money is not the main cause of demosclerosis; votes are. You may be able to limit the money that the sugar farmers' lobby can give to a Louisiana congressman. But that lobby can still deliver the votes of the people in its industry; it can still organize get-out-the-vote drives and "we suggest a contribution" campaigns; it can still run phone banks and buy ads supporting its friends; it can still inundate its enemies' offices with mail; it can do a hundred other things. Ornstein suggests imagining, as a thought experiment, that there were *no* interest-group money flowing to politicians. He doubts that lobbies would work any less hard to defend their interests, or that legislators would be any more eager to enrage constituent groups. In fact, outcomes might not be very different at all. "There simply are no data in the systematic studies that would support the popular assertions about the 'buying' of the Congress or any other massive influence of money on the legislative process," writes the political scientist Frank J. Sorauf. "Even taking the evidence selectively, there is at best a case for a modest influence of money."

The root problem is that the groups with the money represent millions of American voters, and those millions *like* their benefits and subsidies and anticompetitive deals. In politics, money is just one kind of political weapon. To attack demosclerosis, you need to weaken the groups, or else they just pick up another weapon.

Advocates of limiting money in politics argue that such reforms can at least make the process more equal. Today, they say, the system favors rich interests that hire slick lobbyists, whereas limits on spending would level the playing field. The trouble with this argument is that it's about three decades out of date. Environmentalists, unions, small businesses, veterans, the elderly—those groups and the multitudes like them are not "the rich," they are us, and they are all busy lobbying. In fact, it's partly *because* the fat cats lost control that the lobbying process has entered its debilitating spiral. For just that reason, limiting donations from interest groups or political action committees may actually tilt the playing field *toward* the fat cats and insiders. Groups such as unions and environmental organizations are agglomerations of little people who become a political force by pooling their money; stop them from collecting and disbursing money, and the advantage may shift toward large companies and Mr. Bigs who don't depend on political action committees for their clout.

Don't get me wrong: money reforms should be tried. Partial public financing of campaigns won't cure demosclerosis, but it should make politicians less obsessed with the ceaseless search for cash, a change for the better. Disclosure rules for lobbyists are also a good idea, because they let people know who is seeking what goodies, at what cost, and who is doing the bargaining.

Experiment with such measures, by all means. But don't expect much. Reforms rejiggering the rules for campaigns and lobbying may be a part of coping with demosclerosis, but only a small part. Since the early 1970s, at least half a dozen political-finance reforms and lobbying laws have been enacted, and those obviously haven't solved Washington's problems.

People who believe that the root of the problem is the professional political class suggest another kind of reform: term limits. Here the idea is to make the government less beholden to lobbies by reducing politicians' stake in their jobs. Instead of being in business for themselves—pandering to entrenched interests in order to protect their lifetime political careers—politicians will be real people with real lives who will make independent, sensible decisions, and then return to their hardware stores in Dubuque.

Term limits might help. Their advocates, such as Edward H. Crane of the Cato Institute in Washington, argue plausibly that political careerists wind up representing the interests of government itself, rather than those of the constituents back home. Term limits might weaken the culture of professional politics, in which politicians and lobbyists and groups run in circles to create jobs for each other. On the other hand, term limits also might hurt. Politicians might enter one office and immediately begin scheming and jockeying for the next. No sooner might a House member be elected than he might begin pandering in order to prepare a Senate bid. Instead of getting careerists out of politics, term limits might just shorten their attention span. More fundamentally, term limits don't much change the equation that confronts every sitting politician who must decide whether to defy organized favor-seekers: vote against the lobby and weather a blizzard of hate mail, or vote with it and reap its "Honorary Dairyman of the Year" award.

That is not to say that term limits are necessarily a bad idea. They ought to be tried, preferably at the state level to see how they work. (California, which adopted term limits for the state legislature in 1990, is conducting one experiment right now.) If the limits put a damper on the culture of political careerism, then they will have achieved something worthwhile. At bottom, though, the roots of demosclerosis lie not in Washington's careerist culture but in the transfer-seeking logic that shapes and drives that culture. To see term limitation as a solution is to pin large hopes on what may be merely a step sideways.

The ultimate problem with all process reforms is that lobbies are us, and you can't isolate a democratic government from its own society. If society divides and redivides into more groups seeking benefits, government can't be cut off from those groups' influence by clever campaign-finance rules. Process reforms can at best add a few buffering layers. While extra buffering layers are worth having (as long as they don't make the government numb), in the end they are no solution, and they divert attention from substantive reforms that go deeper and offer more hope.

LOCKING AWAY THE GOODIES

We Americans organize into lobbies because government can feed us. Some libertarians and conservatives would solve that problem in the most direct way. They would put the food out of reach. That is, they would make the whole transfer-seeking business illegal.

In advancing their idea, they take up a line of thought that goes back to the founders. James Madison was aware of the dangers of transfer-seeking, and warned against "speculators" who earn profits by brokering government subsidies and favors. "The sober people of America . . . have seen with regret and indignation that sudden changes and legislative interferences, in cases affecting personal rights, become jobs in the hands of enterprising and influential speculators, and snares to the more industrious and less informed part of the community," Madison wrote in *The Federalist.* "They very rightly infer, therefore, that some thorough reform is wanting, which will banish speculations on public measures." Madison's idea was that government should have little power to reassign property, so that "speculators on public measures"—transfer-seeking entrepreneurs— would have little to buy and sell. Thus does the Bill of Rights say, in no uncertain terms, "No person shall . . . be deprived of life, liberty, or property without due process of law; nor shall private property be taken for public use without just compensation."

For decades the Supreme Court more or less held to the Madisonian vision, slapping back government's efforts to move private wealth around. In the last third of the nineteenth century, however, the courts began upholding transfer laws. "From 1877 to 1917 the Constitution was altered in numerous ways that made transfers much easier to obtain," write Terry L. Anderson and Peter J. Hill. "Except for the income tax amendment [of 1913], all of these changes came through [judicial] interpretation." During the New Deal, after a period of resistance, the Supreme Court yielded more ground by blessing

President Roosevelt's interventionist economic program. Since then, constitutional restraints on transfer-seeking have been few.

Suppose you went back to something more like the state of affairs before the New Deal. Suppose, that is, you reduced the government's power to reassign resources. If the government took money from someone, or passed a regulation reducing the value of someone's property, or restricted someone's use of his property, it would have to compensate him for the loss. If Smith wanted to put a billboard on his beachfront property or pave over his wetland, the government could stop him only by buying his property or compensating him in some other way, rather than just passing a law. Necessarily, then, the government would have a much harder time giving away favors to people who wanted benefits at Smith's expense.

This is the general approach favored by members of the so-called economic rights movement, who believe that government's ability to grant transfers at will has gotten out of hand. Their approach has a big advantage and a big disadvantage. The big advantage is that it would work. There is no point lobbying a government that can't do anything for you. When Washington loses its power to give favors to groups, groups will stop seeking favors from the government. Those groups' lobbyists will go away and get real jobs. Capital which had been captured by the parasite economy will be set free again.

The big disadvantage is that any plan that restricts the government's ability to subsidize merchant mariners will also restrict its ability to run a Social Security program or enact environmental laws. Everything the government does, right down to such core functions as law enforcement and national defense, requires the power to take tax money from one place and put it somewhere else. To strip government of its power to transfer wealth is to "solve" government, not demosclerosis.

Unfortunately, it's impossible to allow only good or important redistributive laws while forbidding the "special-interest" ones, because no one agrees on which kind of law is which. I believe that the Small Business Administration is silly, but some people think it's vital to the nation. There is no longer any clear consensus on what government shouldn't do—which means that there is no accepted middle ground between allowing virtually no government transfers (the original system) and allowing virtually unlimited transfers (the current system). It's worth searching for such a middle ground, but as of now none has been discovered, much less agreed upon. So on to more practical suggestions.

SCATTERING THE GOODIES

One of the reasons Washington is suffocating under the swarm of interest groups is that Washington is an irresistible target. You can go there for almost any kind of benefit you want, and it's the only game in town. There are no other federal governments around that might undercut you or favor your competitors behind your back. Washington is one-stop shopping for the parasite economy.

If central government is so big that it attracts every manner of opportunistic interest, while being too unwieldy to adapt as it should, why not decentralize? Why not devolve whole functions to lower levels of government?

Although states and cities aren't immune to demosclerosis, there are a lot more of them around. Decentralization would mean that lobbies would need to spread their resources across more governmental units. Imagine the problems that lobbies might face trying to seek subsidies in each of fifty states. Just as important, different states and localities offer the possibility of running different programs that would compete with one another. If Hawaii discovers a better kind of health-care program, or Michigan a better way to finance schools, it will gain an advantage over less effective states. Variety and competition can give each jurisdiction the opportunity and the incentive to learn from the successes and failures of the others. And if, in the end, a local government does turn sclerotic, people can leave. They're not stuck with every program forever—a big advantage. Meanwhile, back in Washington, if the federal government is given less to do, then it may be able to do its job better.

A thoughtful plan to rearrange responsibilities was proposed in 1992 by the Brookings Institution economist Alice M. Rivlin, who went on to serve as deputy director of the Clinton Administration's Office of Management and Budget. By the 1970s, Washington "resembled a giant conglomerate that has acquired too many different kinds of businesses and cannot coordinate its own activities," she wrote in her book *Reviving the American Dream*. "The federal government has taken on too much responsibility and should return some of its functions to the states. A clearer division of responsibilities between the states and the federal government could make both levels operate more effectively."

Under Rivlin's plan, the feds would be in charge of the health-care system and broad social-insurance programs like Social Security. Washington would cede to the states control of most or all programs in education, job training, economic development, housing, transportation, social services, and some other fields. One result would be programs that were better adapted to local conditions, and thus more effective. Other results would be clearer accountability and sharper competition. "Once clearly in charge," Rivlin argued, "the states would compete vigorously with each other to improve services and attract business by offering high-quality education, infrastructure, and other services."

Decentralization has been batted around for years; President Eisenhower named a commission to study it, and more than a decade later President Nixon named another. In 1981, Bruce Babbitt, the Democratic governor of Arizona (and later President Clinton's secretary of the interior), called for a rearranging of roles. "Congress ought to be worrying about arms control and defense instead of potholes in the street," he wrote. "We just might have both an increased chance of survival and better streets." President Reagan touted a "new federalism." Yet, through it all, nothing happened, except that the federal government's elephantiasis grew worse.

As of now, no one has agreed on which functions to strip from the central government, or how to rewrite its charter. And, of course, lobbies will fight to keep their federal holdings. So re-sorting local and federal roles is a project that will take decades. But it's also a project worth doing and long overdue, especially for those who want the federal government to succeed in the long run.

In the meantime, we need measures that help manage demosclerosis in the nearer term. So, again, skip ahead, this time to what I think is the most promising class of options.

HAMMERING THE PARASITES

We can't stop each other from forming interest groups and lobbying. We can't shut groups and activists out of politics. We can't repeal the Olsonian laws which dictate that, left to themselves, lobbies accumulate over time. But we don't have to leave lobbies to themselves. What if we can subject them to forces that soften them up? What if we expose them to a kind of chemotherapy, which weakens their grip? I believe it can be done. And there are many ways to do it. In roughly ascending order of importance:

PIT LOBBIES AGAINST EACH OTHER

I mentioned earlier that it would be nice if parasites could be used to neutralize each other. In a more perfect world, for instance, the sugar growers' lobby and the sugar users' lobby might fight each other to a perpetual standstill, and then finally give up and go home.

Although it's hard to push groups into direct confrontations, it might be possible to change the rules in a way that forces groups to spend more energy attacking each other. The answer might be a zero-sum rule—a rule requiring that every addition be balanced by an offsetting subtraction.

As a thought experiment, imagine a rule saying that, henceforth, Congress and the president may not add a single word, *on net,* to the federal statute books. If you wanted to pass a forty-page law, you would have to find forty other pages to get rid of. At first, legislators might just go through the books pruning verbose language—a worthwhile result, if you think about it. But eventually, when Congress wanted to add a new law, it would need to begin looking for an 1872 mining statute or a 1922 insurance statute to get rid of. Like the man who decides his donkey can't carry any more, Congress would have to start unloading as well as loading.

That isn't quite a serious suggestion. In practice, something as crude as a no-new-words rule might encourage politicians to write underdrafted, overvague laws. (A very succinct banking-reform law: "All bankers shall be liable for up to life in prison if they don't do the appropriate thing, as determined by the relevant authorities.") But it's the principle that counts. Today, new subsidies and programs are just piled on top of old ones, and there is no reward for getting rid of anything. A zero-sum rule might harness the energies of interest groups to hunt for anachronisms to get rid of. One result might be to force at least somewhat more adaptation. Another result might be to force seekers of new favors into conflict with defenders of old favors, thus weakening both.

The most common species of the zero-sum genus is the balanced-budget amendment to the Constitution, which is well intended but probably too easy to circumvent with gimmickry and schlock artistry. If you tell politicians to balance the budget without also reducing the appetite and power of transfer-seekers, all you do is invite everyone to juggle the books and skirt the law, thus corrupting the budget and weakening the Constitution itself. (States balance their operating budgets, but less for the sake of their constitutions than of their credit ratings, which provide real-world financial discipline.) A more promising approach was tried in 1990. That year, a deficit-reduction law included a pay-as-you-go rule, requiring that program increases be financed with offsetting tax hikes or spending cuts. The rule seemed to help and, indeed, was renewed by President Clinton and Congress in 1993.

The potential downside is that zero-sum rules may end up actually reducing government's flexibility. The reason is that a requirement to get rid of *some* old program doesn't translate into a mandate to get rid of any *particular* program, and each one is defended. On an overcrowded boat, if you add one person, you must push someone else off, but government doesn't work that way. If all we do is tell the government to push out "some" old program, we may cause either of two perverse outcomes, or some of both.

First, we may add to the already formidable advantage that ancient programs and entrenched interests enjoy at the expense of fresh approaches and new needs. To some extent, this seemed to happen under the 1990 rule. "Pay-as-you-go protects existing programs while requiring new ones to pay their own way," wrote Allen Schick, an expert on the federal budget. "While old programs have been frozen into the budget, new ones have been frozen out." In that case, a zero-sum rule may hasten calcification.

Or, second, the zero-sum rule might only push out the program with the weakest lobby, instead of the one with the weakest claim. The winner would be, not the best program, but the one whose interest group sent out the most computerized mail, donated the most cash to politicians, and spent the most on lobbying. In that case, the zero-sum rule would give groups a reason to redouble their investment in lobbying—since, after all, no group wants to be the unlucky loser who gets pushed off the boat. Government might become even more besieged than it is already.

In the right environment, a zero-sum rule might help; but if you just pass a zero-sum rule without doing anything else, it won't do much good and might actually hurt. The missing ingredient is to make substantive choices about what the country needs and what the country can live without. Time, then, to talk about choosing.

STOP THE RAIDS ON THE FUTURE

The first thing to do is to stop interest groups and complicit politicians from eating the unborn. Closing the budget deficit is not only morally imperative, it's also tactically important. When parasites can't feed on the future, they must fight over a relatively smaller budget in the present. That makes their lives more difficult, while putting the nation's savings off limits. Above all, balancing the budget forces today's voters to reckon the full price if they play a game of grabbing goodies from the next guy.

Conservatives often insist on balancing the budget by cutting spending alone. That would be better than doing it by raising taxes alone, but it has proved to be politically impossible. Once a program or benefit is locked into place, it's usually so fiercely defended that, given a choice, politicians would rather buy it on credit than chop it out or even cut it.

"Well," say conservatives, "if you give politicians more money, they'll just spend it, and the deficit won't go down. Keeping a lid on taxes is the best way to control spending and restrain deficits. So we'll oppose all new taxes, period." The trouble with this argument is that it shuts its eyes to the whole experience of the last decade, which showed that restraining taxes does not, in fact, restrain the growth of government or the piling up of deficits. On the contrary, in the 1980s taxation as a share of the economy was held about constant, but deficits and spending didn't fall—they set new peacetime records.

That stands to reason. If a government spends $1.5 trillion but collects only $1.2 trillion in taxes, it offers benefits to the public at a 20 percent discount. And when you offer benefits at a discount, the public demands more of them. In turning modern conservatism into the First Evangelical Church of No New Taxes Ever, right-wingers have convinced themselves that they're constraining the supply of government benefits, when actually they're stoking the demand for them.

The American public today is like a glutton whose overeating makes his *descendants* obese. You can explain until you're blue in the face why he ought to diet, but only when he himself sees and feels the full burden of his gluttony will he curb his appetite. There is no solution but the old-fashioned one. In order to reduce the deficit, taxes must go up, probably a lot. The sale on subsidies and benefits must be ended. To make sure that new tax money isn't shoveled back out the door to hungry interest groups, taxes need to be coupled with reductions in spending.

Raising taxes while cutting spending is no one's idea of fun. It is, in fact, precisely what the voters and their groups have not allowed politicians to do—not, at least, on a scale nearly big enough to do the job. Voters believe that if politicians would just stop "wasting" money, the deficit would go away. One reason the voters believe this is that opportunistic conservatives keep saying it. With their no-new-taxes dogma, American conservatives have managed to pander to public greed ("You deserve more") while simultaneously blaming someone else for the deficit ("It's big spenders' fault"). Their neat political trick has turned modern conservatism into a partner of demosclerosis and an unwitting handmaiden of Big Government.

So here is a way in which the theory of demosclerosis renders American politics-as-usual obsolete. It suggests that conservatives must retreat from their antitax histrionics and actively support tax increases (provided those are tied to spending cuts). Doing so ultimately serves conservative purposes: as people begin to feel the full cost of government, they will be readier to contain their transfer-seeking appetites and make choices about what they want from Washington.

In the late 1970s, led by Ronald Reagan and the slaphappy supply-siders, conservatives discovered that the key to popularity was to offer tax cuts as the solution to every problem. Now the question is whether they can change their pander-and-blame ways.

CUT THE LOBBIES' LIFELINES

Now we come to tougher medicine still—tough but effective. *Eliminate subsidies and programs*—including tax loopholes, which are subsidies administered through the tax code. Get rid of things to make room for things. Cut entire programs loose and pitch them overboard.

Once resources are pried away from entrenched lobbies, they can be used for innovation or deficit reduction or, best of all, both, restoring some measure of vitality to government. Killing low-priority programs and ancient subsidies also weakens demosclerosis itself, by shutting off the money that sustains lobbies. When the subsidies stop flowing, the lobbyists seem less worth paying and their clients have less money to pay with. Why is there a sugar lobby? Because it defends a sugar subsidy. Get rid of the subsidy, and the lobby, while perhaps it won't vanish overnight, is weakened.

The strategy can work, but only on a relatively big scale. No group wants to be singled out (that's "unfair"), and isolated hits don't save any visible amount of money anyway. Why take on a powerful lobby for a lousy half-billion dollars? Even if you succeed, the voters won't notice the difference. The key, instead, is to round up as many programs as possible—hundreds, preferably—and shove them all over the cliff together. Then you save real money and create real maneuvering room.

It's difficult, but it can be done. In fact, it was done recently. By the mid-1980s, the federal tax code had become a sprawling mess of handouts and favors and gimmicks and shelters, a deluxe condominium for parasites. As the code descended further into incoherence and overcomplexity, enlightened

Democrats began calling for reform. Republicans, not wanting to lose the issue, jumped on board. In 1985, the Reagan Administration proposed sharply curtailing loopholes and using the money to reduce tax rates. In 1986, with a hard push from the president, the tax-reform bill passed. At one blow, it swept away years' worth of accumulated tax breaks that had distorted the economy and acted as a full-employment program for tax lobbyists.

No, the tax reform was not a giveaway for the rich. Before the reform, there were so many tax shelters that people with $100,000 incomes were actually paying only half the official 50 percent marginal rate on their last dollars of income. After their loopholes had been plugged and their rates reduced, they paid as much as ever, and the poor paid less. Rather, tax reform was a takeaway from the lobbying industry. With tax rates lower, people had less reason to lobby for loopholes. After all, once your top tax rate is cut from 50 percent to 25 percent, a tax shelter is only half as valuable to you—so a tax lobbyist is only half as much worth hiring. It's probably no coincidence that, in the wake of tax reform, the number of lobbyists registered with the Senate dropped sharply, albeit temporarily.

In all, the 1986 tax reform was the most brilliant antiparasite stratagem of our time. That's the good news. The bad news is that lobbies never give up, and politicians can never resist buying votes by offering tax breaks to favorite lobbies. In 1988, George Bush promised fistfuls of tax breaks in his election campaign—for capital gains, for oil and gas, for rural development, you name it. Luckily, he mostly didn't deliver. Bill Clinton was even worse, proposing bunches of new tax breaks (many of which Congress, fortunately, refused to enact).

Over time, the 1986 tax reform has gradually eroded, but even so, it proved a point. Politicians *can* do a big housecleaning, if they arm themselves with determination and a big package.

To get the job done requires three ingredients. First, leadership from the very top. The president is the one politician with a stronger professional interest in the whole government and the whole nation than in any particular piece of either. Second, savvy packaging and presentation. One possibility is a specially appointed commission of graybeards to build a big package of subsidy reductions and program eliminations, which, if given the president's blessings, would be presented to Congress for an up-or-down vote on an expedited schedule. It's a gimmick, but if it helps, so much the better.

The third ingredient is a coherent set of guiding principles. Anyone can talk about "cutting programs" and "attacking lobbies" in the abstract. The question is, *which* programs and *which* lobbies? In the overcrowded boat, you need some ground rules for deciding who goes overboard, or else you wind up with a melee that throws the weakest people into the sea or even capsizes the whole vessel. Similarly, in an environment where every program is "necessary" and getting rid of anything is "unfair," you need some principles for deciding what goes and what stays. Because demosclerosis tends to turn government reactionary and maladaptive, the principles should be forward-looking and pro-adaptive. I suggest the following:

- *Favor the poorest.* Does a program serve the poorest of the poor? Then give it special consideration—not a safe-conduct or an exemption from critical scrutiny, but a leg up.
- *Favor the diffuse.* Does a program serve a class of people—consumers, say, or the unemployed—who are too broad and diffuse to lobby? Then give it special consideration. (But be skeptical of lobbies that claim to represent the broad public interest; they are just as likely to be in business for themselves as is any other lobby. Self-styled consumer groups often advocate policies—overregulation, for instance—which are bad for consumers but good for consumer groups; same for many groups claiming to represent taxpayers or the planet or whatever.)

- *Favor the young.* Does a program primarily benefit children (a classic diffuse constituency, unable either to vote or to lobby)? Then give it special consideration. But, again, beware. Adults have been known to collect subsidies by claiming to speak for children.
- *Favor investment over consumption.* Does a program have a *strong* claim to be a long-term investment? Then give it special consideration. But be tough-minded and selective, because everyone calls his favorite program an "investment."
- *Disfavor organized interests.* Does a program benefit an identifiable group, profession, or region? Then it deserves, at best, suspicion.
- *Don't do what markets can do.* Does a program provide a service that markets could provide or beneficiaries could pay for? Then it's a good candidate for the trash can.
- *Don't give without demanding.* Does a program give something for nothing? Then take a dim view of it, unless it serves children or the poor. Instead, favor programs whose costs are covered in some substantial share by the people enjoying the benefits. The whole idea behind transfer-seeking is to capture benefits at cost to someone else, and so a good way to discourage transfer-seekers is to make them pay for more of what they get, either in money or in public service.
- *Don't do things just because they seem nice.* Is the main justification for a program sentimental? Does a program "protect a way of life" (agriculture subsidies) or "save a treasured institution" (Amtrak passenger-train subsidies, Small Business Administration subsidies) or just seem like a nice thing to do (arts subsidies)? That's not a reason to fund it. Chances are, either the program is subsidizing goods or services that would have been available anyway (there was no shortage of art in America before the National Endowment for the Arts came along), or else the

program is fundamentally reactionary in character, keeping alive that which adaptation decrees should die.

- *When in doubt, do without.* Remember, saying yes to organized groups usually seems harmless in the short run, but the demosclerosis that you feed by saying yes is devastating in the long run. Even inexpensive subsidies become havens for thousands of beneficiaries, whose entrenchment compounds demosclerosis. Arts subsidies become the property of regional arts-council administrators and grant-wise artists, who join up to become a permanent national lobby. To break the debilitating cycle, one must behave like a disciplined dieter: never say yes to anything just because it's small.

- *Always apply the scratch test.* No matter what the program is, ask of it: If the program didn't already exist, would we start it from scratch? If the answer is no, whet the ax.

Truth be told, most of the Great Society and a fair piece of the New Deal—not to mention the bulk of the tax laws—would go out the window if you applied these tests rigorously. However, you don't have to apply them to the maximum possible extent, and, in fact, you couldn't if you tried. Reasonable people can and should debate how much to prune. The important thing is to have pruning principles and use them. Otherwise, the federal garden becomes a weedpatch.

In fortifying one's resolve as interest groups shriek, it may help to remember that the reason to prune and chop is not to kill government, or even to shrink it, but to restore its flexibility and effectiveness. The point is to break the stranglehold of entrenched claimants and to clear ground for new ventures. By making room for adaptation and unloading an overburdened system, you make government likelier to work. And that is good for liberals, above all.

So here is a second way in which the theory of demosclerosis renders American politics-as-usual obsolete. Liberals will need to take the lead in scouring for programs to get rid of. *They* must put their shoulder to the work which, until now, mainly antigovernment types have talked about.

For many liberals, that kind of work seems foreign, if not downright immoral. Now the question is whether liberals can free themselves from the prison of retroliberalism, which never met a program it didn't like (except defense), and which sees killing and cutting domestic programs as callous and reactionary.

DOMESTIC PERESTROIKA

Lobbies live to lock money in and competition out. Their fondest love is a monopoly claim on public funds or private markets. Insurance companies defend rules keeping banks out of the insurance business. Fruit growers defend rules letting them limit the number of lemons that can be sold. Cable-television companies defend regulations keeping phone companies out of the entertainment-transmission business. Peanut farmers defend a licensing system that lets them shut out new growers. Taxi companies defend rules that prevent the number of cabbies from increasing. Public-school employees, postal workers, and welfare administrators fend off competition from private providers of services.

How to weaken them? Strip away their anticompetitive protections and let competition hammer them. Not only does competition help make the economy more efficient, it also weakens entrenched lobbies. It forces transfer-seekers to sink or swim according to their skill at producing goods or services, rather than their skill at lobbying in Washington.

Domestic perestroika starts with removal of government restraints on competition. Jimmy Carter's deregulation of transportation industries and interest rates, though imperfectly executed, was an antiparasite move to set beside the 1986 tax reform. Deregulation created some turmoil in the marketplace (which was, of course, just the point), yet it produced better deals for travelers and small savers, greater efficiency in the transportation and financial markets, and, for the most part, better service. After the passage of the Air Cargo Deregulation Act of 1977 and the Airline Deregulation Act of 1978, airfares fell (after adjusting for inflation) by more than 20 percent, the number of passengers doubled, and air accident rates fell by almost half (with, yes, *more* nonstop service). A Brookings Institution analysis estimated that consumers saved roughly $100 billion in the first decade of deregulation. The railroad deregulation of 1980 saved shippers as much as $5 billion a year, with lower accident rates. After trucking was deregulated in 1980, the number of carriers more than doubled, trucking jobs increased by a third, and the economy saved on the order of $8 billion a year. Such are perestroika's blessings—not unmixed, to be sure, yet more than worth the trouble.

Much remains to be done: banking and financial perestroika, agricultural perestroika, communications perestroika, energy perestroika, health perestroika. Deregulation isn't always wise, and each case needs to be judged on its particulars. But the point is to hunt aggressively for opportunities to tear out anticompetitive franchises, and thus to pursue what the writer James Fallows has called the reopening of America.

No less important than exposing coddled private interests to competition is to expose coddled *government* interests to competition. Today the public sector, not the private sector, is the biggest haven for monopolistic deals and franchises. In the private sector, monopolies are the exception, but in the public sector they're the rule. In America there are dozens of ways to send overnight mail and packages, but only one way to send a first-class letter. In each city there are thousands of places to get groceries, but only one place to get a welfare check. In most places, if you want your household trash collected, you had better pay the government's rate. And so on.

A blind spot of postwar American liberalism has been its failure to understand that a monopoly or cartel administered by a public authority is at least as likely to be backward and abusive as one administered by a private company. "It is one of the enduring paradoxes of American ideology that we attack private monopolies so fervently but embrace public monopolies so warmly," write David Osborne and Ted Gaebler, the authors of *Reinventing Government*. Both kinds of monopolies are likely to produce high prices, poor service, slow innovation, and entrenched arrogance. And both kinds breed lobbies whose mission is to see that the coddling never stops and that newcomers never enter.

By creating havens for lobbies, monopoly power weakens government over the longer term. And because government monopolies are notoriously careless about their customers' welfare, they arouse ill will among the public, weakening government still further. "Our public sector can learn to compete," write Osborne and Gaebler, "or it can stagnate and shrink, until the only customers who use public services are those who cannot afford an alternative."

Wherever possible, then, bring perestroika to the public sector. Force government providers to compete against other government providers, or against private competitors. To cite one well-known example, the city of Phoenix forced its trash-collection agency to compete with outside bidders, with notable success. Various studies, note Osborne and Gaebler, show that "on average public service delivery is 35 to 95 percent more expensive than contracting, even when the cost of administering the contracts is included."

Bringing competition inside the stale confines of government agencies is already catching on in America—in fact, in the White House. The Clinton Administration glowingly talked up the idea in its 1993 government-reform report (which David Osborne helped write): "By forcing public agencies to compete for their customers—between offices, with other agencies, and with the private sector—we will create a permanent pressure to streamline programs, abandon the obsolete, and improve what's left." At this writing, at least fifteen states have passed laws letting private operators run roads and railways. Abroad, Britain, New Zealand, and other countries are trying out plans that force some government bureaucracies to provide their services competitively.

Allowing competition within government is a promising path. But it's no substitute for the kind of public-sector perestroika that counts the most. Where possible, government monopolies should be swept away altogether.

The schools are a good example. In Washington, D.C., a truant boy told his grandmother he was afraid to go to school: "They have guns and knives at school." In Boston, where four in ten graduates of public high schools can't read at ninth-grade level, students are stabbed and principals threatened. In Houston, a poll found that 85 percent of parents said their kids were unsafe in school. In Chicago's housing projects, children will go live with relatives in other neighborhoods or states, or even try to flunk eighth grade, to avoid the terror of the public high schools. In New York City—well, that point is too obvious to belabor. The wealthy can flee dysfunctional and dangerous public schools, and have been doing so for years. The poor are left behind to take their chances, all in the name of "saving the public schools"—meaning, saving the jobs of the people who run them.

The public-school interest groups—teachers' unions, principals' associations, school boards' groups—argue that their monopoly claim on taxpayers' money is in the national interest. But, like so many monopoly franchises, this one serves its holders better than its captives. It also resembles other monopolies in its black-hole-like ability to suck in money without noticeably improving performance. Over the entire period since World War II, spending per public-school student, after adjusting for inflation, has increased about 40 percent a decade, doubling every twenty years. Average class sizes have fallen; more teachers hold master's degrees than ever before. Yet test scores have sunk, and horror stories about what students don't know are legion. Public schools aren't under pressure to perform, because most of their "customers"—students and parents—can't vote with their feet.

If you hand every parent—or, at the very least, every lower-income parent—a ticket applicable toward school tuition and say, "Take your tax money and go find the best school you can," you allow buyers of education to circumvent the interest groups which have overgrown every cranny of public education. You force entrenched providers to fight for their paychecks. Do that, and many of them will rise to the challenge and improve. While competition is not an educational panacea, there is every reason to think that it will make the schools better—in both sectors, private and public, as all schools work to attract students. The benefits will flow especially to the poorest, who are now trapped in the worst schools. And the country will gain politically by prying the education industry loose from the lobbies' grip.

Not every private company or government agency can be forced into competition. Building three private airports in Cincinnati and forcing them into competition might not work (though, on the other hand, it might). Yet the lobby-weakening potential of market-opening moves is large and still largely untapped. A good rule of thumb is this: where you see a government restraint on private competition, look for a way to get rid of it. And where you see a government agency sheltered from competition, look for a way to expose it. In every case, you will weaken interest groups and stimulate adaptation.

FOREIGN COMPETITION

Left to itself, the accumulation of groups and cozy deals never stops. To fight back requires a counterforce capable of weakening entrenched interests and cozy deals day after day, year after year. Foreign competition is such a counterforce.

In 1992 and 1993, as Americans pressed the Europeans to

open their heavily protected agriculture markets, French farmers—one of the world's most sanctimonious yet thuggish lobbies—threw rotten eggs at cabinet members, blocked Paris's
rush-hour traffic, dumped fresh produce in town squares,
burned American flags, and vandalized a McDonald's in Paris,
among other antics. "Don't kill the French farmer!" they cried.
Actually, knocking out their subsidy props would only have
killed the more inefficient of the French farmers, but in doing
so it would have reduced farmers' numbers, thus reducing their
political power—which was strong. The voracious European
farm lobby has all but controlled the parliaments of Europe,
eating $40 billion a year in direct subsidies, and much more in
indirect costs to European consumers and American farmers.
What does Europe's farm lobby fear and hate most of all? Foreign competition.

By taking on the French farmers—something that French
politicians weren't inclined to do—the Americans were doing
the whole world (and especially the French) a favor. The Japanese so heavily rely on foreign pressure of this type that they
have a word for it, *gaiatsu*. Economic *gaiatsu*, from Japan and
other countries, is one of the great progressive forces in America (and the world) today.

People who bemoan the rise of Japanese auto imports in
America forget what Americans were actually driving in the
1970s, when the Big Three complacently ran what their critics
argued was a kind of loose cartel. Think how much better cars
are today, thanks in no small measure to Japanese competition.
People who worry about the rise of Japanese steel may not
realize that Japanese competition and investment have sharp-
ened the American steel industry after decades of disinvest-
ment and obsolescence. "Without Japanese investment,
technology, and manufacturing organization, we would likely
find ourselves with a much smaller domestic steel industry, if
any at all," Richard Florida and Martin Kenney, two academics
who study the industry, wrote in 1991. "The power of Japanese

industry to transform American steel has been astonishing. Major strides have been made in an industry that was viewed by many as an unsalvageable 'basket case' not more than a decade ago."

Trade introduces new actors and new technologies, which help keep the economy flexible and vital. Just as important, since there is no World Congress to lobby, the job of winning anticompetitive goodies on a worldwide scale is almost impossible. When you expand trade, therefore, you almost automatically weaken local interest groups that thrive within sealed borders.

In this context, the single best parasite-weakener in the world is the General Agreement on Tariffs and Trade. The GATT is all but unknown to most Americans, yet it is the most effective form of global *gaiatsu* going. Under it, more than a hundred countries regularly negotiate to reduce their trade barriers and market subsidies. The conventional arguments for GATT and other free-trade negotiations are economic. "Trade makes us wealthier," the economists say: it hones productivity on the whetstone of competition, it lets people anywhere take advantage of economic efficiencies everywhere, it allows larger economies of scale and speeds countries up the learning curve. While all of that is true, the most important benefits of trade-opening measures like GATT are not economic but political. By weakening lobbies, trade can help invigorate democratic government—not just in the United States, but all over the world.

That would be impossible if all countries had the same interest groups and the same cozy deals. But they don't. If Europe's farm protectionism is steeper than America's, and if America's maritime protectionism is steeper than Europe's, then the Europeans can attack the American shipping interests and the Americans can attack the French farming interests— and both can attack the Japanese securities cartels. Even within sectors, countries can engage in mutual cozy-deal disarmament

("We'll open our wheat market if you'll open yours"). Under GATT, dozens of countries join the circle and attack each other's lobbies. In effect, governments pick off each other's parasites.

The lobbies fight back. They scream, they shriek, they kick and buck. They say that trade liberalization is unfair and that it will be their ruin. They wrap themselves in the flag and sing the national anthem. When the French farmers blocked the streets and trashed McDonald's, they claimed to be representing France's national heritage. Manufacturers insist that defending their markets (and profits) from foreign "threats" is vital to the national interest, to the technology base, the job base, whatever. Unions insist that foreign competition destroys American jobs and reduces American incomes. Green groups protest that competing against dirtier countries undercuts environmental standards at home. Their arguments, being seductive, are worth a moment's examination.

As for environmentalists, they often worry more about trade than they need to. Trade makes nations richer, and richer nations are the ones that can afford environmental standards in the first place. "A growing body of evidence suggests that the more open a country is in terms of trade and investment, the greater the likelihood of its achieving faster economic growth as well as improved environmental performance," writes Sally A. Shelton of Georgetown University. Yes, a dirtier country may enjoy some advantages in competing with a cleaner one, but it may also suffer from many disadvantages—higher medical costs, a sicker workforce, inefficient resource use, and so on. There is no empirical or historical reason to think that dirtier countries "win" in trade and cleaner ones "lose"; if they did, then it wouldn't be the case that the United States, with the world's most extensive environmental laws, accounted for a *higher* share of the developed countries' industrial output in the early 1990s than in 1970, when the Environmental Protection Agency first opened for business.

Moreover, the discipline of foreign competition helps keep environmental rules economically sensible. If you know that General Motors must compete with Toyota, you'll be more careful to reduce GM's tailpipe emissions in a relatively efficient way, and not past the point where tailpipe emissions aren't worth reducing. You can focus your environmental energies where you get most bang for the buck. That's good for the environment and it's good for the economy—though it is bad for extremist activists and single-issue lobbies, because it restrains the demands they can attain at the expense of the economy as a whole.

Unions' calls to save American jobs and wages are appealing but misguided. True, trade puts painful pressure on unions—*if they're uncompetitive*. Effective and flexible unions can make their companies more productive. The unions that need to worry are the ones that defend archaic work rules, engage in featherbedding, block productive cooperation with management, or try to fix wages at levels that markets won't support (thus feeding inflation and currency devaluation). But this is exactly the boon of trade: it puts competitive pressure on cozy arrangements that benefit entrenched groups but rigidify the economy as a whole.

The impassioned debate over the North American Free Trade Agreement in 1993 brought front and center one of the most common objections to foreign competition, namely that it sucks jobs out of America. That charge is flat wrong—no more sensible than claiming that Illinois loses jobs by trading with New York and California. The period since World War II was marked by trade liberalization, yet it saw dramatic increases in employment, in the United States as well as abroad. Imports have doubled as a share of the American economy since the early 1970s, growing faster than exports, but over that same period the economy added 35 million new jobs and the percentage of the population that was employed rose rather than declined. And that stands to reason. Suppose you buy a foreign car which is just as good but $1,000 cheaper, or which costs the same but saves you $1,000 in repair costs. You have "earned" an extra $1,000, which you will spend or invest elsewhere in the economy, putting people to work and giving yourself what amounts to a raise. Meanwhile, foreigners selling in the U.S. market earn dollars, which they spend by buying American exports and (especially when there's a trade deficit) investing in the American economy. Either way, trade is a win-win game for the economy as a whole.

The problem isn't that foreign competition destroys American jobs on net, but that it often shifts jobs from one sector to another in ways that benefit the economy as a whole but sting specific groups—which in turn organize lobbying efforts to block the change. And that, again, is the point: foreign competition hurts entrenched interest groups. Sympathize with them, help them with adjustment when necessary, but *expose them to competition*.

Companies and business groups that argue for protection from foreign competition, whether in steel or agriculture, never fail to invoke the national interest and the threat of foreigners' "taking over" some important sector. What they don't say is that you necessarily protect one American industry at the expense of many others. Protect American car makers, and their higher prices hurt thousands of American businesses that buy cars; protect American manufacturers of flat-panel computer displays, and you hurt the competitiveness of American computer makers, who need the best displays at the lowest prices; protect American sugar growers, and higher sweetener costs hurt food manufacturers of every description. Every business lobby claims to be especially vital to the economy or the nation, but you can't protect them all. When the reshuffling game is over, the winners are the ones with the sharpest lobbyists.

An example: some business lobbies have argued for years that the country should subsidize their efforts to find new export markets. And, indeed, the U.S. government offers such subsidies. But not all exports can be subsidized, and the big winner turns out to be, not high-tech goods or pharmaceuticals or machine tools, but food products. In 1991, a single Agriculture Department program—the Market Promotion Program—spent more than all Commerce Department export-promotion programs combined. The promotion program was passed in 1985 as a gimme for California agriculture interests, which otherwise weren't keen to support that year's farm bill. In 1991, the program spent $465,000 subsidizing foreign ads for Chicken McNuggets, and $450,000 helping to promote V-8 juice in Asia and Argentina. Millions went to the wine industry, the orange industry, the almond industry—all of which were politically strong in California. Not coincidentally, the Bush Administration, which needed friends in California, supported the program. So did the Clinton Administration, which also needed friends in California. Despite the program's help, however, U.S. farm exports increased only half as fast as nonfarm exports; and an Agriculture Department study found that the program's benefits to the agriculture sector were offset by its costs to American consumers and taxpayers.

In short, the United States was subsidizing potato-chip exports instead of computer-chip exports, a policy which made political sense instead of economic sense and seems to have had little effect anyway. The story was typical. In the business-subsidy game, everyone claims to speak for the national interest, but the winners tend to be the ones with political clout and hotshot lobbyists. And, of course, the subsidies and lobbyists are hard to get rid of once they're put in place. Demosclerosis deepens. On paper, the occasional business subsidy or protection may make sense, but the gains are trivial compared to the toll that demosclerosis takes on government.

America's relative openness to outside competition—foreign goods, foreign money, foreign people, foreign ideas, all of which destabilize entrenched interests and cozy deals—is her best insurance against lobbies' sealing off the economy and then carving it up. In India, in the former Communist bloc, in Mexico before Salinas, in Brazil, in many other countries, closed economies gave interest groups the run of the place, with sad results. Openness is America's best hope that it won't happen here.

If you want to keep barnacles off your boat, head for white water. Americans should seek at every turn to expose lobbies to foreign competition, rather than sheltering them. They should exploit every chance to tear down trade barriers (of which America has plenty), and they should welcome foreign investment—the more, the better.

I don't want to oversell foreign competition. It isn't a magic potion. Interest groups that aren't directly involved with trade—the veterans' lobby or the American Association of Retired Persons, for instance—aren't much affected by foreign competition one way or another. Still, of all the countermeasures in the arsenal, foreign competition may offer the best combination of effectiveness and accessibility. We know it helps, and we have the means to pursue it. Above all, it works every day. As the tax-reform experience showed, if you scatter parasites just once they soon reassemble. But foreign competition pounds them all the time. It is a sentinel that never sleeps.

THE MISSING LINK

At this point in the discussion, after I've put my stack of suggestions on the table, people usually register two complaints. Unfortunately, both are sound.

The first is that the medicines seem a little weak, compared with the scope of the disease. On the one side, there are powerful ossifying forces that come up from deep within society and that operate on the whole government all the time. And on the other side—free trade? America does a lot of trading already; will doing more of it solve the problem?

I'm the first to agree that the "solutions" to demosclerosis seem a bit pallid compared to the problem. At this stage, demosclerosis is like Alzheimer's disease, or like some forms of cancer: we have a better understanding of how it works than of how to stop it. One cannot overstress that as of now there is no magic bullet, no six-step reform plan, that makes the problem go away so that we can worry about something else. For just that reason, I believe that figuring out how to cope with demosclerosis is the greatest challenge now facing American government. Indeed, the very fact that we don't yet know the answers makes searching for them all the more important. Almost certainly, there are powerful countermeasures yet to be discovered. Clearly, we can do better than we have done so far.

The second complaint is just as reasonable. "Sure," people say, "the kinds of measures you suggest might help. But the whole problem is that groups organize to stop those measures. You've established that cutting protective subsidies is important for keeping government flexible, but the whole problem is that one *can't* cut them, or at least can't cut them quickly or deeply enough to adapt to change. The lobbies fight subsidy reductions, tax increases, decentralizing moves, trade liberalizations—they fight everything you advocate. Just how are we supposed to use competition to weaken lobbies when the whole problem is that the lobbies are blocking competition?"

To an extent, this objection is fair. Exhorting the voters to oppose the very lobbies that the voters willingly join and finance does seem circular. The same goes for exhorting the political system to change the policies that the system seems less and less able to change. But there is more to the story. In America, lobbies are not all-powerful. If they were, the 1986 tax reform could never have happened; neither could the popularly maligned, but nonetheless useful, 1990 budget agreement between President Bush and Congress; neither could any number of trade-liberalizing agreements; neither could many other things. Lobbies are not monolithic. Newcomers benefit when entrenched interests are forced to compete, and shrewd politicians can find and mobilize some of those newcomers.

Moreover, with a suitably large package politicians can divide the lobbies and then charge through them. That was how they passed the 1986 tax reform, which pitted lobbies that lost tax breaks against lobbies that gained from lower rates. Finally, lobbies can be steamrolled if voters or politicians push reform to the top of the national agenda. That doesn't happen often, but it does happen. Many lobbies preferred leaving the health-care system alone, but in 1992 the voters routed them.

The point is that demosclerosis may be an impersonal and inexorable tendency of the political system, but *it is still only a tendency.* Fighting it depends on that most personal and fickle of counterforces: political leadership.

The strategies that I've talked about so far try to reduce the supply of transfer-seeking groups or reduce their strength. At least as important, in the long run, is the demand side of the equation. As long as the people continue to form more groups and hatch more demands for benefits, the problem continues. Successful management of demosclerosis depends, in large measure, on persuading the public to pull back from the transfer-seeking game.

Partly, that requires education: showing people the long-term costs of transfer-seeking. Until the voters come to see through the illusion that the benefits they demand are free gifts, the transfer-seeking game will expand. Realistically speaking, however, the broad public can't easily take the lead in fighting lobbies. The cost-benefit calculus of transfer-seeking is such that, for any given individual or group, investing in lobbying almost always seems to make sense: put in a little money, and maybe you can take out a lot of money, and, anyway, as long as others are playing, you had better play also.

Success must depend, then, on political leadership. It depends on the emergence of politicians who understand demosclerosis, have a grasp of what must be done, and will sell their case to the public. It then depends on persuading the public to elect politicians who will administer the medicine.

There have been some encouraging, if spasmodic, signs. In 1992, Jerry Brown, a former governor of California, ran for the Democratic presidential nomination and, despite his renowned weirdness, waged a surprisingly tenacious campaign. Brown focused wrathfully on the parasite class, which he denounced as "the people who always figure out a way to prosper even as more Americans suffer" (read: transfer-seeking professionals). Brown offered two pieces of an antiparasite regimen. One was reform of lobbying and campaign-finance laws. The other was a flat-tax proposal, which he touted as an assault on "the crooked Washington fund-raising machine that routinely auctions off loopholes to the highest bidder." His flat-tax plan was criticized as being bad for the poor, though actually that would have depended on its design. But the plan would certainly have been bad for the transfer-seeking professionals who make a living by lobbying and lawyering the tax code, and who win no matter who else loses. Which was Brown's point.

After Brown's campaign collapsed, Ross Perot's even more remarkable campaign arose in its wake. Like Brown, Perot railed against special interests and Washington corruption, offering his own partial antiparasite program in the form of deficit reduction. Alas, Perot was both too authoritarian and too provincial to understand demosclerosis; he seemed to think he could fix it by ordering the "special interests" to shut up and go away, and he seemed to believe that openness to foreign competition was nothing better than a sellout of American interests to conniving foreign lobbyists. Still, Perot's astonishing performance at the polls—19 percent, the highest draw for a third-party candidate since Theodore Roosevelt ran on the Bull Moose ticket in 1912—signaled that a constituency might be built for a reform candidacy.

There were other signs that politicians were getting the message. Senator Robert Kerrey, a Nebraska Democrat who ran for president in 1992, announced that if elected he would reduce the number of cabinet departments by half and cut nonentitlement domestic spending by a quarter. Later, in opposing the elevation of the Environmental Protection Agency to cabinet status, he said, "Government is simply too big and inefficient and something must be done. So what does Congress do? We make our problem bigger by proposing to establish another department in the bureaucracy before any comprehensive reform is taken." Coming from a right-wing Republican, that would have been political blab-as-usual; but coming from a centrist Democrat whose roots were in the party's liberal wing, it looked like a sign of growing awareness.

Kerrey was the first Democratic candidate to fold in 1992. Brown folded, too, and Ross Perot seemed satisfied to turn into a professional motormouth. Instead, the voters chose a self-proclaimed "new Democrat," a professional politician who had spent his career trying to make government work. The man who landed the job of managing demosclerosis was William Jefferson Clinton.

8

THE
CLINTON EXPERIMENT

I N AUGUST OF 1993, after the president's economic plan finally passed, a drizzle of disappointment settled over Washington. To win, President Clinton had used every ounce of
energy, yet disaster came frighteningly close. In the House,
after a frantic scramble for support ("No Reasonable Offers
Refused as Administration Bargained," said one headline), he
won without a vote to spare. In the Senate, six Democrats de-
fected and a harrowing roll call ended with fifty votes in favor,
fifty opposed. The vice president broke the tie. Clinton had put
the economic-reform plan at the center of his campaign—"It's
the economy, stupid" was the campaign's informal motto—and
now the plan was law.

Yet no one seemed jubilant—least of all the president. A
week after his victory on the economic package, when he spoke
to the National Governors' Association, he sounded exhausted
and almost heartsick. "Now, I miss—I miss you," he said to the
people who, a year ago, had been his political colleagues. "I miss
the way we make decisions. I miss the sort of heart and soul and
fabric of life that was a part of every day when I got up and went
to work in a state capital. Somehow, we've got to bring that back
to Washington."

In February, soon after Clinton's inauguration, Senator Bill Bradley, the prominent New Jersey Democrat, had called for broad, even breathtaking, reforms. "I urge President Clinton to put on each legislator's desk the vote of that legislator's lifetime," Bradley had said. Now, six months later, he looked at the final product and said dryly, "I don't think that this is the vote of our lifetimes. The people out there want real, fundamental political reform, economic reform, and social reform. This is only the beginning." Senator Robert Kerrey, the Nebraska Democrat who had demanded that Democrats kill subsidies and close cabinet departments, was no more enthusiastic about the economic package (though he, like Bradley, voted for it). "It is impressive in its honesty, but there is none of the radical change in structure that needs to occur," Kerrey said. "It is the same old stuff, in my judgment, in that it allows bureaucracies to continue to grow and doesn't make the kinds of spending cuts that everyone who walks around up here knows we need."

Washingtonians agreed that what had passed wasn't negligible. What they disagreed on was its importance. One group— call them the reformers—looked at the size of the problem and found the new economic plan sadly lacking. "There has been no conceptual breakthrough here," said Will Marshall, the president of the Progressive Policy Institute, a centrist Democratic think tank with which Clinton himself had been closely associated. "There's no question but that this exercise has conformed to the usual logic of Washington politics. I think what we're seeing is the awesome power of the Washington *nomenklatura*. It's the power of the political class in Washington to thwart change and innovation."

Another group—call them the realpolitikers—looked at the limits of Washington politics and found the economic-reform plan full of hopeful signs. "Considering what the president was up against, there's quite a bit to be proud of here," they said. "You can't change everything overnight, and the new administration actually got quite a bit done." If anything, the headlines declaring (in the words of the *National Journal*) "Gridlock: It Hasn't Gone Away" were too harsh. In Clinton's early months, a deficit-reduction plan passed. The student-loan program got an administrative overhaul. Congress agreed to auction off access to television and radio frequencies, instead of just giving it away. The rural electrification program was reformed. A new national service program was adopted. Objectively, things were getting done.

So who was right, reformers or realpolitikers? Neither, really. Neither group was asking the right question.

The reformers' disappointment was understandable, but, from the point of view of demosclerosis, it was also somewhat naive. There's little reason to think that switching the faces or parties in Washington will, in itself, lead to "real, fundamental reform" or "radical change in structure," or even make fundamental reform or radical change much easier. There's also little reason to expect that demosclerosis can be quickly or decisively cured with a bold reform that shatters the old rules and liberates Washington; Clinton could no more make a clean sweep of Washington than fly to the moon. Thus the main question by which to judge the Clinton experiment cannot be: Did the Clinton Administration redefine the rules and turn the government around?

The realpolitikers' emphasis on the new administration's accomplishments was fair and partly justified, but, from the point of view of demosclerosis, it was mostly beside the point. Yes, Clinton got some things done. But it's useful to recall, in this context, the difference between demosclerosis and "gridlock." Gridlock posits static immobility: nothing gets done, so the government just sits there. Demosclerosis posits a crippling dynamic imbalance: government gets a lot done—indeed, often works at a frenzied pace—yet problems don't get solved on net. The key issue isn't whether reforms happen or new laws pass; it's whether reforms and new laws *work*—that is, whether they solve more problems than they create. Thus the main question by which to judge the Clinton experiment cannot be: Did the Clinton Administration make things happen?

The right question is something like this: Did Clinton and Congress make a start on cleaning up the environment for government?

For demosclerosis is a kind of environmental problem. If the air is full of acid, it's no good just to breathe harder; you need to make the environment less hostile to your lungs. And if demosclerosis calcifies programs and turns them into obstacles and eternal sinecures, it's not enough just to pass more of them; you need to clean up the environment to make it less hostile to government. That means weakening lobbies or cutting through them, or both.

I'm not pretending to render any kind of final verdict on the Clinton Administration's record; that won't be known for years, if at all. It's not too soon, though, to make some provisional judgments—and, equally important, to consider what the new administration's early months taught about demosclerosis itself.

SCOREBOARD

One lobby-weakening strategy, as I've already argued, is foreign competition. Here was where the new president showed his best side. The 1993 test case was the North American Free Trade Agreement, a treaty reducing barriers to trade and investment between the United States, Mexico, and Canada. NAFTA mattered enormously to the Mexicans, who were fighting to shake off the stultifying effects of decades of xenophobia and protectionism. For the United States, whose economy is twenty times the size of Mexico's, the economic impact of NAFTA promised to be far smaller (though mostly positive). Nevertheless, Clinton understood that a congressional rejection of NAFTA could mean trouble for all future trade deals. He also seemed to understand that America will stagnate if she turns her back on foreign competition. In the finest moment of his first year in office, Clinton found his voice, fought hard, and won a resounding victory in Congress.

As so often happens with demosclerosis, though, the good news came with some bad news attached. Until recently, opposition to trade-liberalizing agreements came mostly from particular lobbies—textiles, for example, or steel—concerned about maintaining particular sinecures. Those lobbies could usually be isolated or bought off. But the picture had changed by the time Clinton came along. The free-trade agreement with Mexico faced organized resistance from hundreds of groups—labor unions, consumer groups, environmental lobbies, churches, community activists, Ross Perot's group, various unhappy industries—that linked up in a phalanx of opposition. "In the U.S.," reported Bob Davis and Jackie Calmes of *The Wall Street Journal* on the day of the NAFTA vote, "the muscle-flexing by the broad antitrade coalition marks the first time since Franklin Roosevelt started reducing tariffs in 1934 that a trade-liberalization measure has been so imperiled." In Oregon, more than fifty local groups, ranging from the state's Sierra Club to the Ecumenical Ministries of Oregon, formed the Oregon Fair Trade Coalition to oppose NAFTA; parallel groups sprouted in dozens of other states, and then coordinated with each other. Although they lost, the leaders of the groups swore, as Joan Claybrook of Public Citizen told the *Journal,* that "this is the beginning—not the end."

The NAFTA battle revealed—and helped to build—a network of antitrade interest groups that no one expects to disappear. On an ideological level, the groups blame foreign competition for every kind of economic ill; on a more workaday level, they have discovered that mobilizing against trade taps deep anxieties and brings in money and members. NAFTA passed, but the job was much harder for Bill Clinton than it had ever been for, say, Harry Truman or Richard Nixon, and it doesn't look likely to become any easier.

Another lobby-weakening strategy is to decentralize. Here there was no significant action, although the National Performance Review—a White House commission on government reform overseen by Vice President Al Gore—did suggest devolving more authority to federal managers in the field and giving states and localities more flexibility.

domestic competition ↘

Another lobby-weakening strategy is to encourage domestic competition. The administration did show interest in forcing some government agencies to compete for business. It proposed requiring the Government Printing Office to compete with private printers, for example, and it suggested that the National Oceanic and Atmospheric Administration try using private ships for its data-gathering work. Those ideas, however, mostly affected the government's internal affairs. The Clinton Administration shrank from broader forms of domestic perestroika that would offend powerful groups: ending the postal monopoly, for example, or letting banks compete with insurance companies and securities houses.

A sad example was what happened on education. The Clinton people steered a mile wide of vouchers. They even renounced experiments. Hell no, said Richard W. Riley, the new secretary of education: "I can't see spending public money to see if something is worthwhile when I'm 100 percent sure it's not." So Clinton was unwilling to go around the status quo by letting public money flow to private schools. Yet he also lacked the wherewithal to build on top of the status quo by giving more public money to public schools. And so, in time-honored fashion, he proposed a set of commissions. If they wanted to, state commissions could write voluntary standards for student performance, school adequacy, or course coverage. Meanwhile, federal commissions would develop standards to weigh the state standards. While the paper was moving back and forth between state and federal study groups, states would get a few hundred million dollars to finance their standard-setting commissions and run some pilot programs. (Is that clear?) "It's sort of the policy wonks' full employment act," said Bruce Hunter, the chief lobbyist for the American Association of School Administrators. "In the Bush Administration they got in the habit of it, and apparently they can't break it."

Another lobby-weakening strategy is to reduce the deficit, and so reduce the interest groups' ability to feed off the future. Here, to his credit, President Clinton made a serious effort—thus providing a real test of his strength against demosclerosis.

THE ICE-CREAM MAN COMETH

Unfortunately, the strength of the challenge was compromised by the weakness of the challenger. In his fight against the deficit, Clinton the president found himself crippled by Clinton the candidate.

A president or Congress that simply accepts the mountainous inheritance of existing programs is condemned to govern at the margins: a symbolic initiative here, an appealing but small "cherry program" there. In the main, that was the way George Bush governed—at the margins. Bill Clinton's mandate was, first and foremost, not to be like Bush.

In Washington, though, an iron law is that genuine change—whether reducing the budget deficit or updating the government's priorities—means pulling the plug on popular programs that are supported by constituents, lobbyists, political action committees, and protective friends in Congress. To overpower them, a president needs the backing of the nation as a whole. He needs to bring antisclerotic policies to the electorate and come back with a mandate.

Bill Clinton talked about change during his campaign, but he never built much real support for it. Instead, he promised more of everything to practically everyone, at no cost except to foreigners and "the rich." He promised a $200 billion "Rebuild America" fund for new infrastructure and human-capital programs. He promised 100,000 new police officers and expanded drug treatment; national job-retraining programs; community-service jobs for welfare recipients; more money for AIDS and schools; more Medicare benefits, including more long-term care for the elderly. He promised an investment-tax credit, a tax break for start-up companies, an expanded tax credit for the working poor, a children's tax credit, a tax reduction for the middle class. He promised, perhaps most astonishingly, to extend health coverage to all Americans *for free*, saying that he could find the money by reducing the cost of care without cutting benefits or reducing quality. He promised a lot of other things besides. And, in addition to promising more spending and lower taxes, he promised to *reduce* the budget deficit.

We had heard something like this before: in 1980, when Ronald Reagan promised to increase defense spending, reduce taxes, and still balance the budget. Asked then how he would do it, Reagan had said he would cut "wasteful" spending (read: someone else's programs) and make the economy grow by reducing burdensome taxes that strangled productivity. That was the original supply-side line. Bill Clinton emulated it. Asked how he would keep his promises, he said he would cut defense spending (that money was real enough), cut "pork-barrel spending" (read: someone else's programs), increase taxes on foreign corporations and the rich, and make the economy grow by spending on federal programs—"investments," as he called them—that would increase productivity. Clinton, like Ronald Reagan, ran on a hot-fudge-sundae diet.

Some other Democrats—such as former senator Paul Tsongas, one of Clinton's rivals for the 1992 presidential nomination—talked about making some hard choices, but Clinton would have none of it. Sacrifice? Pshaw. Except for the wealthy, Americans had already suffered enough—a line that Clinton maintained right up to the moment he was sworn in. "The thing that bothered me about so much of the sacrifice talk during the election," he said the week before his inauguration, "is that the middle class in this country and the poor have been sacrificing

for quite a long time now. They spent the 1980s sacrificing."
After being elected on a promise of more of everything at less
cost, how does a president persuade Congress or the voters to
upset any seemingly worthy group or useful program? (Remember, every program is useful to someone.) Having promised a free lunch, how does he sell hard choices? Not easily—
especially if the president was elected with only 43 percent of
the popular vote, as Clinton was.

During the campaign season, as the stream of more-for-
everybody promises became a torrent, many observers hoped
that Clinton, if elected, would switch from being a panderer
(more goodies, no pain) to being a reformer (real change, some
pain). The hope, said Tsongas, was that Clinton was "bright
enough to understand the implications of the problem once he
gets in office." Clinton was bright enough, and he did understand. But he had not equipped himself with the political weap-
ons to do the job.

Under the circumstances, Clinton acted bravely when he
about-faced after the election and attacked the budget deficit,
pretending to have only just discovered how big it was. ("Early
on we had no idea . . . what the scope of this deficit problem
was.") But the Clinton mandate ("No hard choices") wasn't
much different from the Bush mandate ("No new taxes"). Perhaps, then, no one should have been surprised when Clinton
unveiled a timid deficit-reduction plan. According to the
Clinton Administration's own projections, the plan would reduce the deficit from about 5 percent of the gross domestic
product in 1993 to just under 3 percent four years later—and
then the deficit would once again resume its upward path. The
national debt would continue to rise as a share of the economy;
the massive entitlement programs were barely nicked. More embarrassing, the Congressional Budget Office reported that the
Clinton plan offered only three-fourths the deficit reduction
that President Bush and Congress had patched together in the
budget agreement of 1990, during the putative Era of Gridlock.

It was a measure of the Clinton plan's timidity that Congress, supposedly the Guardian of Gridlock, finally passed a bit *more* deficit reduction than the president proposed. Even so, the final package was tamer than the 1990 budget agreement, after adjusting for inflation and economic growth. Robert Reischauer, the head of the Congressional Budget Office, noted that balancing the budget within ten years would require another antideficit package roughly twice the size of Clinton's. The deficit problem was put on hold for a few more years, until the time came for the next emergency deficit plan like this one.

Beyond reducing the deficit lies that other, more important lobby-weakening strategy: systematically clearing out subsidies and anticompetitive deals that feed lobbies and choke government. Here was where 1993 brought its brightest hope and, in the end, its most bitter disappointment.

STIFFENING SPINES

If you ever get elected to Congress, try this trick: denounce a "wasteful" program, demand a vote on its elimination, and then conveniently lose. You get to be against "waste," but no one in the real world gets stung. An even better trick: the House (or Senate) votes to abolish a program, the Senate (or House) insists on keeping it, and then, ever so reluctantly, the two sides agree in negotiations to let the program continue. (Next year, if they want, the two chambers can switch sides.) One way or another, with plenty of votes and programs to go around, everyone can vote against "wasteful" programs without actually killing any. The politicians are happy, the lobbies are happy, the programs live forever—and the government slowly chokes.

I'm not claiming that a new day dawned in Washington in 1993. Yet there was an unfamiliar and promising scent in the air. More than in the past, Congress seemed to care about killing some programs, instead of just pretending to kill them. In a city where normally everything lives on, some things didn't.

Look at what happened to the wool and mohair program. This was the mid-1950s strategic-fibers policy which failed in the first place and had outlived its rationale by more than thirty years, at a cost of nearly $200 million annually. Far from calling for the program's elimination, in his economic plan Clinton asked only that subsidy payments be capped at $50,000 a year for any one recipient. No hardship there: $50,000 is a third higher than the median U.S. family income. But the wool and mohair program was vulnerable. For one thing, it sounded silly (a subsidy for *what?*). For another, it got a bad press, becoming a symbol of government's inability to end anything; *The New York Times,* for instance, derided the subsidy in an editorial as "the mohair toilet seat," calling it "inexcusable." And so, on July 26, 1993, Senator Richard H. Bryan, a Democrat of Nevada, declared, "A thirty-nine-year raid on the Treasury is long enough," and offered an amendment to kill the program. On a voice vote, the Senate agreed.

According to the standard script, at this stage the House and Senate would go to conference, the agriculture barons in the House would insist that the program continue, the agriculture barons in the Senate would gladly agree, and that would be that. Sure enough, in the House-Senate negotiations all but one senator (Democrat Tom Harkin of Iowa) agreed that the program was vital to beleaguered American wool producers. Two of the subsidy's staunchest Senate defenders were Republican Phil Gramm of Texas, a conservative whose specialty was railing against government waste and big spending, and Democrat Dianne Feinstein of California, a liberal who had been on the outs with her state's powerful farm lobby. Feinstein's support for the wool subsidy didn't go unnoticed. "Big Agriculture is singing the praises of a former nemesis, Democratic Senator Dianne Feinstein," the *Los Angeles Times* reported. "Farm groups . . . have been wowed by her successful efforts to protect the oft-maligned wool and mohair subsidy program." Gramm's support did go unnoticed. At last sighting, this defender of welfare for Angora-goat ranchers was still bawling about spend-thrift government.

Naturally, the program was restored. But the story didn't end. When the deal came back to the Senate in September, Bryan took another shot—and his amendment to kill the wool and mohair subsidy passed again. The Senate wasn't backing down. With the measure back in the House, program support-ers wrung their hands and emptied their mailbags. "I am eight years old and I want to know why the government wants to take away our living," wrote Nelda Corbell, whose parents raised Angora goats in Texas, in a letter to her congressman. The House proposed a compromise. The Senate refused. At last, the House—and the sheep ranchers' lobby—folded, salvaging only a two-year phase-out. Effective on December 31, 1995, the Na-tional Wool Act of 1954 is repealed.

The Senate's decision to stand its ground and bludgeon a program to death seemed encouraging. Even more encourag-ing was that that wasn't the only such incident in 1993. A similar fate befell the forlorn federal honey program, a little $12 mil-lion subsidy set up in 1950 to shield beekeepers from a honey-price decline following the end of World War II. This was the *only* program that candidate Bill Clinton, during the 1992 cam-paign, had promised to get rid of. After its supporters mounted a campaign to save it, however, he backed down and announced that he was satisfied with a $50,000 limit on payments and a reduction in subsidy levels. This was "an important step for-ward," said Clinton amiably.

The deal was done—except that two Republicans, Repre-sentative Harris Fawell of Illinois and Senator Hank Brown of Colorado, snuck up on the honey people with a last-minute killer amendment. "If one dies and goes to heaven and wants to come to earth and have eternal life," complained Fawell, "come back as a federal program." Now, attacks on the honey program were nothing new; the program had been a Republican buga-boo since the days when Senator Dan Quayle denounced it as a "sweet little rip-off," and Brown himself had been hounding it for a decade. This time, though, the opponents won. As always, the Senate and House agreed in conference to restore the program—but the House rejected the deal, demanding the honey program's head. Between them, the American Beekeeping Federation and the American Honey Producers Association brought five representatives to Capitol Hill to lobby for a week—to no avail.

The defunding of the honey-subsidy program wasn't exactly a seismic event. For one thing, the program was tiny. For another, although the beekeepers lost their cash subsidy, they kept their guaranteed access to cheap federal credit, which was something. Besides, lobbies never sleep: by the time the honey program died, the beekeepers were already at work seeking import restrictions on low-cost honey from China. "If we can get that done," said one industry representative, "they can take the honey program." Yet here again, Congress had killed an ably defended program *without* presidential leadership. Surely something was afoot?

And then it happened yet again. The House voted to kill the Advanced Solid Rocket Motor program, a $3.7 billion NASA project that had more than doubled in cost while drifting from one rationale to another. In negotiations with the Senate, the two chambers ritually restored the project, but the House stood firm and sank it. "People are getting fed up around here," said Democratic representative Timothy J. Penny of Minnesota. "People are getting tired of the games." And again: the House killed the Superconducting Super Collider, the controversial atom smasher that interest groups and Texas legislators had saved the year before. The White House hadn't wanted to kill either of the science projects. Suddenly it was Congress that was playing the Terminator.

A cynic could say that Congress killed a few high-profile programs for show and then went on with business as usual. But even if that was so, the very fact that Congress felt pressured to put on such a show was a hopeful sign. More politicians seemed to be "getting it": understanding that their effectiveness was being strangled by their own desire to maintain every program forever. They wanted to kill *something*, if only to show themselves that they could.

The trouble, of course, is that killing two or three random programs a year won't make any noticeable difference. As always, the overwhelming majority of programs lived on, including all but a few of the programs that anyone even bothered to oppose. For instance, the Civilian Marksmanship Program, an archaic 1903 subsidy for target-shooting clubs, easily deflected challenges in the House and Senate. Supporters said the $2.5 million program—originally designed to train marksmen for wartime mobilization—taught gun safety and, in Republican representative Paul E. Gillmor's words, "has enhanced the U.S. position in world competition; nine out of ten clubs of the U.S. Olympic shooting team . . . are from this program." (Convinced?)

It's one thing to throw away the occasional trinket, quite another to do a systematic housecleaning. Turning the new mood in Congress into a program of structural reform required one key element, presidential leadership. And that element was sadly missing.

SMALL CHANGE

At the beginning of his presidency, Clinton faced a choice: govern from the inside, or govern from outside.

Washington power politics depends on three main actors: the president, the Congress, and the public. To achieve anything that isn't strictly routine, two of the three need to act in concert—and, if necessary, gang up on the third. In the "outside" strategy, a president tries to rally the public to win Congress's assent. That was what Ronald Reagan did in 1981: he rallied public support to roll over Congress.

When the outside strategy works, it's a smash. But it's also risky, because it may entail an open declaration of war against the Washington interest groups and Capitol Hill barons. If a president asks the public to rally to him and it doesn't, he becomes a figure of pity or contempt, buffeted by headlines like "Can He Govern?" The inside approach, by contrast, takes the Washington rules and relationships more or less as givens and tries to turn them to advantage. The president works with the Congress and a critical mass of interest groups to build a "do-able" program, and then either sells it to the public or—as with the 1986 tax reform—at least persuades the public not to object.

Reformers, who feared that compromises with Congress and the interest groups would vitiate any major reforms, wanted Clinton to confront the system. "When you want to play with the powers in Congress, you pay a price," the Progressive Policy Institute's Will Marshall said. "When you have even Democratic constituencies souring on government, it seems to me that the challenge for this administration is a fundamental reassessment of government's role."

Realpolitikers, on the other hand, didn't see much choice. Clinton had won with only 43 percent of the vote; whether he could appeal to the public over Washington's head was questionable, to say the least. Besides, the inside strategy seemed to fit best with Clinton's own consensus-building style. The president didn't seem inclined to challenge the power structure. A month before his inaugural, it was already becoming clear that he sought to work with the interest groups, in order to "get things done," rather than work against them. His top appointments were predominantly of two types: on the one side, political professionals and insiders (lawyer-lobbyist Ronald H. Brown at Commerce, veterans' lobbyist Jesse Brown at Veterans Affairs, former senator Lloyd Bentsen at Treasury); on the other side, intellectuals drawn from the Democratic Party's base of interest-group liberals (Donna Shalala at Health and Human Services, Robert B. Reich at Labor). "All in all," said the *National*

Journal, surveying the Clinton cabinet, "a familiar group of Democrats-in-waiting." The interest-group liberals would naturally be eager to get along with the interest groups; and, for pragmatic reasons, the political professionals would counsel Clinton against stirring up trouble.

When budget-writing time came, realpolitik won. "We decided early on that we weren't doing this as an academic exercise," a Clinton adviser told *Time.* "We wanted a program that could get through Congress." And so the Clinton Administration produced an economic plan that contained almost no restructuring of the government.

I've already discussed the size of the Clinton economic plan—that is, how much it reduced the deficit overall. But even more important than the size of the plan were its contents. A $500 billion deficit-reduction plan can make fundamental choices about what government should and shouldn't do, or it can rely on a hodgepodge of budget freezes, administrative maneuvers, accounting tricks, and the like. With rare exceptions, Clinton's plan took the latter route. Of the president's reductions in existing government spending, the vast bulk—five-sixths—came from defense-spending cuts, from snipping the edges of the Medicare and Medicaid programs, from dubious assumptions about lower government interest costs, and from even more dubious assumptions about administrative savings. The budget proposed the elimination of not one major or even middle-sized program, and its offering of mostly trivial terminations accounted for less than 5 percent of the total savings—nothing beyond the routine. In 1992, when Leon Panetta was still a member of Congress, he had said that the Agriculture Department's Market Promotion Program—that weird subsidy for overseas corporate advertising—probably ought to be eliminated. In 1993, Panetta was Clinton's budget director, yet the president proposed continuing the program at its existing level, $150 million a year. By refusing to get rid of anything significant, Clinton was effectively saying that every federal program was essential. To pass his budget would be to leave virtually untouched the accumulated mass of interest-group benefits. Clinton had punted.

Even so, Clinton proposed some reforms: student-loan reforms, broadcast-frequency auctioning, an end to rural electric subsidies, higher fees for grazing and mining on federal land, and a few others. And, where he did propose changes, his track record in Congress was pretty good. True, the rural electrification program never came close to dying. To lobby for it, three thousand rural citizens swooped down on Washington, where they were briefed by the National Rural Electric Cooperative Association's staff, armed with information packets and buttons, then sent up to Capitol Hill to buttonhole members. After a horde of them circled the desk of Representative Melvin Watt, the North Carolina Democrat said, "It's certainly powerful to see this many people visit you on an issue. It's got to have an impact on you." Something else doubtless had an impact, too. In December 1993, only a few weeks after Congress rescued the rural electric program from the president's death decree, the National Rural Electric Cooperative Association announced the name of its new chief executive officer: none other than Representative Glenn English of Oklahoma, who, as chairman of the subcommittee on rural development, was the program's leading protector in the House. ("Throughout his congressional career," sang the association, "he has shared our goals.") Apparently in a hurry to slip through the revolving door, English left halfway through his term to work for the group whose program he had just saved—a cheeky move even by Washington's sad standards. Still, the program was reduced by 40 percent, and, for the first time in its fifty-year history, larger subsidies were aimed at needier borrowers—on the whole, meaningful reforms. Similarly, Congress met Clinton halfway on student-loan reform, and it accepted his broadcast-spectrum reform completely.

That Clinton got a good share of what he asked for made it

all the sadder that he asked for so little. Where the president doesn't lead, Congress can't follow. No surprise, then, that in the final economic package Congress shunned structural change and settled for what Senator Kerrey called the same old stuff. As it had always done in the past, Congress temporized and fiddled and finagled. Instead of tearing out subsidies, Congress nibbled at inflation adjustments—for example, pushing back federal retirees' inflation adjustment by three months. A large share of the savings came from tinkering with payment formulas in Medicare and other programs; for instance, price supports went down on butter and up on nonfat dry milk. Another large share of the savings came from merely extending expiring provisions of current law, such as user fees and short-term taxes. Another large chunk came from extending the overall spending freeze adopted by Bush and Congress in 1990—and spending freezes, of course, just demand that the government do everything it ever did with less and less money. "It's a lot of marginal changes again," sighed Rudolph G. Penner, a former Congressional Budget Office director who had seen Washington produce more than a few such vacuous packages.

Shortly after the election, Clinton had said that his mandate was "an end of politics as usual." That was exactly what the economic plan did not deliver. In the end, what was extraordinary about the 1993 outcome was its ordinariness. It was a standard-issue, made-in-Washington budget deal—one more temporizing move in a long series stretching back to the early 1980s. In fact, in all but the fine print it was a slightly smaller retread of the Bush Administration's notoriously visionless 1990 budget deal: lower defense spending, higher top income-tax rates, snippings from Medicare, a spending freeze, and some creative accounting—all while leaving the federal government's ramshackle structure untouched.

In September 1993, after the budget effort was over, the president's own National Performance Review declared that "the federal government seems unable to abandon the obsolete.

It knows how to add, but not to subtract." Apparently, though, learning to subtract was not a priority for the Clinton Administration. The task force suggested hundreds of ways to improve government management, some of them admirable, some of them a bit—shall we say—wishful. (Recommendation: "Congress must demand less and clarify priorities more." Thanks.) Under the heading "Eliminate Special Interest Privileges," the panel made exactly four suggestions: eliminate highway demonstration projects mandated by Congress (these were often pork), cut unneeded air-service subsidies to small communities, and abolish—you guessed it—the honey subsidy and the wool and mohair subsidy, which were already under heavy fire in Congress. Other eliminations were few and mainly inconsequential.

When someone complained that the task force's four hundred recommendations included only fifteen program eliminations, budget director Panetta replied, "I would kiss the ground and thank God if we could eliminate fifteen." One could sympathize with his plight, even if he wasn't doing much to fix it. Better management of the government is fine as far as it goes, but it's no substitute for weeding out ineffective and unimportant programs. If Ford were still producing almost every car it ever made from almost every factory it ever opened, no amount of tinkering with the management system could save it. Confronted with this problem, Clinton's government-reform effort ducked, just as the economic plan had done.

"He really did have a golden opportunity with the budget to do some radical kinds of things," Penner remarked. But cleaning up the environment for government is messy and, politically speaking, dangerous. Clinton didn't seem to want to get his hands dirty. That was doubly a shame. A new president with a new mandate doesn't come along every day. Opportunities to launch a systematic attack on demosclerosis—not a decisive attack, but a big one, like tax reform—come along only once every decade or two. In 1993, the moment was squandered.

THE PRICE HE PAID

Instead, the president did what others had done before him. He piled his own program on top of every preceding administration's program: tax relief for the working poor and for business investment, spending for urban-development programs (so-called enterprise zones, for example), money for low-income housing and worker training, and so on. Instead of rationalizing the rickety federal government, he dropped a few more pieces on top. In the long term, that wouldn't be good for the government. In the short term, it wasn't good for the president, who saw his dreams of broad change squeezed to near-marginality.

Clinton had staked his campaign on an ambitious plan to make the economy more productive. One could disagree with his plan, but it had the "vision thing" in spades. At its heart was the idea, increasingly popular in the Democratic Party, that the country needs a massive government capital-spending program to improve physical and human infrastructure: roads, bridges, job retraining, smart highways, high-speed rail, electric cars, environmental technologies, information highways. The idea touched all the political bases. For centrist and conservative Democrats, a public-investment program would move the government's focus away from short-term consumption and toward long-term investment. For liberal Democrats, public investment offered the prospect of jobs, development projects, and a renewed mission for government. As a candidate, Clinton was enthusiastic, promising to reduce the deficit "as quickly as I can, but I'm not going to give up another decade of high-wage jobs and investment opportunities." In fact, his ambitious public-investment program was the main plank of his economic platform in 1992: "In the absence of increasing investment in this country, including public investment, you can't get growth going again," he said.

What Clinton did not do during the campaign was talk about a real change in priorities (translation: some group gets less). Instead, he campaigned on a promise to raise $45 billion painlessly by "preventing tax avoidance by foreign corporations," a promise that turned out to be wildly inflated, just as the tax experts had predicted. He promised a windfall from vague and painless reductions in "pork-barrel spending," but that magic lunchbox, too, was empty at budget time. Although Clinton picked up some money by raising top tax rates, he found nowhere near enough to finance a large-scale public-spending program. So his investment plans were strangled by his own inability, or refusal, to throw anything away. After the inauguration, he was trapped with no option but to scale back his "investment" agenda. Congress, demanding more by way of deficit reduction, scaled it back even more. What finally emerged, according to the Economic Policy Institute, a liberal think tank in Washington, was a fiscal 1994 federal budget that included *less* for government investment—that is, for infrastructure, education and training, and civilian research and development—than President Bush had spent the year before.

In the end, the main spending increase that Clinton got was a large increase in the tax credit for the working poor. There was also more for food stamps, foster care, and child immunization. Those increases were significant and laudable, but far short of what Clinton and the liberals had hoped for. Jeff Faux, the president of the Economic Policy Institute, looked at the remnants of the investment plan and declared: "This is not satisfactory. If this is all it is, and Clinton doesn't resuscitate the investment theme and there's no money for it and we end up with a Democratic administration claiming success in the terms of a CPA, this is a failure."

Even more poignant was the fate of Clinton's national service program. More than any other initiative, national service defined his vision of what he had called "our New Covenant":

young people could work for their country to pay back their student loans, learning citizenship and responsibility. "Just think of it," he rhapsodized at the 1992 Democratic convention, "millions of energetic young men and women, serving their country by policing the streets, or teaching the children or caring for the sick. . . . That's what this New Covenant is all about."

A year later, the end product was miniaturized by "fiscal reality," alias demosclerosis. To fulfill Clinton's vision, national service would need to be a broad, national commitment, and not just a showcase for a few lucky applicants. But by February, national service looked more like a pilot program than a defining initiative. That month, Clinton asked for $7.4 billion over four years—"hardly the scholarships-for-all he had initially promised," wrote Steven Waldman in *Newsweek*. "So before Clinton's plan was even introduced to Congress, it had been radically scaled back." Congress scaled it back still further, approving, in the end, only $1.5 billion over three years.

This was still a modestly significant program. But there will be about eighteen million young Americans of roughly "national service" age in 1997; of those, about one-quarter of 1 percent will be enrolled in national service. Attempts to serve more participants ran into bogus federal poverty, partly because existing student-aid programs were viewed as untouchable. Attempts to reward participants more generously ran into opposition from veterans' groups, which believed that their claim to national-service benefits should be second to none. In the end, the program looked more like a new ornament than a New Covenant. Explaining why it settled for something so unrevolutionary, the Clinton Administration at one point brought forward R. Sargent Shriver, John F. Kennedy's brother-in-law and the first director of the Peace Corps. "With the shortage of money now," he said, "one has to be satisfied with achieving modest goals." Imagine—a "poorer" nation than in Kennedy's day, when the federal government's budget, in constant dollars, was only a third the size of today's!

Within the administration's ranks, the reality of demosclerosis was sinking in. In the White House, an official pointed to the continuing freeze on domestic discretionary spending, which is the kind of spending that an activist president cares most about. The freeze didn't even provide enough money to keep programs even with inflation, and it would last until 1998, halfway through the president's *second* term, if he had one. "The freeze will bite harder and harder," the official said. "You either look for fundamental structural reforms or you settle for smaller and smaller quantities of the same old programs. Those are the only two choices."

I asked him what he thought would happen. "If I had to make a bet," he said, "I'd say that, nine times out of ten, the defensive forces of the same old programs will be stronger than the offensive forces advocating new programs."

STILL SLUSHED

None of this is to say that changing presidents and parties has made no difference at all. That would be silly. It is to say that changing presidents and parties isn't enough. In fact, it's far from enough. If the changing of the guard in 1993 did nothing else, it showed that the diminution of government's problem-solving power transcends personalities and partisanship.

When asked why the government worked so poorly in the Reagan-Bush era, many experts pointed to divided control of the Washington power structure. It's a credible explanation: when one party controlled the White House and the other the Congress, each tried to keep the other from succeeding. Accountability was fragmented. Mistrust of the White House prodded a suspicious Congress to micromanage every agency and cling defensively to every program.

Certainly, divided control was part of the story. But divided control ended in 1993, and demosclerosis didn't.

When I asked around at some of the agencies in Washing-

ton, staff people said that relations between their agencies and
Congress had, indeed, become less strife-ridden now that both
branches were in Democratic hands. But the more cooperative
atmosphere, they added, didn't much change the reality that
almost everything is permanent. When I dug into a couple of
agencies' budgets, the numbers confirmed that unified Democratic control did give agencies more flexibility, but not very
much more.

The Agriculture Department budget provided a neat comparison. Every year, Republican administrations would routinely ask for the abolition of more than two hundred little
programs and projects and grants, many of them pork-barrel
research grants, ranging from a rural-technology grant program to a dairy-goat research project. In the last budget he
submitted, President Bush asked to kill about 250 items worth
a total of $230 million. His score was dismal: Congress elimi-
nated only twenty-seven items, saving a trivial $13 million. For
all practical purposes, Bush could kill nothing.

In principle, a Democratic Congress should be readier to
work with a Democratic president on program eliminations,
since the two are more likely to share the same priorities. In
practice, there was some improvement, but not much. President
Clinton asked to kill many of the same items as Bush—more
than two hundred of them, worth a total of $160 million. Al-
though he asked for less than Bush, he got more: three dozen
eliminations, saving about $38 million. So the straitjacket wasn't
quite as tight. On the other hand, it was still very tight: Clinton's
savings amounted to one two-thousandth of the Agriculture
Department's budget.

Or look at the Education Department. There, the Bush
Administration had sought to end about forty education programs, most of them very small. Of those, one—support for a
research institute in New York—was put on a phase-out track.
Again, Clinton asked to kill some of those same items: to be

precise, eleven of them and a handful of library grants, together worth about $200 million, which the administration wanted to rechannel into its national service initiative. As planned, support for the research institute was allowed to die. But none of the other items was killed. State student incentive grants, consumer and homemaking education grants, Ellender fellowships, education grants for native Hawaiians—all of them lived on, funded at the same level. Same stuff, different day.

Numbers like those suggest that the forces defending programs are Olsonian, not just partisan. A look at big-picture politics gives confirmation. Many examples could serve: the lobbying frenzy that destroyed Clinton's broad-based energy tax, the fate of his national service plan, the erosion of education reforms. The new administration was only ten weeks old when western land interests gave Clinton a smacking he wouldn't forget. Grazing fees for government land cost a fraction of the private equivalent, a juicy subsidy even when one factors in that public land tends to be of poorer quality. Similarly, under an old law from 1872, miners could buy rights for as little as $2.50 an acre, with no royalties charged on the ore they extracted. "The time is long overdue to reform a law passed four years before the Battle of the Little Big Horn," said Secretary of the Interior Bruce Babbitt.

In the Reagan-Bush years, when some members of Congress suggested raising land-use charges, ranchers' groups spent heavily to defeat them, laid siege to Capitol Hill, and, for good measure, denounced the reformers as "socialists" promoting "cultural genocide." Now that the president himself was threatening the franchise, the western interests went full bore. Seven Democratic senators from the West met with Clinton to say how much his plan would hurt their states (read: certain organized interests concentrated in their states). Clinton, who needed their support for his embattled economic-stimulus bill, backed down, humiliated. "Another Clinton plan for a bold initiative withers under fire," said *The New York Times* in its news coverage.

It seemed likely that the Clinton Administration would eventually get some land-use reforms enacted, albeit narrower ones than environmentalists and the administration had hoped for. But no one who watched the process in 1993 could think that the election of a new president had solved government's problems. Demosclerosis is anchored to permanent lobbies, not just to passing politics. Changing the faces and reshuffling the chairs in Washington can help (or hurt) at the margin, but it doesn't make the parasite economy shrivel up, and the basic asymmetry of demosclerosis remains as strong as ever. As President Clinton discovered when he took on the western land lobby, withdrawing a subsidy or anticompetitive deal is still much harder than granting one. The imbalance persists.

In an environment that destroys government's flexibility and debilitates the method of trial and error, policy-making becomes a high-wire act. The most dramatic example is health-care reform, one of those unusual agenda-dominating issues created when Congress, the president, and the public all demand change. At this writing, the smart money in Washington is on passage of a giant health-care bill, perhaps the most ambitious reform effort since the New Deal. "So," people will be tempted to say, "demosclerosis isn't such a problem after all." But remember: the main problem isn't adopting programs, it's *adapting* them—revising them *after* they're adopted or, harder still, replacing them after the beneficiaries have built their protective shell. A program as huge and complex as a national health plan—overhauling a seventh of the American economy at one blow!—can't be gotten just right the first time, no matter who is president or how carefully the legislation is drafted. It will need to be adjusted through the process of trial and error. If lobbies calcify the program and block its ability to adapt, after a decade or so it's likely to cause as many problems as it solves, if not more. Instead of trying, failing, and trying again, we might get stuck with our first try for years. In that case, heaven help us if we get it wrong.

That, finally, is why cleaning up government's environment is so important. When the air is full of lead and sulfuric acid, the very act of breathing becomes dangerous. And when the political environment is full of groups that petrify every program and gum up the process of trial and error, the very act of governing becomes dangerous.

AND STILL THEY COME

De Mosclerosis continues

Meanwhile, the governing environment isn't getting any cleaner. The Olsonian forces never quit, which is why it's unwise to miss opportunities to attack demosclerosis. Left alone, groups keep forming and growing; transfer-seekers keep hunting up new subsidies and perks; hyperpluralism becomes more hyper and the parasite economy thrives. The cleanup job left undone this year becomes bigger next year.

Here is a sampling of what was going on quietly in the background as the politicians tussled noisily in the foreground.

• *Lobbies and groups and associations kept streaming to Washington.* The Motor Vehicle Manufacturers Association (now the American Automobile Manufacturers Association) announced that it was moving its headquarters to Washington after ninety-two years in Detroit. The National Association of Independent Schools moved to Washington, saying that, with federal legislation and regulations increasingly affecting private schools, it "wanted to be closer to the source." The Business Roundtable, a chief executives' group, moved its main office down from New York City. MasterCard International moved its government-relations shop from New York to Washington; its competitor Visa, citing a flurry of regulatory and legislative activity that could affect the company, opened a Washington office, headed by a former staff member of the Senate Banking Committee. The Society of Manufacturing Engineers announced it would open a Washington office, citing "increased interest in manufacturing in Washington." The Mille Lacs Band of Ojibwe, a Minnesota-based Indian tribe, opened a Washington office (the Navahos had been the first tribe to do so, eleven years before), and at least two other tribes, the Wisconsin Oneida and the Connecticut Mashantucket Pequot, were considering doing the same. The Christian Coalition, a conservative religious group led by Marion G. (Pat) Robertson, opened a Washington office. Even Major League Baseball came: "We thought we needed a Washington office because baseball has a lot of business going on in Washington."

• *Interest groups kept forming.* A new group called the Taxpayers Defense Committee began placing ads on cable television, urging viewers to call a toll-free number and pay $9.95 to send Mailgrams to their senators and the White House. Two former Justice Department officials (including William P. Barr, attorney general in the Bush Administration) announced a new group to advocate tougher laws on violent crime. The National Coalition for Homeless Veterans, which had been meeting informally for three years, decided that the time was right for a permanent presence in Washington, hiring a three-member staff with a $500,000 budget. The Family Research Council, a socially conservative think tank, said it would set up a group "to do more-direct lobbying work." An assortment of Washington advocacy groups formed the Free Speech Coalition, whose mission was to clean up the image of interest groups and oppose restrictions on lobbying.

Inevitably, the health-care-reform effort launched dozens of groups and fed hundreds (thousands?) of lobbyists. A dozen large companies formed the Corporate Health Care Coalition; a coalition of health insurers and business associations formed the Voluntary Purchasing Cooperative Coalition; sixteen big-city hospitals formed the National Association of Urban Access Hospitals. In preparation for the fight, health-related political action committees sprang up. Two hundred of them were active in the 1991–92 election cycle, of which about four dozen were new; in the six months following the election, at least another ten health PACs registered with the Federal Election Commission. The pathologists formed a political action committee, as did the plastic surgeons, the anesthesiologists, and others.

• *The parasite economy kept expanding and the transfer-seeking sector kept creating jobs.* "The players in the [health-care] reform debate seem afraid not to hire scads of consultants," wrote Julie Kosterlitz in the *National Journal,* adding that "consultants, naturally, are ecstatic." "It's unmanaged competition," crowed one overjoyed public-relations executive. Former Democratic representative Mervyn M. Dymally of California, the recently retired chairman of the House subcommittee on Africa, set up a Washington consulting business and gathered clients from Africa and Europe. Arter & Hadden, a law firm based in Cleveland, decided the time had come to get into lobbying and hired former representative Tom Loeffler. Winston & Strawn, a law firm based in Chicago, was busy expanding its own lobbying shop, in short order hiring, among others, former Democratic representatives Beryl F. Anthony and Dennis E. Eckart, as well as Charles Kinney, who had been chief floor counsel to the Senate majority leader. After stepping down as staff director of the House Ways and Means Committee, Robert J. Leonard formed a new legal and lobbying firm with Thomas M. Ryan, a former top aide to the chairman of the powerful House Energy and Commerce Committee. Les Francis, a former executive director of the Democratic Congressional Campaign Committee, gave a reception at a plush Washington hotel to celebrate the opening of his own new lobbying and public-relations firm. And so on. And on. And on.

UNFINISHED BUSINESS

Demosclerosis isn't impervious to treatment, but it is difficult to treat. The president, the Congress, and the public need to try very hard, and they can't expect that the problem will just go away. Instead, they need to go after the disease with determination and persistence. That has yet to happen.

Undoubtedly, 1993 offered hopeful signs. The president's successful support for the North American Free Trade Agreement, in the face of an unprecedented array of organized opponents, was encouraging. So was Congress's increased willingness to kill programs, if it really was a sign of new understanding instead of just a passing mood. Also undoubtedly, 1993 was in no sense decisive. The battle against the deficit ended in yet another draw. The battle to systematically strip away subsidies and anticompetitive deals was never joined. From the point of view of demosclerosis, 1993 was better than some years, worse than others, but in no sense a breakthrough.

As a candidate, Bill Clinton promised goodies to everybody at no cost; as president-elect, he used his election-night victory speech to launch a hackneyed attack on "special interests"; as president, he bungled his first and maybe best chance to clear out some of the underbrush that is choking government. Yet he seemed to understand as well as any politician alive why government is dying. In the opening weeks of his term, he spoke passionately and often of experimentation. In his inaugural address, he declared, "Let us resolve to make our government a place for what Franklin Roosevelt called 'bold, persistent experimentation.' " So important to him were Roosevelt's words that he repeated them in his first national address to the public, a few days before the State of the Union message: "Our every effort will reflect what President Franklin Roosevelt called 'bold, persistent experimentation,' a willingness to stay with things that work and stop things that don't."

And then, in his 1993 economic address, before the Congress, the cabinet, the Supreme Court, the diplomatic corps, the public, and the Almighty, President Clinton ad-libbed a passage of crystalline comprehension. "I have to say that we all know our government has been just great at building programs," he said. "The time has come to show the American people that we can limit them, too, that we can not only start things, but we can actually stop things."

That job remains ahead of us, in its entirety.

9

WILL WE SUCCUMB?

IN 1993, AS WASHINGTON THRASHED in its tightening strait-jacket, I caught up with Marvin Leath. Leath was the Democratic congressman from Texas who, in 1985, had risen to condemn the endless finger-pointing between liberals and conservatives. "We all know who is to blame," he had said. "Liberals and conservatives and all in between are to blame. The people are to blame for believing all the garbage they get bombarded with through the mail raising money from both parties and a thousand special-interest lobbies." After twelve years in Congress, Leath had disgustedly given up politics in 1990. "I came up here because I really wanted to solve problems, and when that stopped being possible, I just got out," he later explained.

Wanting to know how the world looked to him eight years later, I went to see him in his office on Capitol Hill. He had become a professional lobbyist, representing defense contractors, a soft-drink association, a few others.

In the soft light of a Washington morning, I found a man who had almost given up hope. "It's gotten to where no one can govern this country," he said. "That's the systemic problem that exists. How do you govern?"

It's kind of sad, I said, to hear you talk that way. "Sure, it's sad," he said.

Leath had started in politics during the 1960s. When he worked as a staff member on Capitol Hill in the early 1970s, he said, things were better. You could sit down with reasonable people and solve just about any problem. But those were simpler days, long gone. Now, twenty years later, Leath ached for the Clinton Administration to make the system work again. If anyone could do it, he thought, Bill Clinton—bright, articulate, interested in governing well rather than in selling ideology—was the man. But Leath wasn't encouraged. "He's in a job that's just overwhelming," he said, slumped in his chair. "I don't really see us solving any problems yet. I still get so damn frustrated watching this system."

In 1993, Congress passed a deficit-reduction package—granted, just one of a long series. The president announced a government-reform program—granted, also one of a long series. The politicians seemed to be getting serious about major reforms of the health-care system (though whether the reforms would work remained to be seen). Congress seemed more willing to dump programs. Maybe Marvin Leath was too gloomy. An optimist could reasonably see room for hope, even for cautious enthusiasm. American government was still capable of taking on big issues and making big decisions. No, governing wasn't easy. But it wasn't supposed to be easy.

A pessimist wouldn't be convinced. "Yes," he might retort, "some reform happens. Some reform *always* happens. But look what the reformers had to deal with—not just checks and balances, but rust and barnacles! Look how excruciatingly difficult it has become to do anything that irritates any entrenched lobby.

"And remember: reform—adaptation, to be more precise—tends to become more difficult over time. If you don't think things are bad enough, just wait. Demosclerosis is directional. Government officials are like gardeners whose tools get rustier and rustier. As hard as problem-solving has been for Bill

Clinton, it will tend to be harder for his successor, and harder still for *his* successors, if other things are equal."

"*If* other things are equal," replies the optimist. "But other things are never equal. After all, more is happening in the world, and in politics and government, than just the accretion of interest groups and old programs. Besides, the fact that gravity always tends to pull you downward doesn't mean you can't climb uphill. Countermeasures are available and human beings are inventive, and to speak of decline as inevitable is not only wrong but saps the will to fight back. We know there are ways to manage demosclerosis. So let's get to work!"

"Managed decline," retorts the pessimist, "may be better than the other kind, but it's still decline." He would doubt that a counteroffensive would really be persistent enough to overcome the size and appetite and sophistication of the parasite economy. Anyway, the effects of reforms are likely to be temporary. Interest groups will always tend to accumulate over time; if shaken off, they will reaccumulate. "The termites are always there," Mancur Olson himself has said. "The clock keeps ticking."

Actually, Olson is less pessimistic than his theory. In 1982, he ended *The Rise and Decline of Nations* on a hopeful note. "Ideas certainly do make a difference," he wrote. "May we not then reasonably expect, if special interests are (as I have claimed) harmful to economic growth, full employment, coherent government, equal opportunity, and social mobility, that students of the matter will become increasingly aware of this as time goes on? And that the awareness eventually will spread to larger and larger proportions of the population? And that this wider awareness will greatly limit the losses from the special interests? That is what I expect, at least when I am searching for a happy ending."

He is still searching for that happy ending, and he reports being optimistic three days out of five. If the public figures out what's going on, and grows angry enough or exasperated enough, then politicians may risk the wrath of the constituent groups.

"We do see growing recognition of the problem," he says, "and history does show examples of thoroughgoing reform." Mexico, which was long stifled by cozy deals between interest groups and the ruling party, has opened its economy and begun to breathe. Several South American nations have moved away from the domination of military elites and powerful interests. Even the obstinate government of India has recently taken steps toward opening up. And, of course, the former Communist bloc, which was once the wholly owned property of a deeply entrenched parasitic class, is now striving to create competitive markets at home and to join them abroad.

Yet hope can be matched stride for stride by doubt. Mexico, South America, India, the former Communist states—all of them turned to broad reform only after approaching, or actually reaching, economic meltdown. That's not particularly encouraging, if the whole idea is to avoid meltdown. Anyway, America's economy is open enough so that it probably never will reach that point. Without the prod of calamity, can America escape the logic of the transfer-seeking game? Examples of countries that vigorously scrubbed away accumulated subsidies and anticompetitive deals without first entering crisis are few. Margaret Thatcher had only limited success in Great Britain. Perhaps Australia, New Zealand, or Italy will fare better, but the juries there are still out.

Short of calamity, suppose American voters do get angry. So what? Generalized voter anger against "the system" does not translate into votes against particular programs or groups. No one gets reelected to Congress for voting against maritime subsidies or peanut growers. "In Congress, we don't get to vote on the abstraction," Republican representative Vin Weber told *Time* in 1992, shortly before retiring from office. "We have to vote for or against actual programs." In America, the general desire for a housecleaning has not translated into anything like a consensus on whose furniture and knickknacks should be tossed out.

Yes, yes, all right. But the optimist isn't defeated. "Never assume that people are unintelligent or ineducable," he replies. "Voters in democratic societies have consistently defied predictions that they couldn't rise to confront their problems or their enemies. They can confront demosclerosis, and confront it they will. At a minimum, they can certainly learn to manage it, instead of letting it manage them."

Who is right? Maybe the optimist, maybe the pessimist. The best conclusion, for now, may be this: demosclerosis is manageable, but it is not self-managing. To hope lazily that something will turn up is a fool's strategy. Either we deal with demosclerosis, or it deepens.

I don't pretend that the implications of demosclerosis have yet been deeply fathomed by me or anyone else. What's clear, however, is that Americans will need to do some rethinking about what they expect from government and where they stand in relation to it. For liberals, for conservatives, above all for the broad public, the time has come for some attitude adjustments.

WHY LIBERALS AND CONSERVATIVES WILL BE UNHAPPY

As the reality of demosclerosis sinks in, it is bound to make many traditional liberals uncomfortable. American liberals tend to believe that government's problem-solving capacity is large and expandable. Programs solve problems; more problems require more programs. Many liberals have long assumed that government can do almost anything it puts its mind to, if only the right people are in charge.

Demosclerosis says otherwise. It posits, instead, a necessary trade-off between what government tries to do and what it *can* do. By creating programs that create lobbies that lock in programs, government can choke itself on its own output. And this problem can't be wished away. Programs, like medicines, can do good things, but if you don't take the inherent side effects into account you can wind up dead. Like a careful doctor meting out drugs carefully, government needs to stay constantly aware of the limits on how much it can do. Too often, liberals have failed to do that.

Some liberals will dismiss demosclerosis as conservative cant: just another attack on government (and on liberals). That would be unfortunate, a counterproductive act of denial. Another, more common, form of denial is "Yes, but never mind." A few weeks before Bill Clinton took office, I met with a Clinton adviser who advocated a fistful of targeted federal investment programs and industrial policies. Demosclerosis implies that it's almost impossible to insulate such programs from interest groups that capture the benefits and then hoard them. How, I asked, would you get around that problem? He said he had no firm answer, instead saying, "We *have* to make this kind of thing work."

That's "Yes, but never mind": "Yes, organized interests take over programs and engrave them in stone, but we'll keep on acting as though they didn't." Demosclerosis means that "Yes, but never mind" won't do. It means that liberals who want to start a new program or expand an old one ought, at least, to offer along with it a mechanism to protect it from calcification. I'm not sure that such an insulating mechanism is possible, but it might be. Maybe a program could be designed to end automatically if it didn't achieve specified goals in a specified period. (The problem, of course, would be seeing that the program actually died, given that organizations and political patrons would spring up to protect it.) Or maybe a program could measure its own performance and phase itself out. Given the difficulty, probably impossibility, of stopping lobbies and politicians from defending programs that are dear to them, I'm not hopeful that anyone will soon invent a reliable mechanism to keep programs flexible. But if one can be found, liberals, who care about making government work, are the best people to find it.

Until they do, their hope of using government in ever clev-
erer ways is fanciful and, ultimately, self-defeating. Visions of
sharp-eyed government entrepreneurs making cutting-edge
investments, or of agile officials fine-tuning innovative social
programs, are mirages. That isn't to say that government needs
to be dismantled. It is to say that government's effectiveness is
naturally self-limiting, and that those who deny or defy government's natural limits are making its situation worse, not better.

Demosclerosis spells the end, not of liberalism, but of liberalism without limits. If politicians and the public pick their shots
carefully, they can solve a handful of problems pretty well. But
if they try to solve every problem at once—which is what they
have done—they energize every possible lobby and every potential group, thus feeding the very process that destroys government's ability to adapt. My own frustration is that too few
liberals are yet ready to understand this. They cling to a kind of
unlimited governmentalism which, for example, undertakes to
restore rural economies, revitalize inner cities, and shore up
suburbs all at once.

In a sense, they're loving government to death, which really
means they're loving liberalism to death, because liberalism re-
lies on government to solve problems. When government fails,
liberalism fails. And that is the story of the last twenty years.

Conservatives, who dislike government to begin with, will be
happier than liberals with the government-limiting implications
of demosclerosis. But they won't be all that happy. Demosclerosis, if it goes on unchecked, turns government into more and
more of a rambling, ill-adapted shambles which often gets in the
way but can't be gotten rid of. From a conservative point of view,
demosclerotic government just sits there, like a big boulder in
the middle of the road. If it fails to serve a liberal agenda, it is
equally likely to block a conservative one. Liberals may not get
new poverty programs that work, but conservatives also can't
get rid of archaic banking regulations.

Conservatives would thus be foolish to think that demosclerosis is a victory for them. They, too, need to fight it. That means raising taxes and throwing coddled business lobbies out into the cold. It means saying no to financiers and insurance executives and manufacturers and Farm Bureau members and many other subsidized interests who are important parts of the conservative political base—and who don't at all mind subsidies and cozy deals that benefit themselves.

Most of all, it means cutting benefits to (among other people) the broad portion of the American middle class that votes for conservatives, grouses about "big government," and yet reaps a golden harvest of tax breaks and subsidies. The message for those people is: this means you. Government transfer payments are now a sum equivalent to a quarter of all wages and salaries earned by Americans—and that's before counting such massive tax breaks as the deduction for interest on mortgages. "As far as federal expenditures are concerned," writes Herbert Stein, a former chairman of the Council of Economic Advisers, "[the] welfare state for the not-poor is about five times as big as the welfare state for the poor." Tax breaks and regulatory protections are even more heavily skewed toward the not-poor. In 1991, notes former commerce secretary Peter G. Peterson, an average household whose income was over $100,000 collected almost twice as much in government entitlement and tax benefits as did a household earning less than $10,000. (If the government's goal is to equalize incomes, he says, "it would do a better job if it. . . simply scattered all the money by airplane over every population center, to be gathered at random by passersby.") No one is off the gravy train—certainly not conservatives.

Conservatives have talked a good game about "limiting spendthrift government," but the Reagan years showed clearly that they are more interested in talk than action. Real countermeasures against demosclerosis imply real attacks on real subsidies defended by real interest groups and enjoyed by real voters. So far, conservatives haven't had the stomach.

Can either side adjust? It's not easy, partly because their ideologies stymie each other. Conservatives hate to say no to their subsidized friends, or yes to tax increases, because they believe that liberals will just take the money and spend it on new benefits for big-city mayors and welfare bureaucrats. Liberals hate to say yes to program reductions because they believe that conservatives will just take the money and spend it on tax cuts for the rich. So neither side gets anywhere. Government stays too big for conservatives and too inflexible for liberals. It neither solves problems nor goes away.

WHY A DREAM MUST BE BURIED

Let's suppose things don't change very much. Suppose that, instead of thoroughgoing reforms that sweep away entrenched subsidies and anticompetitive deals en masse, all that the political system can manage is a steady dribble of temporizing moves: a numbing series of deficit-reduction packages that never put the problem to rest, a constant scramble to patch existing programs and keep them lurching along, an annual search for dribs and drabs of money to finance trivial new initiatives. Plus, every decade or so, there might be a broader reform, like tax reform in the 1980s or transportation deregulation in the 1970s—something comprehensive and worthwhile, but not decisive.

That's more or less what happens now. If I had to guess, I'd say it's the likeliest scenario for the indefinite future: more of the same.

That would not be a disaster. Though it's true that demosclerosis makes government gummy, the Social Security checks will still go out, the budget will still be passed (most years), patchwork reforms and emergency bills will still be approved. When a program goes totally haywire, it will be stopped from exploding altogether. Farm programs are rarely abolished or even fundamentally rethought, but when some of them spun out of control in the early 1980s and started pricing American farmers out of world export markets, the 1985 farm bill corrected the worst excesses. When Medicare costs began running away willy-nilly, Washington was able to tinker with the program to tame the worst excesses (albeit by shifting many of the costs to the private sector, and so displacing the health-cost problem rather than solving it).

If demosclerosis continues unchecked, it implies that the normal process of government will become steadily less about anticipatory problem-solving and more about last-minute crisis control. Already, like a man holding a flamethrower in his left hand and a firehose in his right, government often finds itself rushing to deal with emergencies that are largely of its own making—the budget deficit, for example, and the savings-and-loan crisis and, to a lesser extent, the health-care crisis. Still, the very fact that government can temporize saves it from seizure and total collapse. True, it tends to get stickier and less adaptive. But that's a prescription for frustration, not death. And frustration with government, as Americans know from experience, is something they can live with if they need to.

Yet learning to live with a sclerotic government is, for many Americans, a shock. Not so long ago, the promise of American government seemed boundless, at least if you were anywhere to the left of the anti-Roosevelt Republicans. The federal government, indeed, seemed the most promising social tool ever invented. In practice, of course, Washington still fell short. But most of us assumed that the governmental tool kit would be refined to make more and more problems soluble. Government, like technology, would improve rather than decline with age, learning how to run programs that would solve poverty, dampen business cycles, and so on.

Instead of becoming stronger, government became feebler. Instead of improving its grip on national problems, it lost traction. Yet even today many Americans are unwilling to give up on the idea that government can be the tool of their dreams. They call upon it to fix low productivity, high hospital bills, inner-city crime, cable television rates, you name it. The depth of the public's disillusionment and cynicism about government is itself a sign that many people still expect Washington to do everything but wash the dishes: you don't rage in disappointment when you don't expect a lot.

Perhaps Americans always expected too much from Washington; in the age of demosclerosis, at any rate, they certainly do. Unquestionably, if Americans undertake a housecleaning of unprecedented scope they can restore more vitality to government. If they work at it, they can slow the accretion of new groups and weaken the existing ones. And that is absolutely worth doing. But there is no point in indulging fantasies. Government's current problems are almost certainly not temporary. Given the mostly irreversible buildup of lobbies over the last few decades, it's unlikely that large, centralized government will ever work much better than it does now.

That doesn't mean that government is dead. Demosclerosis, though damaging, is probably not fatal. It does mean that, although Washington will plod on, the government of our dreams is dead.

WHY IT'S NOT THE END OF THE WORLD

Must we, then, conclude that the country will slide down the tubes? That America will rot? No. Government sclerosis is not the same thing as national sclerosis.

Americans tend to be obsessed with government. Liberals hunt for a governmental solution for every problem. Conservatives hunt for a governmental cause for every problem. Liberals scheme day and night to expand government; conservatives, to shrink it. All of them are governmentalists, in the sense that they define their ideologies and social passions in relation to government. If you're a governmentalist, then demosclerosis must appear to be the ultimate national crisis. In fact, many people's first impulse is to think that if American government calcifies, so must American society.

It isn't necessarily so. One way or another, social change finds ways to flow around obstacles and obsolescence. Technology and ingenuity work to undercut anachronisms and monopolies. The postal service's monopoly on first-class mail has not stopped the onslaught from fax technology, to say nothing of electronic mail and the Internet. American sugar interests managed to restrict sugar imports, but they couldn't fend off NutraSweet.

Besides, there are lots of ways to solve problems, lots of tools besides government. It's a shame when government gets rusty, but people won't wait around sitting on their hands until Washington turns into a creative dynamo. When General Motors found that its workers couldn't read and add well enough to run a new high-tech plant, it started teaching them. Today, many corporations are delivering education that the public schools are not. Others are providing child care and family services for their workers. Haggar Apparel discovered that premature births among its employees were contributing to its rising health-care costs. The company began offering prenatal health classes and took steps to encourage preventive care, with good results. Black & Decker did something similar. Sunbeam-Oster Appliance Company set up a program offering free pregnancy testing and bimonthly maternity classes.

People who need to solve problems are inventive. Blocked in one direction, they will try another. Environmentalists are no strangers to the arthritic pace of government bureaucracy and the excruciating cost of litigation. "The legislation-regulation-litigation sequence is painfully slow," writes Jessica Mathews of the World Resources Institute. The Center for Resource Economics, an environmental research organization, conducted a study of the Environmental Protection Agency and found that the agency had been so hobbled by underfunding, mismanagement, and outside political intervention that it "has been unable to accomplish its mission [and] cannot ensure that American communities and industries are in full compliance with a single federal environmental law." So environmentalists have begun going around the transfer-seeking swamp. "Environmentalists and industries have recently been looking for alternatives to the regulatory straitjacket," writes Mathews, citing "notable instances of cooperation," as when McDonald's and the Environmental Defense Fund worked together to reduce the company's production of solid wastes. In a similar way, many companies that are fed up with the Chinese water torture of litigation have turned to private arbitration instead.

Such ad hoc arrangements may not be as good as a government that works well. But the point is that government calcification does not necessarily mean that problems don't get solved. Other institutions can compensate, at least to some degree. To a large degree, they probably will. If demosclerosis gets worse instead of better, we'll just need to think harder about nongovernmental ways to solve problems.

That's no cause for complacency. A boulder in the middle of the road can be driven around, built over, maybe even used as a billboard, but leaving it there is hardly one's first choice. Similarly, calcified government can be gotten used to, but its costs are real. If government loses its problem-solving capacity or, worse yet, becomes an obstacle to solving problems, the country will be much the poorer.

WHY THE POLITICS OF BLAME IS OBSOLETE

Demosclerosis is a version of what economists have called the tragedy of the commons, a problem that appears where you have a limited resource that's open to all comers. Suppose, for instance, you have a common forest and many independent loggers. Each logger will rush to cut down and sell as many trees as possible, before everyone else takes all the lumber. The forest is badly overlogged. In fact, chances are that it's soon destroyed.

We see this problem again and again; the overhunting of the buffalo was a classic and devastating case, or, more recently, the overhunting of elephants in Africa. In a common-resource situation, if everyone tries to win, everybody loses.

Something similar happens with a run on government. The universe of public policies is a kind of commons. If you see others rushing to get favorable laws and regulations passed, you rush to do the same so as not to be left at a disadvantage. But government can only do so much. Its resource base and management ability are limited, and its adaptability erodes with each additional benefit that interest groups lock in. So if everybody descends on Washington hunting some favorable public policy, government becomes rigid, overburdened, incoherent. Soon it's despoiled. Everybody loses.

In the case of the forest, there are a few possible answers. One is private ownership, another is government stewardship (by the Interior Department, for instance). Obviously, neither of those is an option in the case of the government. A third option is an agreement between loggers to take only so much wood and to replant after cutting. That can work. But it won't happen if the loggers cling to the get-mine-first, blame-the-next-guy mentality.

Look what happens if the loggers cling to the blame game. As the forest begins to thin, every logger blames the other loggers for cutting down too many trees. Hostility reduces the prospects for cooperation. Then, as the supply dwindles, each logger begins to fear that other loggers will collude to shut him out of the forest. Afraid of being the odd man out, everybody rushes all the faster to cut down trees and grab his "fair share." Moreover, a suspicious logger is unlikely to join a compact to limit his harvest, because he'll worry that opportunistic operators will cheat on the deal and cut down even more trees. So the blame game just makes the situation worse.

Now look at demosclerosis. As Americans organize into groups and associations, as they hire lawyers and lobbyists and

MISTRUST

politicians to seek benefits from government, the government begins to break down and its problem-solving capacity—a common resource—shrinks. As the people become angrier, the groups and associations and lawyers and lobbyists and politicians tell them, "Those fiendish special interests are behind it! Hire me to protect you before they rob you blind!" The bitter words of Senator Alan Simpson ring true: "One of the things that we do here so beautifully is the use of fear, raw fear. You can do a lot with raw fear with oil and gas workers. You can do a lot with raw fear with veterans. You can do a lot with raw fear with Social Security recipients." As the politics of fear and scarcity takes over, everybody rushes all the faster to get goodies. Suspicious interest groups can't make a common deal to limit their take, because each fears that others (or newcomers) would violate the pact. As with the forest, so with the government's problem-solving capacity: instead of being marshaled to preserve its usefulness over time, the resource is ravaged. The citizenry despoils government's ability to work. The blame game makes the situation worse, not better.

To have any hope of making the situation better, the public needs to see that the blame-someone-else, don't-touch-mine mentality is self-defeating. The public needs to understand that each and every consumer of government benefits is a party to the transfer-seeking game and all its effects, however well justified any particular benefit or beneficiary may seem. The problem lies not in any individual program or benefit-seeker, but in the collectivity of programs and benefit-seekers. And only in the collective can it be managed. It requires a broad, common agreement to limit transfer-seeking appetites and demands on government—a kind of arms-control pact for transfer-seekers.

America today is richer than any country in human history, including its prior self. It is more secure than at any time in a century. And yet the electorate in 1992 was petulant and self-pitying. It felt it was owed more from its government, not less. Its tone was whinier than at any time in memory—a fact which can only be deeply embarrassing for anyone who pauses to reflect on the millions of people who would give everything to be in America. Can a rich and spoiled American electorate break away from the politics of entitlement and blame? Possible, yes. Easy, no.

Politicians can lead, but it's risky. In America, the standard political model is to assure the middle class that it's being suckered by some evil other. Americans are addicted to being told that they are deprived of their fair share by "the rich" and corporations and right-wing scrooges and the Japanese (according to liberals), by welfare cheats and pork-barrelers and left-wing social engineers and the Japanese (according to conservatives), and by "special interests" (according to everybody). The standard message from politicians and lobbies, who earn fees on every transaction, is: you deserve more benefits and transfers than you're getting. In other words: "Cut down some more trees." And the public replies: Yes! Faster!

WHO DECIDES?

When he left office some years ago, an American president delivered a warning which hardly anyone noticed. "Today, as people have become ever more doubtful of the ability of the government to deal with our problems, we are increasingly drawn to single-issue groups and special-interest organizations to ensure that, whatever else happens, our own personal views and our own private interests are protected.

"This is a disturbing factor in American political life. It tends to distort our purposes, because the national interest is not always the sum of all our single or special interests. We are all Americans together, and we must not forget that the common good is our common interest and our individual responsibility."

Those words were true when Jimmy Carter spoke them in his farewell address in 1981, and they are still true today. I'm the first to admit that pious appeals to a "national interest" are of little help in a game whose incentives all lie on the side of taking as much as possible before the other guy takes first. Yet the game is destructive. It corrodes economic welfare, destroys government, and robs the unborn. If it cannot be ended, it must at least be contained.

Monkeys will ransack the forest for medicinal plants that kill intestinal worms. Dogs will gnaw through fur and flesh to get rid of ticks or fleas. So the American body politic instinctively flails against the parasite economy, casting votes for politicians who claim to be "outsiders" or who promise to fight "special interests." Who will repudiate the politics of blame and tell the people the truth? Who will tell them that they—*we*—are the special interests? That transfer-seeking, like any good con game, depends on its victims' greed? That transfer-seeking is not a game for tycoons or welfare queens, but a dangerously addictive national hobby?

As more people understand how the transfer-seeking game works, they may begin to back away from it. They may elect officeholders whose mandate is to say no. At present, that hope seems naive and wishful, because it first requires that the broad American electorate stop feeling sorry for itself. But it is also necessary.

Who is the cause of demosclerosis? Not villainous lobbyists or wicked insiders or crafty foreigners. Look in the mirror. John Kennedy told Americans to ask what they could do for their country, not what their country could do for them. They adored him and ignored his counsel. Now they must listen, or pay the price.

A NOTE ON SOURCES

To avoid burdening the reader with footnotes and the like, I have tried to cite sources in the text. Following are more details on sources used.

Chapter 1. Alan Simpson's Senate speech, which still repays reading, was given on February 22, 1985, while Senate leaders negotiated the confirmation of Edwin Meese III as attorney general. The speech can be found beginning on page S 1797 of that day's *Congressional Record.* Marvin Leath's speech in the House of Representatives was delivered on May 23, 1985, and is in the *Record* beginning on page H 3646.

The Everett Carll Ladd quotation is from "Why Are So Many People So Pessimistic in So Many Different Countries?" in *The Public Perspective,* March/April 1993.

Chapter 2. Mancur Olson's *The Logic of Collective Action* was published by Harvard University Press; *The Rise and Decline of Nations,* by Yale University Press. The American Motors executive speaking in 1976 about General Motors was quoted by John A. Barnes in "A Sad Day for GM Proves That the Market Rules," *The Wall Street Journal,* February 25, 1992. W. Hampton Sides's piquant description of the bicycle couriers Suicide and

Scrooge can be found in the December 21, 1992, issue of *The New Republic.*

Chapter 3. For the historical material on lobbying, I have gratefully drawn on Jeffrey H. Birnbaum's book *The Lobbyists: How Influence Peddlers Get Their Way in Washington* (Times Books, 1992). It is the best account I know of the life of a lobbyist. Also useful is Birnbaum's article "Lobbyists: Why the Bad Rap?" in *The American Enterprise,* November/December 1992.

For the coinage "the advocacy explosion" and much helpful data on the expansion of lobbying, see Jeffrey M. Berry's book *The Interest Group Society* (Scott, Foresman/Little, Brown, 1989). On the advocacy explosion, another valuable source of data and analysis is Allan J. Cigler and Burdett A. Loomis, eds., *Interest Group Politics,* third edition (CQ Press, 1991). The "typical study" in 1985 of public-interest groups is by the Foundation for Public Affairs and is discussed by Ronald G. Shaiko, "More Bang for the Buck: The New Era of Full-Service Public Interest Organizations," in Cigler and Loomis. The data on growth of environmental groups are from Christopher J. Bosso, "Adaptation and Change in the Environmental Movement," also in Cigler and Loomis.

Robert Wright's quotation is from his article "Democracy's Impending Demise" in *The Sciences,* November/December 1985. Dean Robert C. Clark's quotation is from "Why So Many Lawyers? Are They Good or Bad?" in *Fordham Law Review,* Vol. 61, No. 2 (November 1992). On the formation of farm groups in this century, I have drawn on John Mark Hansen's book *Gaining Access: Congress and the Farm Lobby, 1919–1981* (University of Chicago Press, 1991). Terry L. Anderson's *New York Times* op-ed piece discussing the socioeconomics of environmental-group members is from June 28, 1993.

Chapter 4. The estimates by David N. Laband and John P. Sophocleus of investment in criminal transfer-seeking were published in their article "An Estimate of Resource Expenditures on Transfer Activity in the United States," *Quarterly Jour-*

nal of Economics, Vol. 107, No. 3 (August 1992). I am indebted to David Laband for the term "transfer-seeking" (among economists, the rather obscure term "rent-seeking" is more common).

The quotations in this chapter from Cigler and Loomis are from their introduction to *Interest Group Politics,* cited above. Marc Galanter's figures on state judicial activity—and much other data on legal activity—may be found in "Law Abounding: Legalisation Around the North Atlantic," *The Modern Law Review,* Vol. 55, No. 1 (January 1992). Herbert Alexander and Monica Bauer's figures on political spending—converted by me into constant 1987 dollars—are from their book *Financing the 1988 Election* (Westview Press, 1991); the 1992 estimate was communicated to me by Professor Alexander. For an eye-opener on the interest-group industry, no one should miss the *National Journal*'s regular surveys of group executives' pay and perks; I have drawn upon the survey of January 23, 1993. David E. Rosenbaum's astute analysis of tax-law churning ran in *The New York Times* on December 8, 1992.

Chapter 5. James DeLong's article on the family-leave bill was in *The New Republic,* April 19, 1993. For the maritime lobby's subsidies and political donations, see Rob Quartel, a former member of the Federal Maritime Commission, writing on the op-ed page of *The Washington Post,* December 15, 1992.

The RAND overview of tort litigation is by Deborah R. Hensler, Mary E. Vaiana, James S. Kakalik, and Mark A. Peterson, in *Trends in Tort Litigation: The Story Behind the Statistics* (RAND, 1987). The Saul B. Shapiro quotation is from his op-ed article "Clumsy? Sue New York City" in *The New York Times,* September 30, 1992. Peter Huber's book, detailing the impact of litigation on manufacturers of vaccines and small airplanes, is *Liability: The Legal Revolution and Its Consequences* (Basic Books, 1988). The extended quotation from Dan Dobbs is taken from "Can You Care for People and Still Count the Costs?" in the *Maryland Law Review,* Vol. 46, No. 1 (1986). For tort-litigation costs, an important source is Tillinghast's *Tort Cost Trends: An International Perspective* (I drew upon the 1992 edition).

For estimates of the costs of international farm subsidies, the key source is the Organization for Economic Cooperation and Development's annual *Agricultural Policies, Markets and Trade;* I quote the total cost of subsidies in 1992, as given in the 1993 edition. The RAND estimates of employment effects of laws restricting firing are in James N. Dertouzos and Lynn A. Karoly, *Labor-Market Responses to Employer Liability* (RAND, 1992).

The findings on fancy restaurants in state capitals are from the paper by David N. Laband, Frank Mixon, and Robert Ekelund, Jr., in *Public Choice,* Vol. 78, No. 2 (February 1994). The $1 trillion estimate of transfer-seeking investment in 1985 is from the article by Laband and Sophocleus cited above.

Chapter 6. On the sugar program's costs and beneficiaries, see the U.S. General Accounting Office's report *Sugar Program: Changing Domestic and International Conditions Require Program Changes* (April 1993). On the rural electrification program, a good sketch of the politics is in James Bennet, "Power Failure," *The Washington Monthly,* July 1990 (to which I am indebted for the quotation from the former government official who said that opposing the program was hopeless). On the peanut program, see the General Accounting Office's *Peanut Program: Changes Are Needed to Make the Program Responsive to Market Forces* (February 1993).

Freeman Dyson's invaluable perspective on finding the right size, along with many other powerful insights, is in *Infinite in All Directions* (Harper & Row, 1988). I also quote briefly from Dyson's *From Eros to Gaia* (Pantheon, 1992).

On Roosevelt's New Deal, I am indebted to Michael Barone, *Our Country: The Shaping of America from Roosevelt to Reagan* (Free Press, 1990). On the economic effects of the federal budget deficit, see the General Accounting Office's June 1992 report *Budget Policy: Prompt Action Necessary to Avert Long-Term Damage to the Economy,* which contains estimates of long-term costs of large deficits.

Chapter 7. Norman Ornstein's quotation is from his article "Money in Politics," *The Ripon Forum,* July/August 1992. Frank J. Sorauf's is from *Money in American Elections* (Scott, Foresman, 1988). James Madison's statement is from No. 44 of *The Federalist.* On the Supreme Court and transfer-seeking, see Terry L. Anderson and Peter J. Hill, *The Birth of a Transfer Society* (Hoover Institution Press, 1980).

Alice Rivlin's provocative book *Reviving the American Dream: The Economy, the States, and the Federal Government* was published in 1992 by the Brookings Institution. Also on the subject of reallocating federal and state roles, Bruce Babbitt (then governor of Arizona) wrote in *The New Republic,* January 24, 1981. Allen Schick's analysis of pay-as-you-go budgetary rules is in his essay "Deficit Budgeting in the Age of Divided Government," in Marvin H. Kosters, ed., *Fiscal Politics and the Budget Enforcement Act* (American Enterprise Institute, 1992).

The Osborne and Gaebler statements are from their book *Reinventing Government: How the Entrepreneurial Spirit Is Transforming the Public Sector* (Addison-Wesley, 1992). For a detailed account of how Japanese investment and know-how have revitalized American rust-belt industries, an indispensable source is Martin Kenney and Richard Florida's *Beyond Mass Production: The Japanese System and Its Transfer to the U.S.* (Oxford University Press, 1993). Sally A. Shelton is quoted from her article "Perot's Sound Bites Miss the Point; Mexico's Environmental Activism Is Rising Fast," *The International Economy,* July/August 1993.

Chapter 8. Education Secretary Richard W. Riley's renunciation of school-voucher experiments was from his confirmation hearings, quoted in *Education Week,* January 20, 1993. Representative Timothy J. Penny was quoted by Jeffrey L. Katz in *Congressional Quarterly,* October 9, 1993. Representative Melvin Watt was quoted by Kevin Merida in *The Washington Post,* May 8, 1993. The estimate of investment spending in Clinton's first budget is from Todd Schafer, "Still Neglecting Public Investment: The FY94 Budget Outlook," Economic Policy Institute briefing paper, September 1993. Steven Waldman's report on the national-service initiative's fate is in *Newsweek,* September 20, 1993.

Chapter 9. On welfare for the not-poor, see Herbert Stein's "Who's Subsidizing Whom?" in *The Wall Street Journal,* September 15, 1993, and Peter G. Peterson's "Facing Up" in *The Atlantic Monthly,* October 1993. Jessica Mathews was writing on the op-ed page of *The Washington Post,* November 9, 1992. The Center for Resource Economics study of the EPA was reported in *The Washington Post,* May 24, 1993.

INDEX

NOTE: Italicized page numbers indicate figures, tables, and charts.

ABOUT THE AUTHOR

JONATHAN RAUCH, a contributing editor of the *National Journal,* has been writing on government and economic policy for more than a decade. He is the author of two previous books, *The Outnation: A Search for the Soul of Japan* (1992) and *Kindly Inquisitors: The New Attacks on Free Thought* (1993), and his work has appeared in many publications, including *The New Republic, The Atlantic Monthly, The New York Times, The Wall Street Journal,* and the *Los Angeles Times.* He takes modest pride in the fact that his articles on the federal honey subsidy and on the wool and mohair subsidy figured in both programs' eventual demise.